STAR WARS®
SHADOWS OF THE EMPIRE™
EVOLUTION

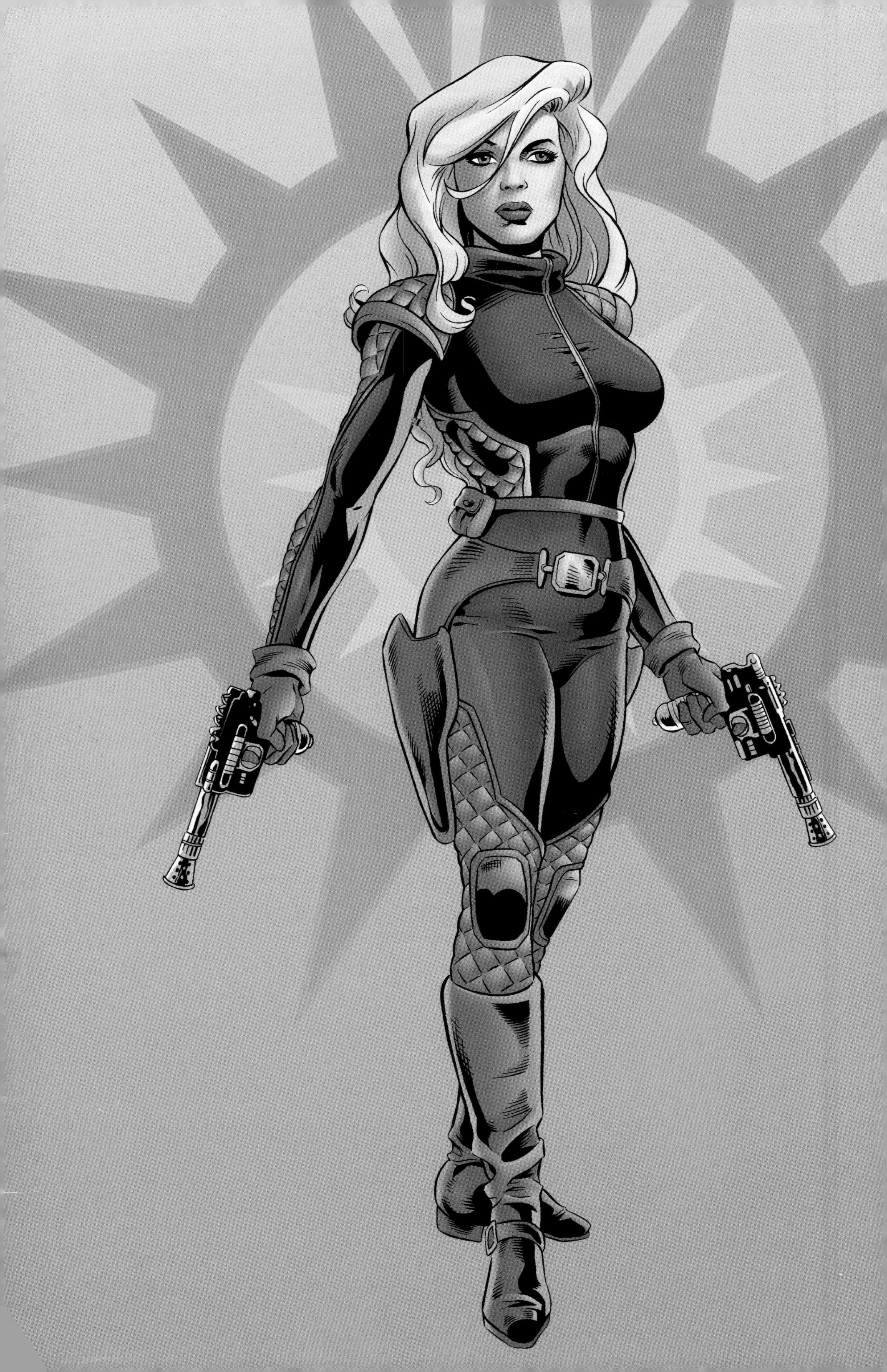

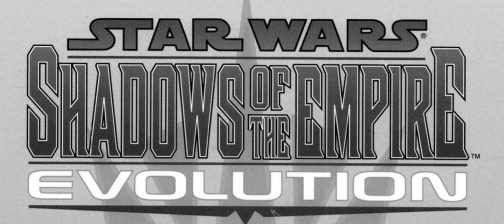

STAR WARS
SHADOWS OF THE EMPIRE
EVOLUTION

story
STEVE PERRY

pencils
RON RANDALL

inks
TOM SIMMONS & RON RANDALL

colors
DAVE NESTELLE

lettering
STEVE DUTRO

cover art
CHRISTOPHER MOELLER

DARK HORSE COMICS®

publisher
Mike Richardson

series editors
Bob Cooper & Peet Janes

collection editor
Chris Warner

collection designer
Lia Ribacchi

art director
Mark Cox

special thanks to
Allan Kausch and ***Lucy Autrey Wilson***
at Lucas Licensing.

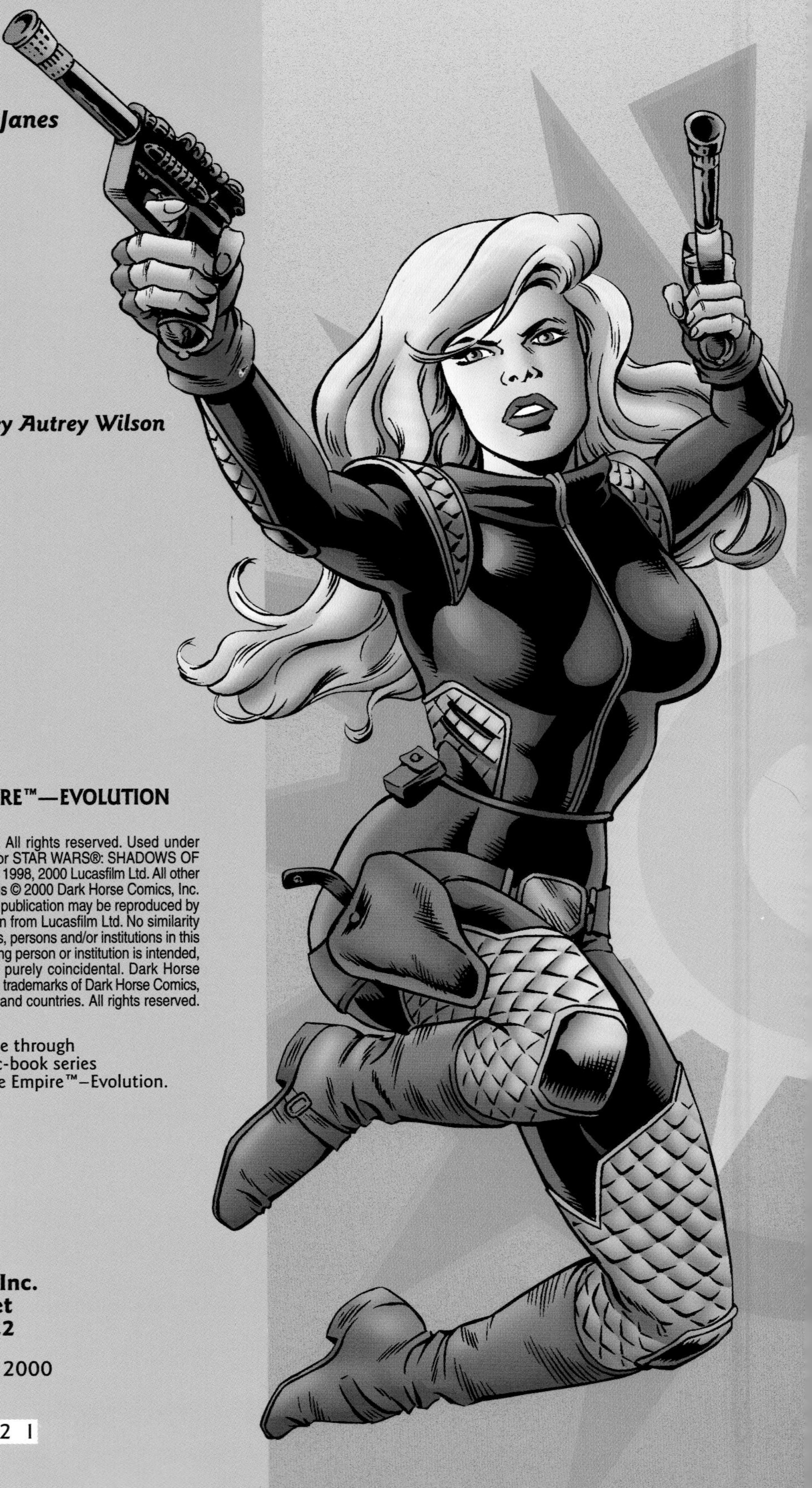

STAR WARS®:
SHADOWS OF THE EMPIRE™—EVOLUTION

This book collects issues one through five of the Dark Horse comic-book series Star Wars®: Shadows of the Empire™—Evolution.

Published by
Dark Horse Comics, Inc.
10956 SE Main Street
Milwaukie, OR 97222

First edition: February 2000
ISBN: 1-56971-441-X

10 9 8 7 6 5 4 3 2 1

Printed in Canada

STAR WARS® TIMELINE

5,000 BSW4 - 3,986 BSW4	TALES OF THE JEDI
32-0 BSW4	STAR WARS (Monthly)
32 BSW4	STAR WARS: EPISODE I THE PHANTOM MENACE
10-5 BSW4	DROIDS
10-0 BSW4	*CLASSIC STAR WARS: HAN SOLO AT STARS' END*
10-0 BSW4	BOBA FETT: ENEMY OF THE EMPIRE
SW4	STAR WARS: EPISODE IV A NEW HOPE
0+ ASW4	*CLASSIC STAR WARS: THE EARLY ADVENTURES*
0+ ASW4	VADER'S QUEST
0+ ASW4	SPLINTER OF THE MIND'S EYE
0+ ASW4	RIVER OF CHAOS
0-3 ASW4	*CLASSIC STAR WARS*
3 ASW4	STAR WARS: EPISODE V THE EMPIRE STRIKES BACK
3+ ASW4	SHADOWS OF THE EMPIRE
4 ASW4	STAR WARS: EPISODE VI RETURN OF THE JEDI
4 ASW4	**SHADOWS OF THE EMPIRE: EVOLUTION**
4 ASW4	THE JABBA TAPE
4 ASW4	MARA JADE: BY THE EMPEROR'S HAND
4+ ASW4	*CLASSIC STAR WARS: THE VANDELHELM MISSION*
4+ ASW4	X-WING ROGUE SQUADRON
9+ ASW4	THE THRAWN TRILOGY
10 ASW4	DARK EMPIRE
10+ ASW4	DARK EMPIRE II
10+ ASW4	BOBA FETT: DEATH, LIES, AND TREACHERY
11 ASW4	EMPIRE'S END
11+ ASW4	CRIMSON EMPIRE
11+ ASW4	CRIMSON EMPIRE II
13+ ASW4	JEDI ACADEMY
20+ ASW4	UNION

Shadows of the Empire — Evolution

En route to Tatooine following *The Empire Strikes Back*, hoping to rescue Han Solo from his carbonite imprisonment at the hands of Boba Fett, the Rebels are discovered by an Imperial fleet intent on capturing Luke Skywalker alive for Darth Vader. Vader is convinced he can sway his son over to the dark side of the Force. Unbeknownst to Vader, the Falleen Prince Xizor, ruthless and cunning leader of the Black Sun criminal organization, intends to kill Luke and implicate Vader — hopefully gaining the trust of the Emperor and becoming his new right hand in the process. Part of Xizor's plan, playing both sides against the middle, includes insinuating himself and his personal assassin, the human replica droid Guri, into the good graces of the leaders of the Rebellion — then turning on them.

Luke travels with his Rebel friends from Gall to Tatooine in an unrelenting effort to free Han, unaware that he's caught in the middle of a deadly game being played out by two struggling factions of scoundrels — one ready to capture him in order to deliver him to Vader alive, the other dead set on killing him. Luke is eventually captured by bounty hunters and taken to Xizor's castle on Coruscant. He narrowly escapes Xizor's clutches with the help of Lando Calrissian, Dash Rendar, and the droids. The Rebels manage to destroy Xizor's castle in the skirmish — and as Xizor retreats to his skyhook above the planet, an angry Vader arrives with the Imperial navy, threatening to destroy Xizor's skyhook if he doesn't call off his personal fleet. The skyhook is destroyed during the battle, and it's assumed that Xizor is dead.

Now, with Xizor ostensibly out of the picture, Black Sun is floundering. But there's certainly no lack of eager lieutenants ready to step up and assume a leadership role — including at least one mysterious figure whom no one in Black Sun was aware of before. Meanwhile, Guri is every bit as confused as the rest of Black Sun as to her future — not the least of which is due to her uncertainty about just how much "human" there is in a human replica droid.

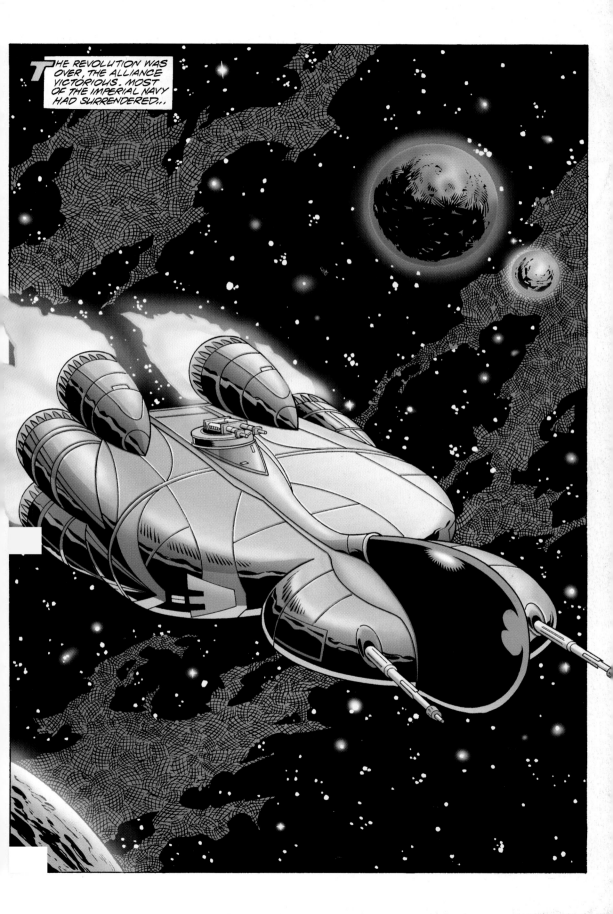

THE REVOLUTION WAS OVER, THE ALLIANCE VICTORIOUS. MOST OF THE IMPERIAL NAVY HAD SURRENDERED...

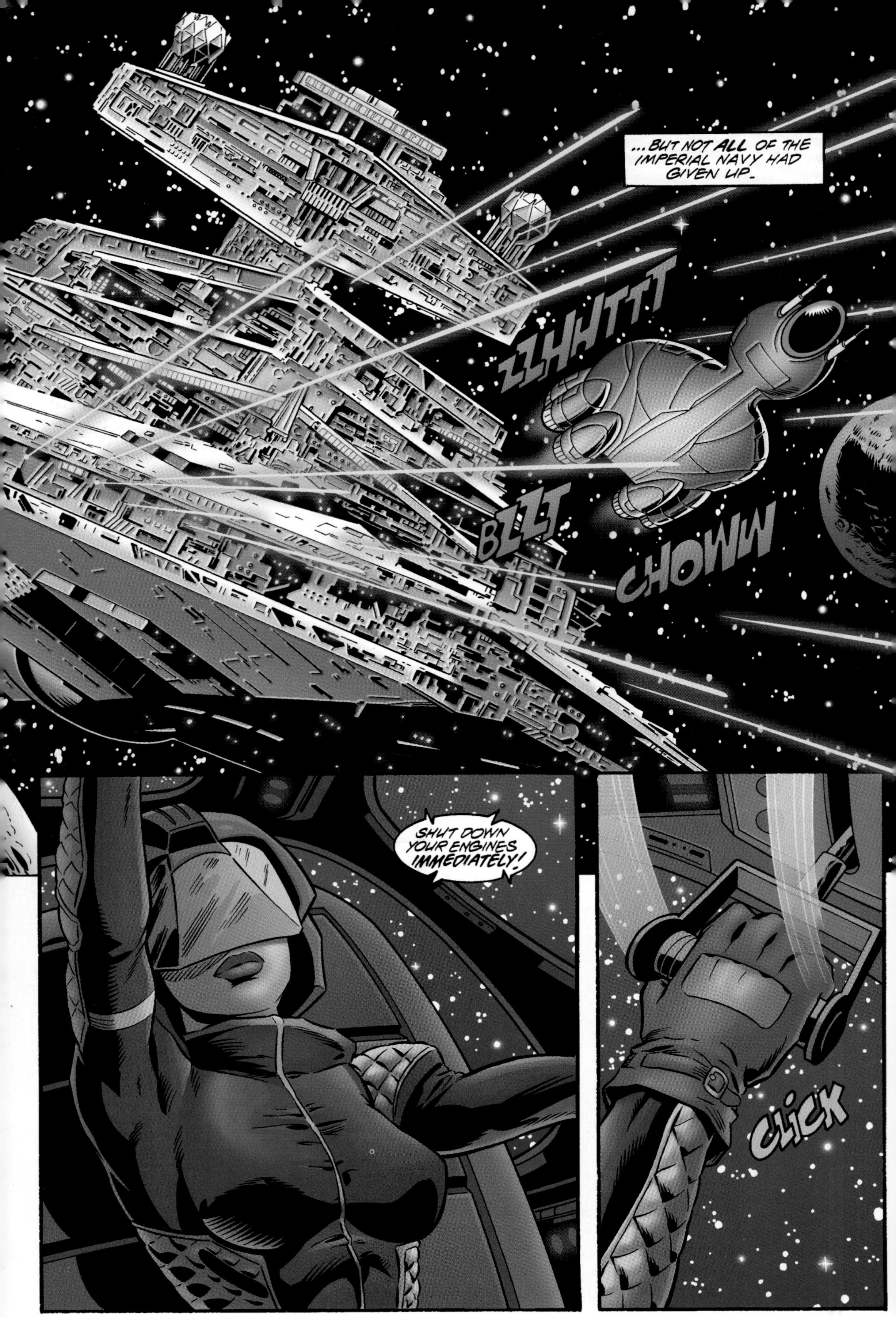
...BUT NOT ALL OF THE IMPERIAL NAVY HAD GIVEN UP.
ZZHHTTT
BZZT
CHOWW
SHUT DOWN YOUR ENGINES IMMEDIATELY!
CLICK

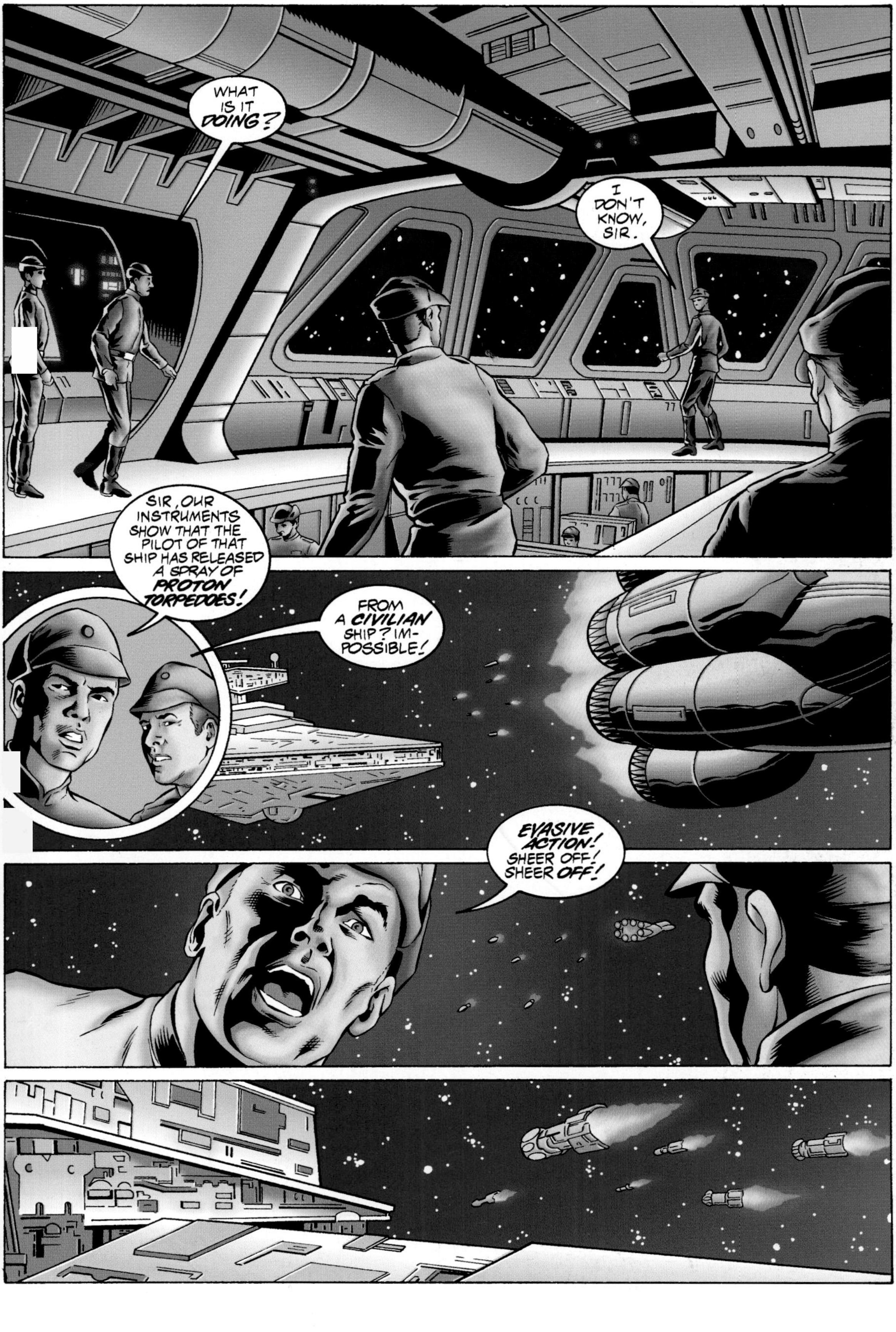
WHAT IS IT DOING?
I DON'T KNOW, SIR.
SIR, OUR INSTRUMENTS SHOW THAT THE PILOT OF THAT SHIP HAS RELEASED A SPRAY OF PROTON TORPEDOES!
FROM A CIVILIAN SHIP? IM-POSSIBLE!
EVASIVE ACTION! SHEER OFF! SHEER OFF!

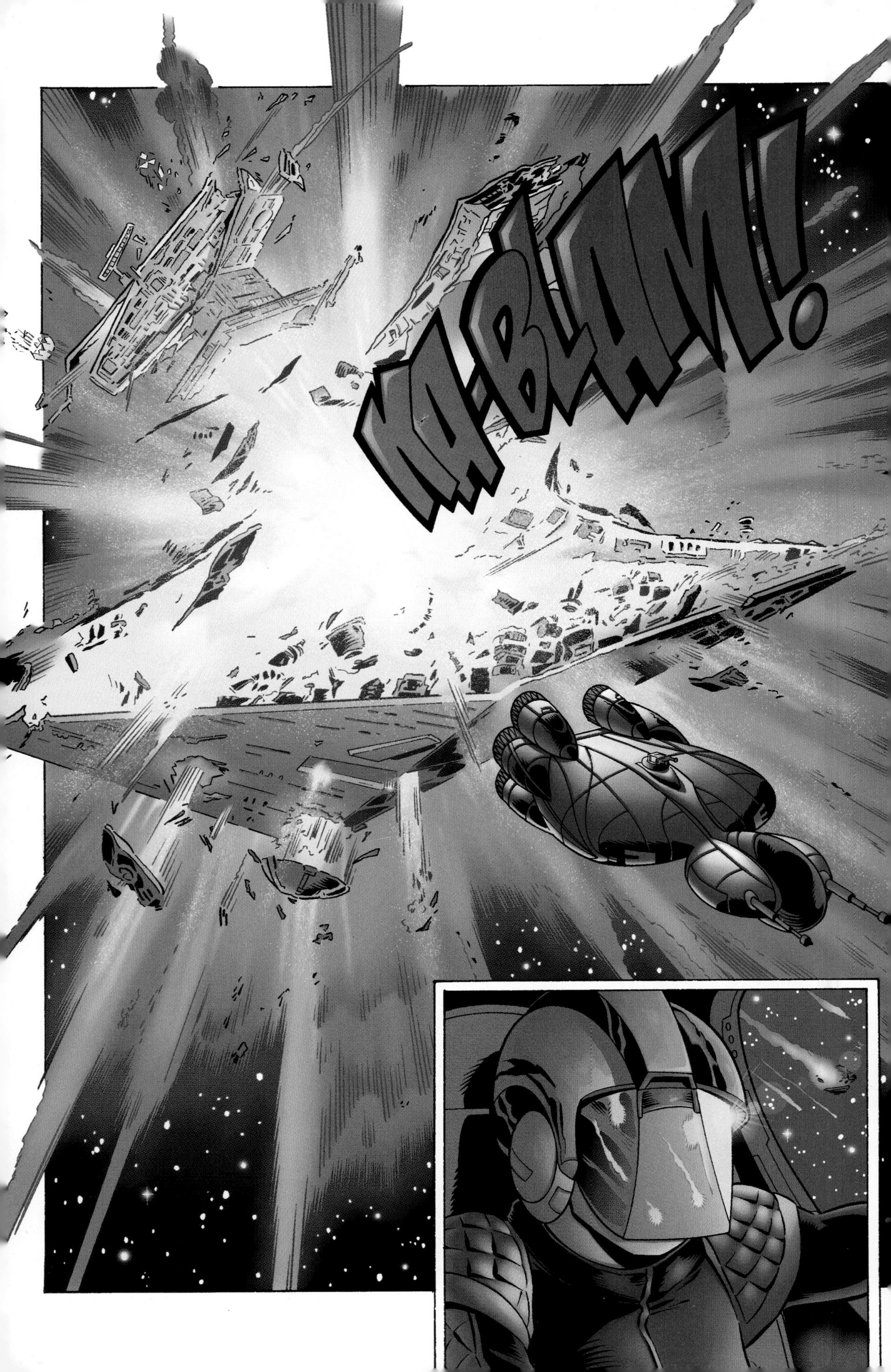
KA-BLAMM!

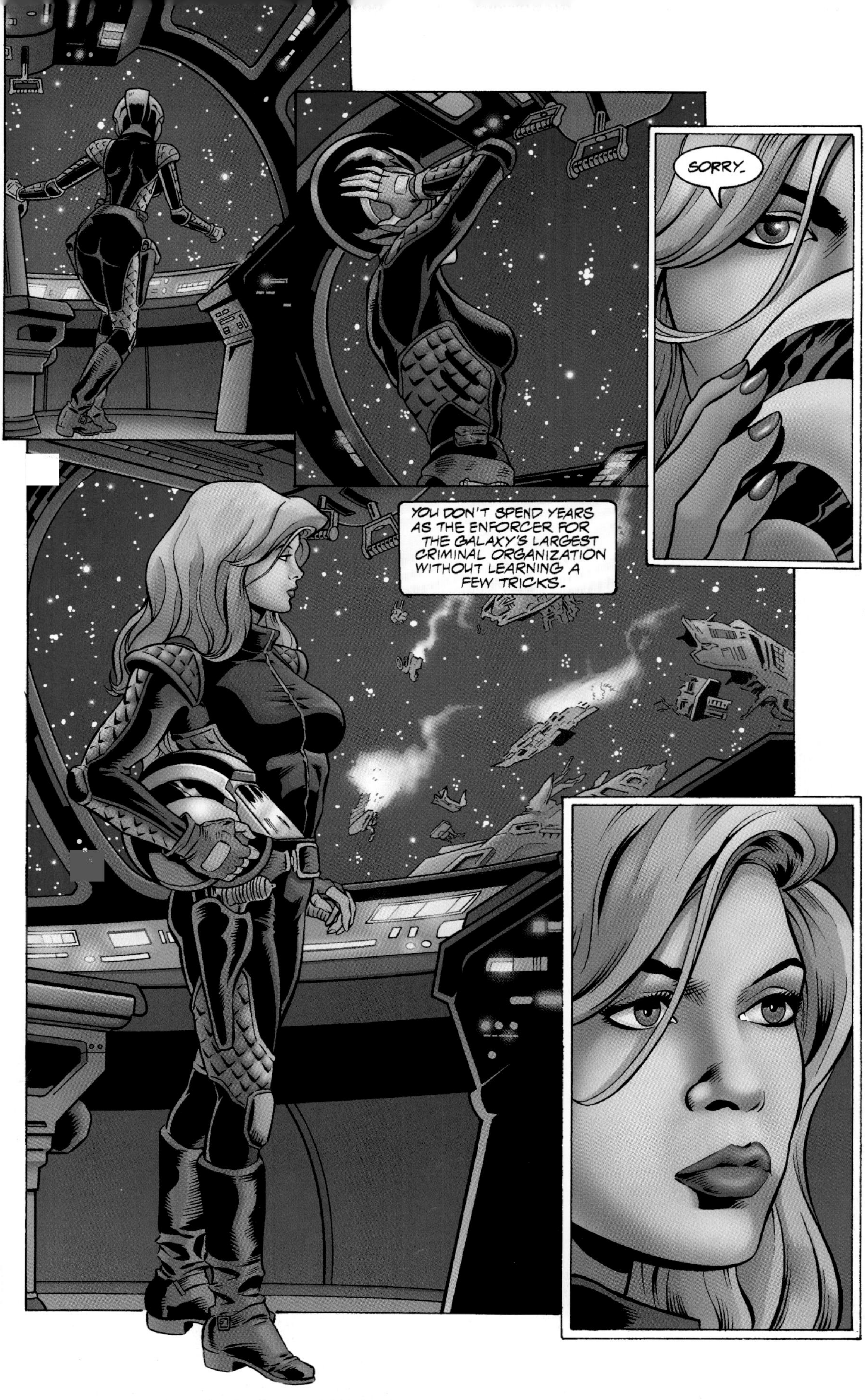
SORRY.
YOU DON'T SPEND YEARS AS THE ENFORCER FOR THE GALAXY'S LARGEST CRIMINAL ORGANIZATION WITHOUT LEARNING A FEW TRICKS.

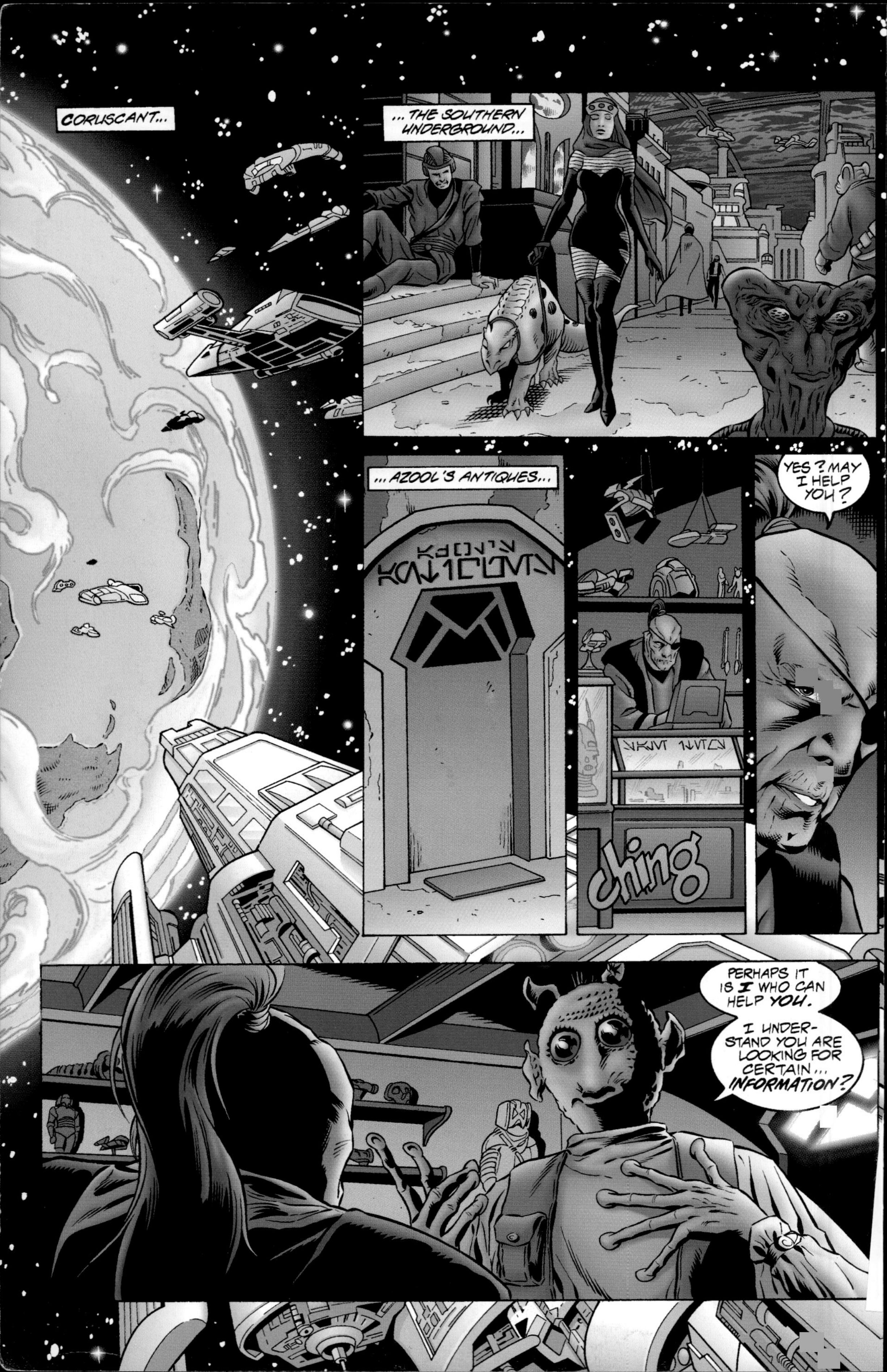
CORUSCANT...
...THE SOUTHERN UNDERGROUND...
...AZOOL'S ANTIQUES...
ching
YES? MAY I HELP YOU?
PERHAPS IT IS I WHO CAN HELP YOU.
I UNDERSTAND YOU ARE LOOKING FOR CERTAIN... INFORMATION?

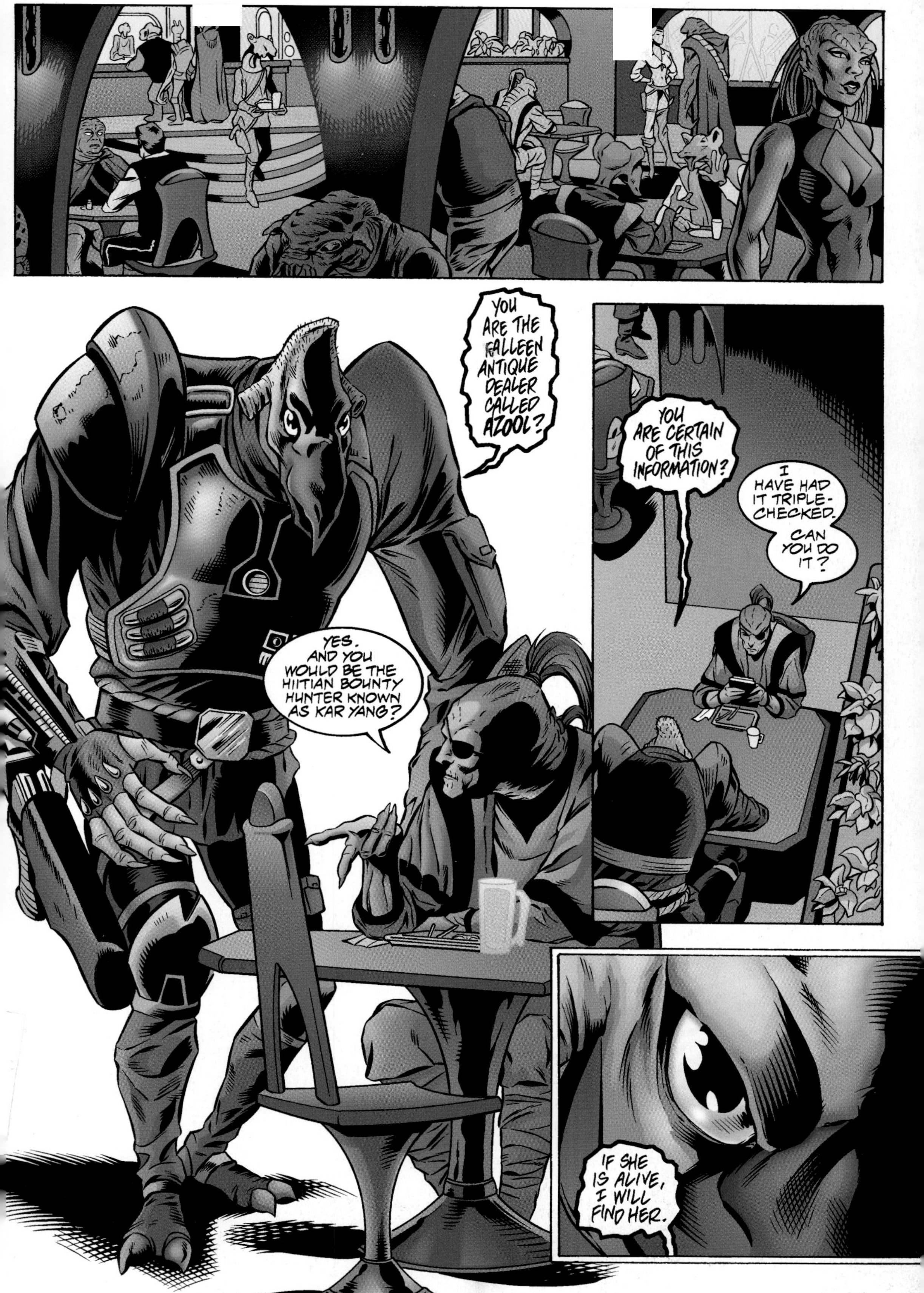
YOU ARE THE FALLEEN ANTIQUE DEALER CALLED AZOOL?
YES. AND YOU WOULD BE THE HIITIAN BOUNTY HUNTER KNOWN AS KAR YANG?
YOU ARE CERTAIN OF THIS INFORMATION?
I HAVE HAD IT TRIPLE-CHECKED.
CAN YOU DO IT?
IF SHE IS ALIVE, I WILL FIND HER.

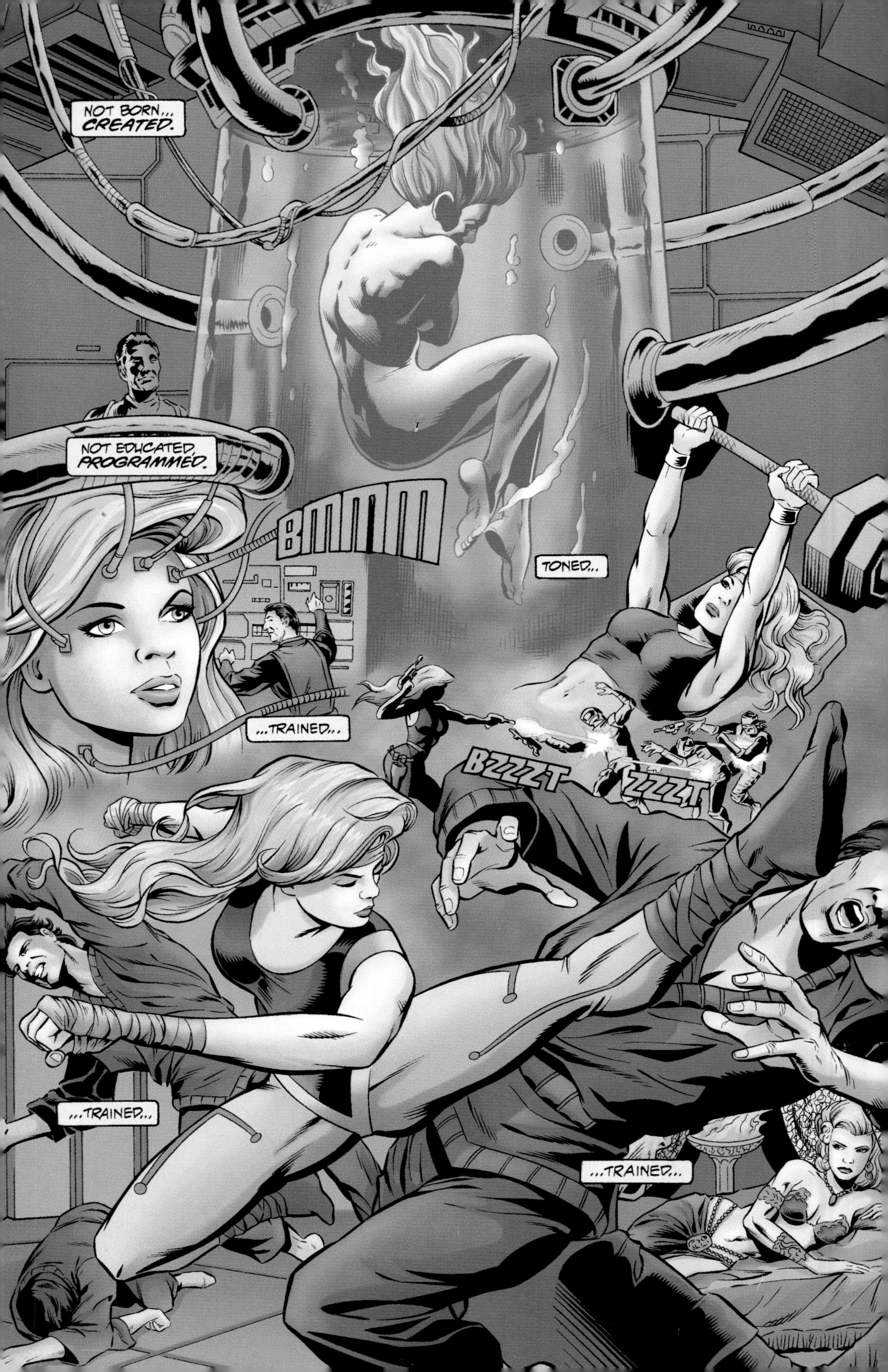

NOT BORN...
CREATED.
NOT EDUCATED
PROGRAMMED.
BMMM
TONED...
...TRAINED...
BZZZT
ZZZZT
...TRAINED...
...TRAINED...

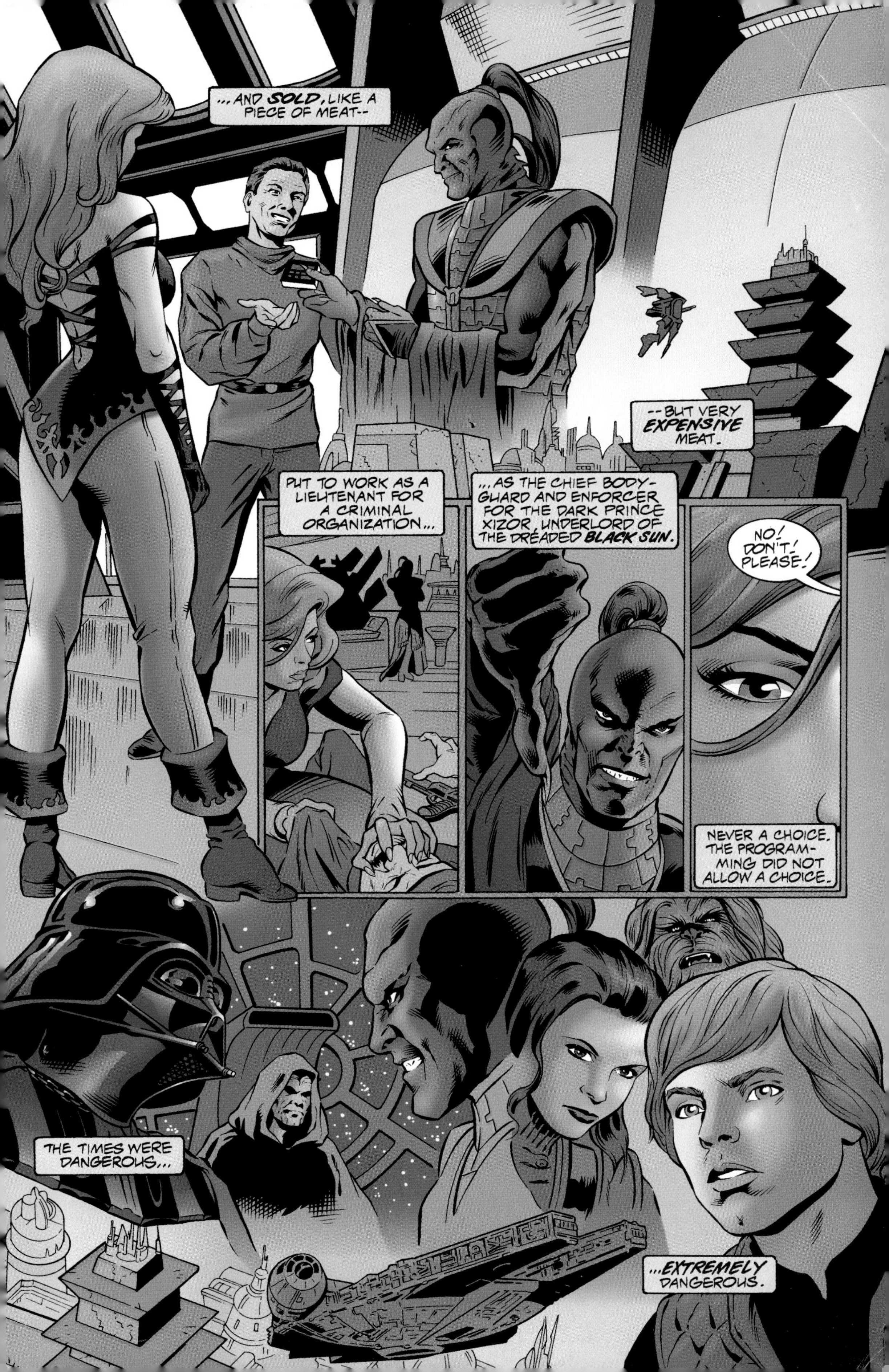
...AND SOLD, LIKE A PIECE OF MEAT--
--BUT VERY EXPENSIVE MEAT.
PUT TO WORK AS A LIEUTENANT FOR A CRIMINAL ORGANIZATION...
...AS THE CHIEF BODY-GUARD AND ENFORCER FOR THE DARK PRINCE XIZOR, UNDERLORD OF THE DREADED BLACK SUN.
NO! DON'T! PLEASE!
NEVER A CHOICE. THE PROGRAM-MING DID NOT ALLOW A CHOICE.
THE TIMES WERE DANGEROUS...
...EXTREMELY DANGEROUS.

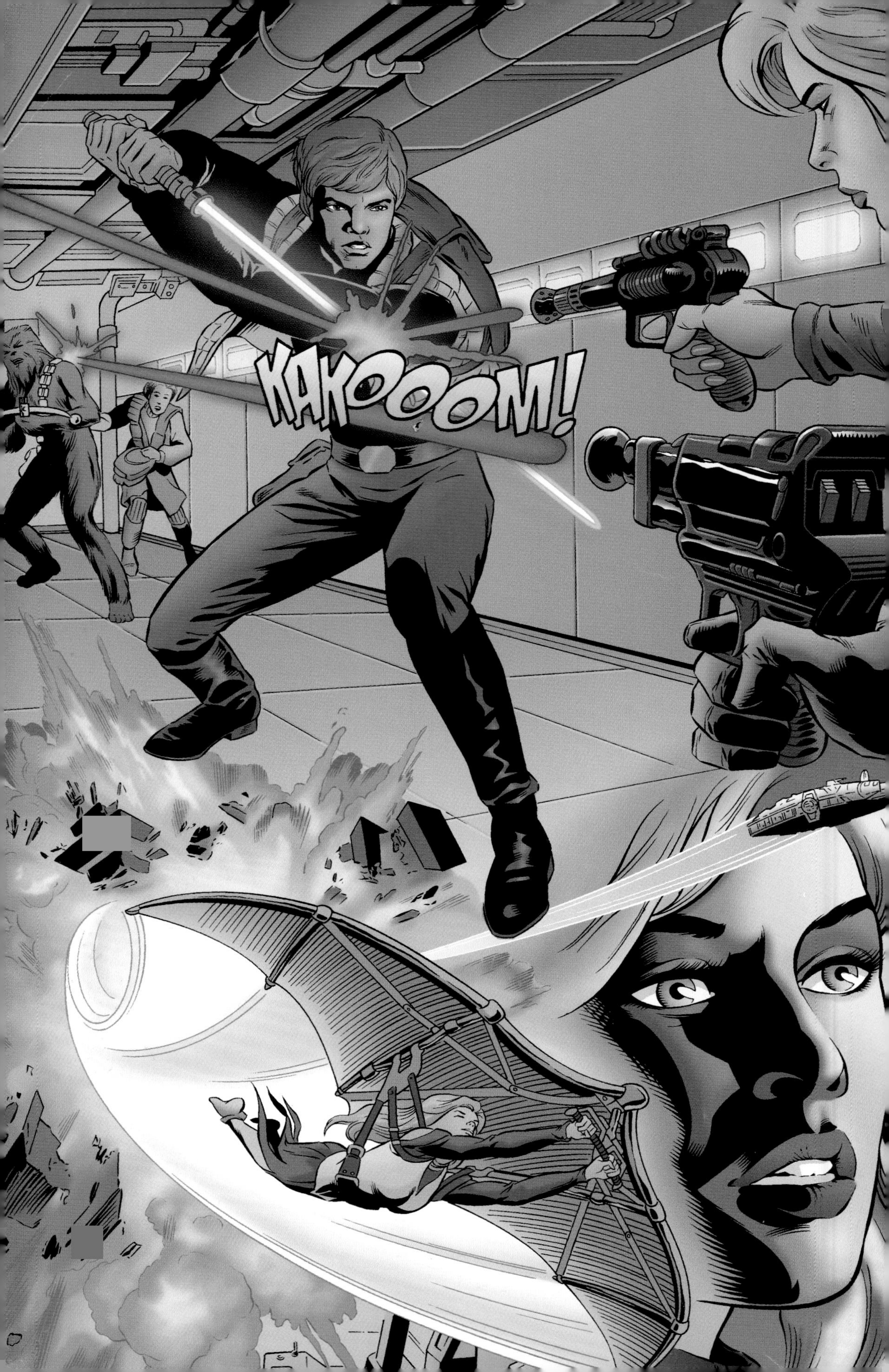
KAKOOOM!

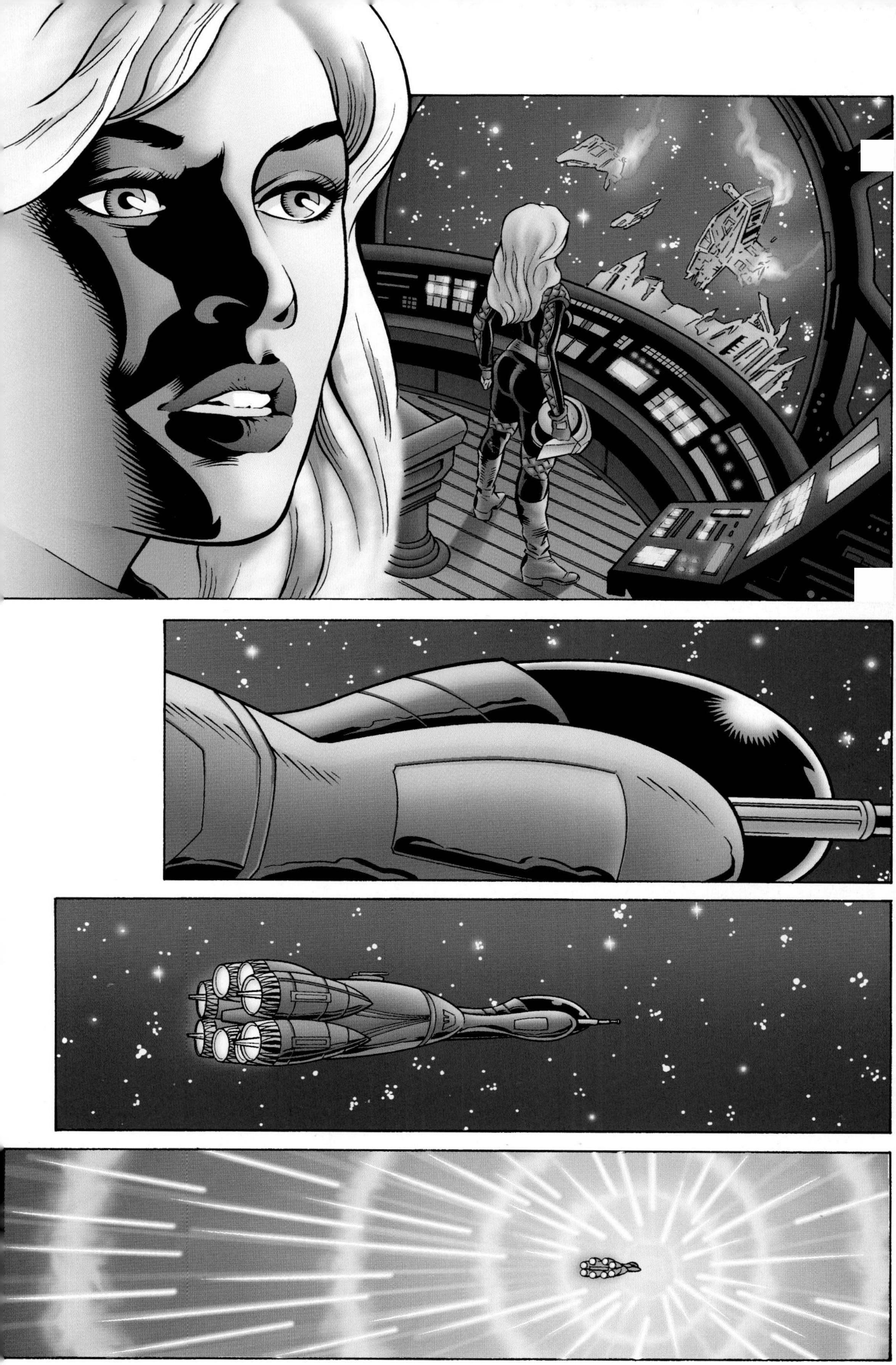

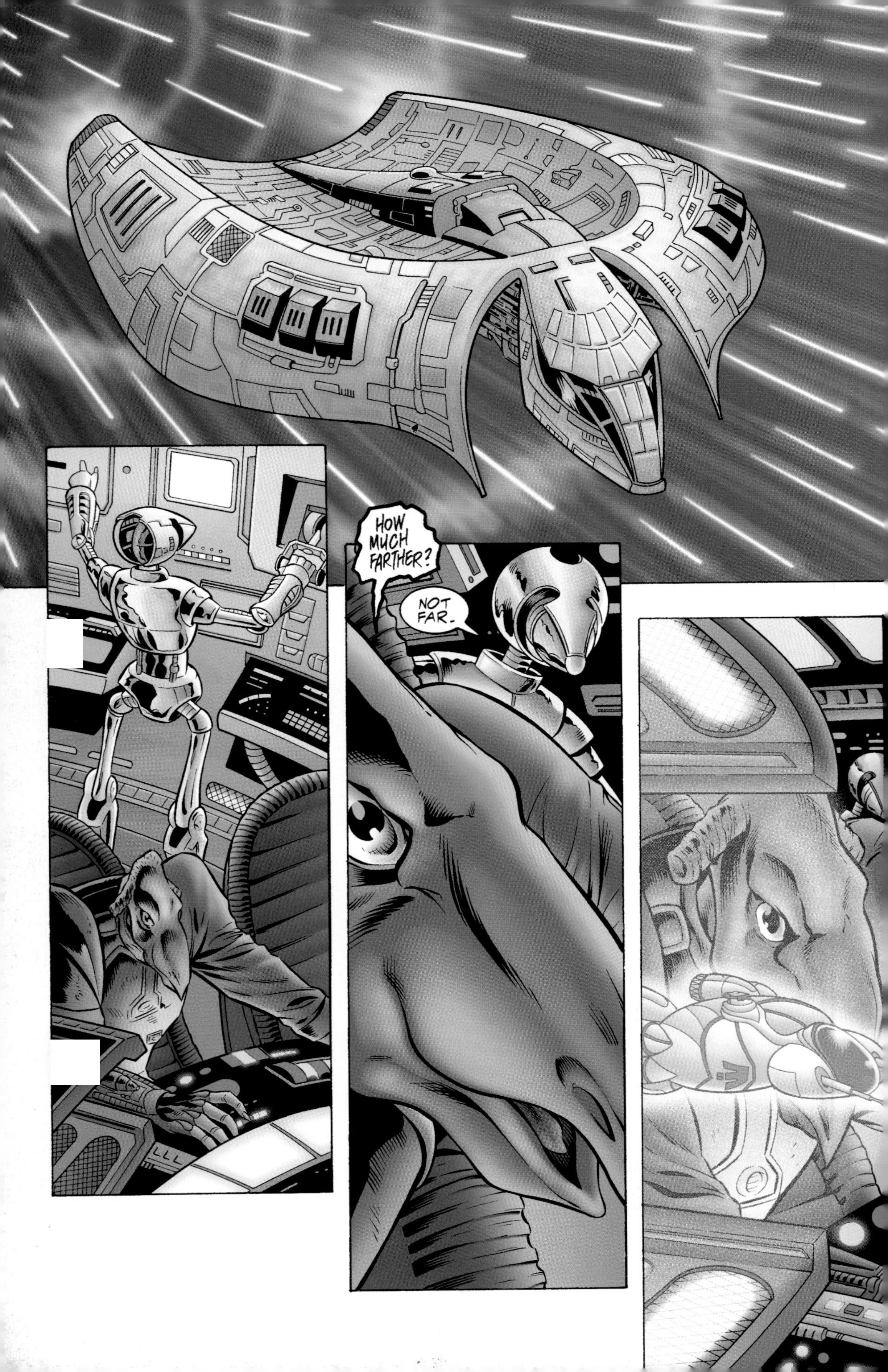
HOW MUCH FARTHER?
NOT FAR.

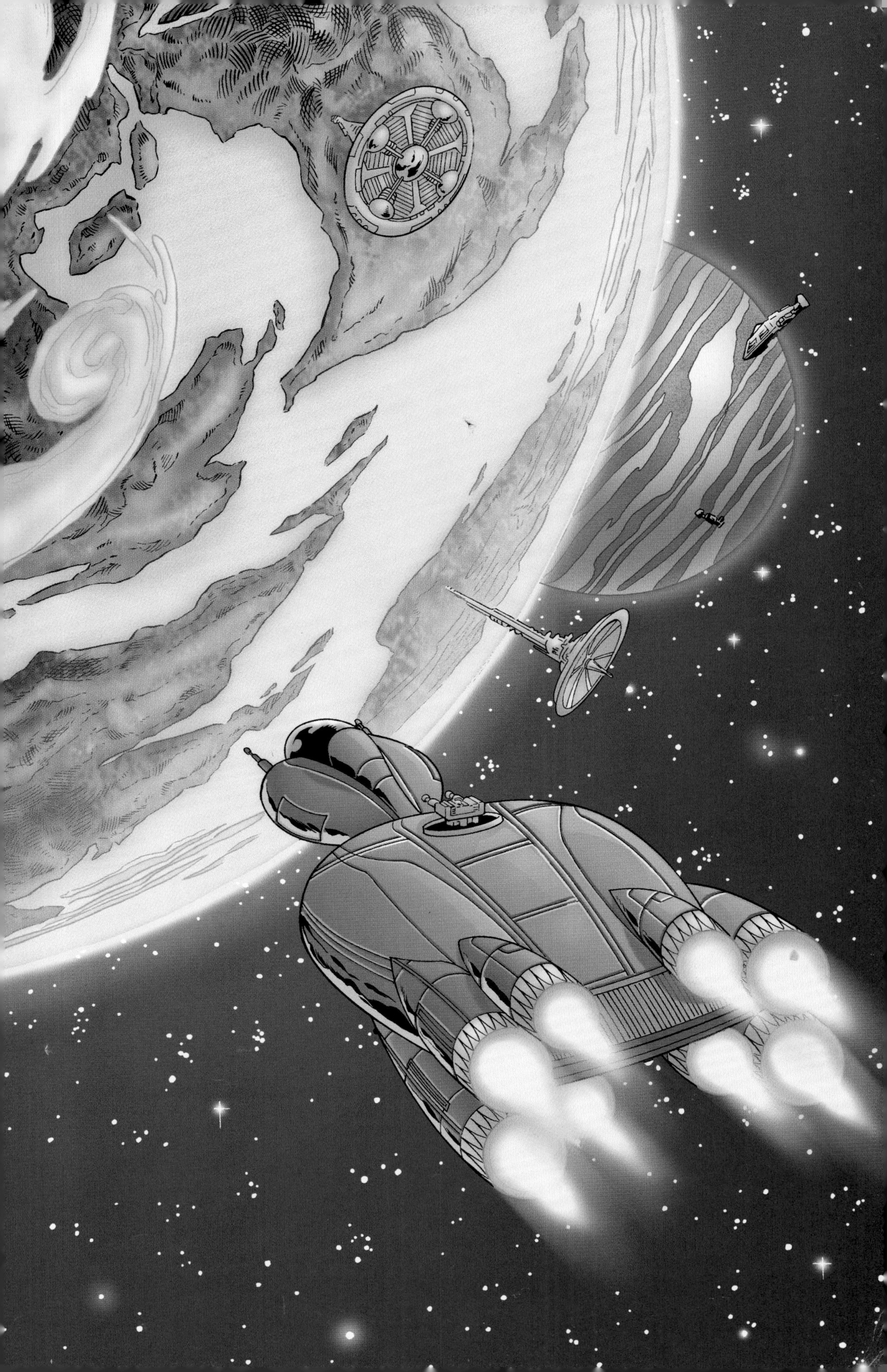

YOU ARE CLEARED FOR LANDING.

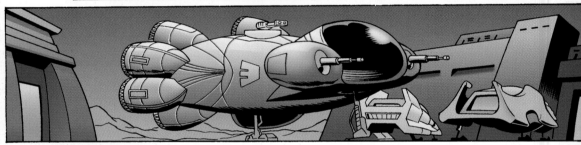

WELCOME TO HURD'S MOON. YOU ARE REQUIRED TO CHECK BLASTERS OR OTHER WEAPONS.

THEY WILL BE RETURNED WHEN YOU DEPART.

I'M NOT CARRYING ANYTHING I CAN CHECK.

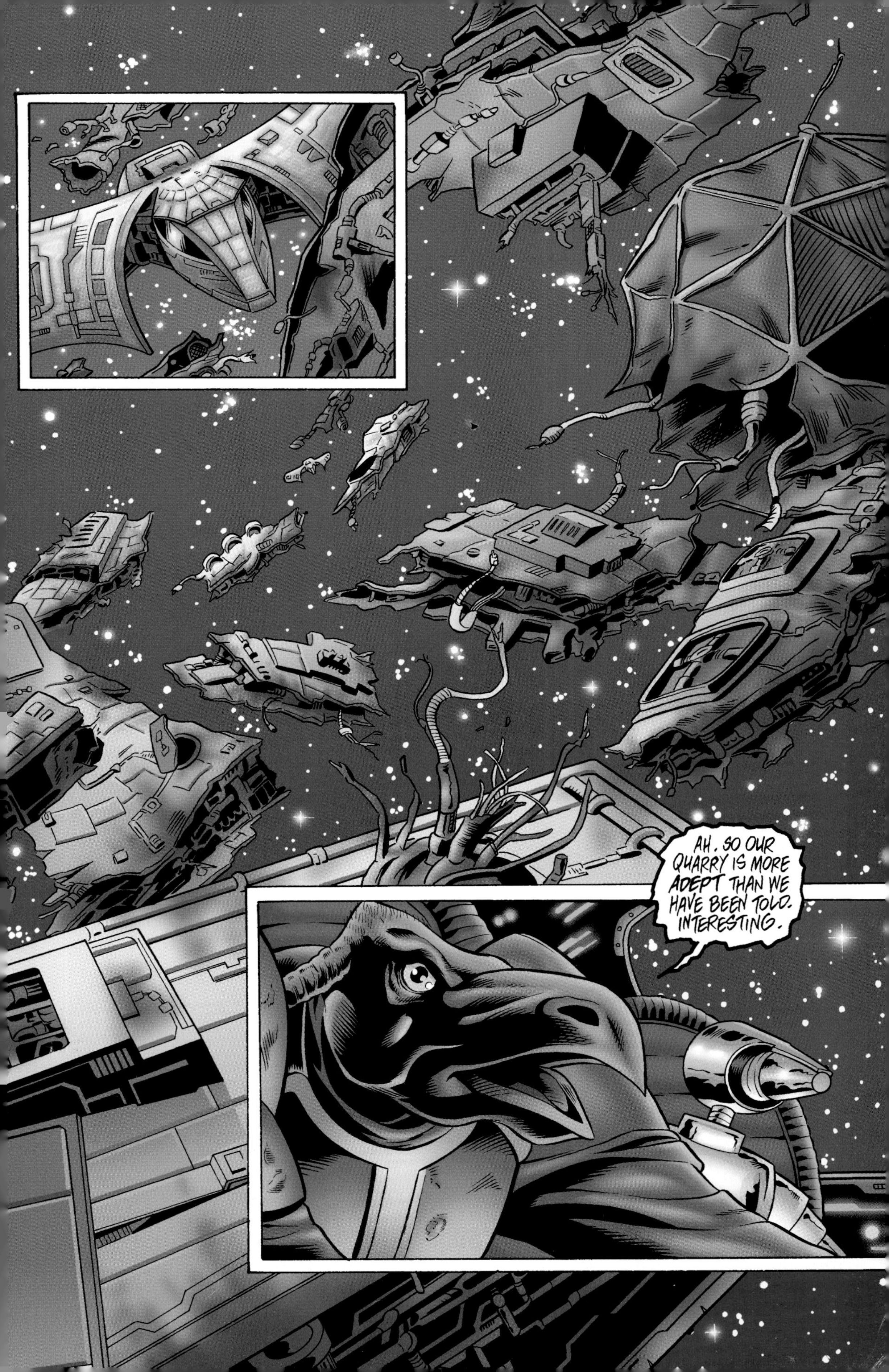
AH. SO OUR QUARRY IS MORE ADEPT THAN WE HAVE BEEN TOLD. INTERESTING.

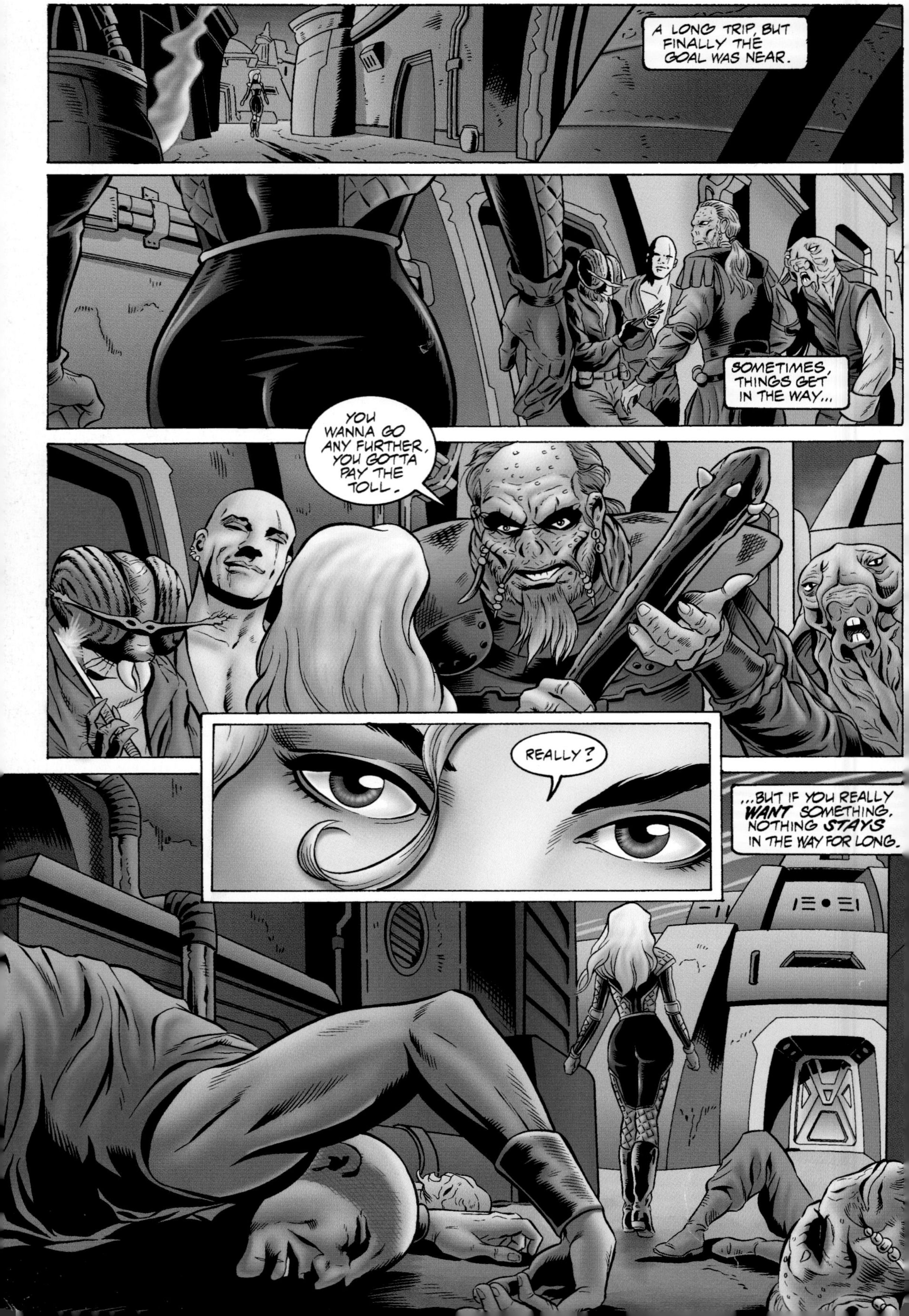
A LONG TRIP, BUT FINALLY THE GOAL WAS NEAR.
SOMETIMES, THINGS GET IN THE WAY...
YOU WANNA GO ANY FURTHER, YOU GOTTA PAY THE TOLL.
REALLY?
...BUT IF YOU REALLY WANT SOMETHING, NOTHING STAYS IN THE WAY FOR LONG.

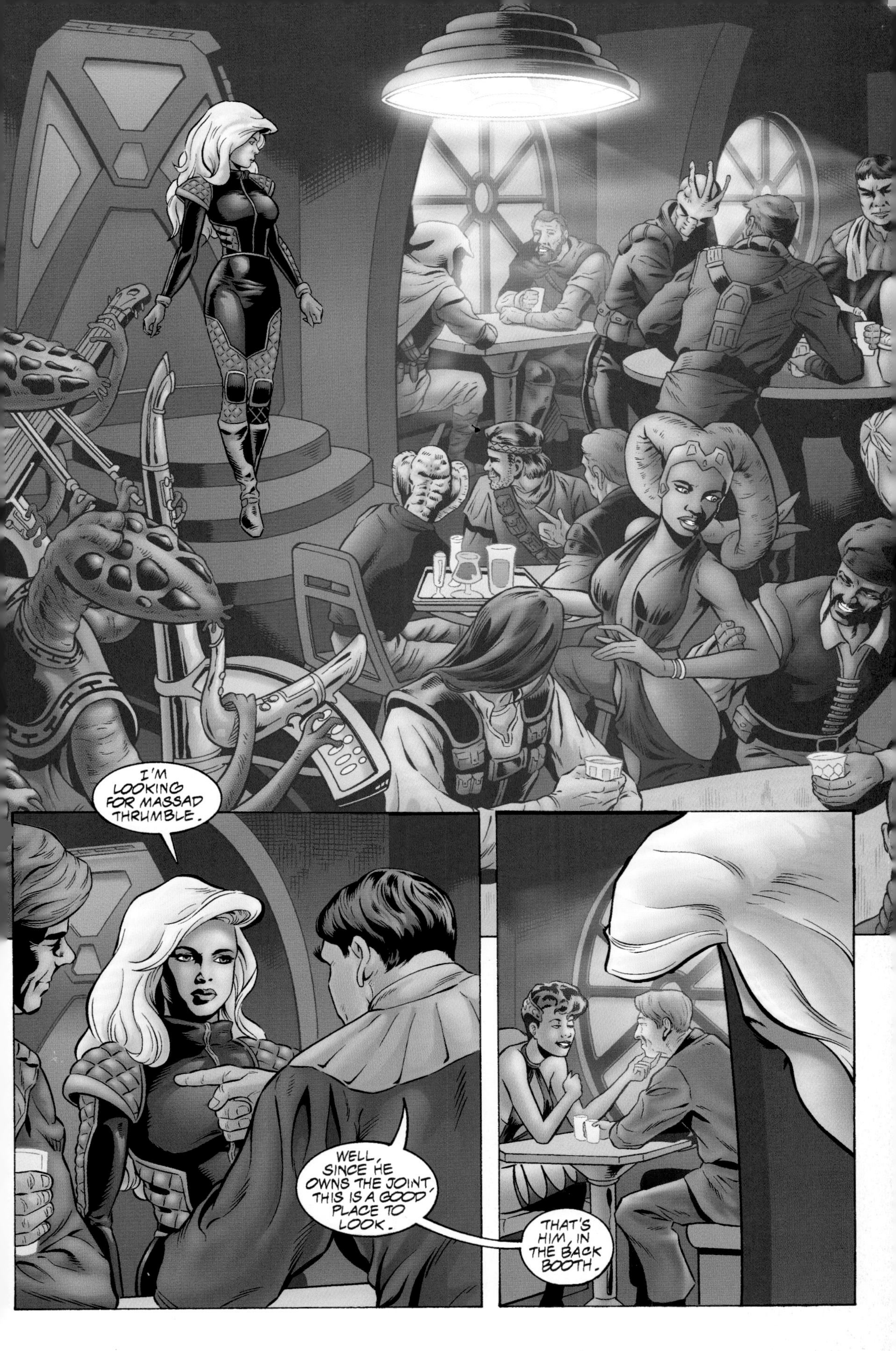
I'M LOOKING FOR MASSAD THRUMBLE.
WELL, SINCE HE OWNS THE JOINT, THIS IS A GOOD PLACE TO LOOK.
THAT'S HIM, IN THE BACK BOOTH.

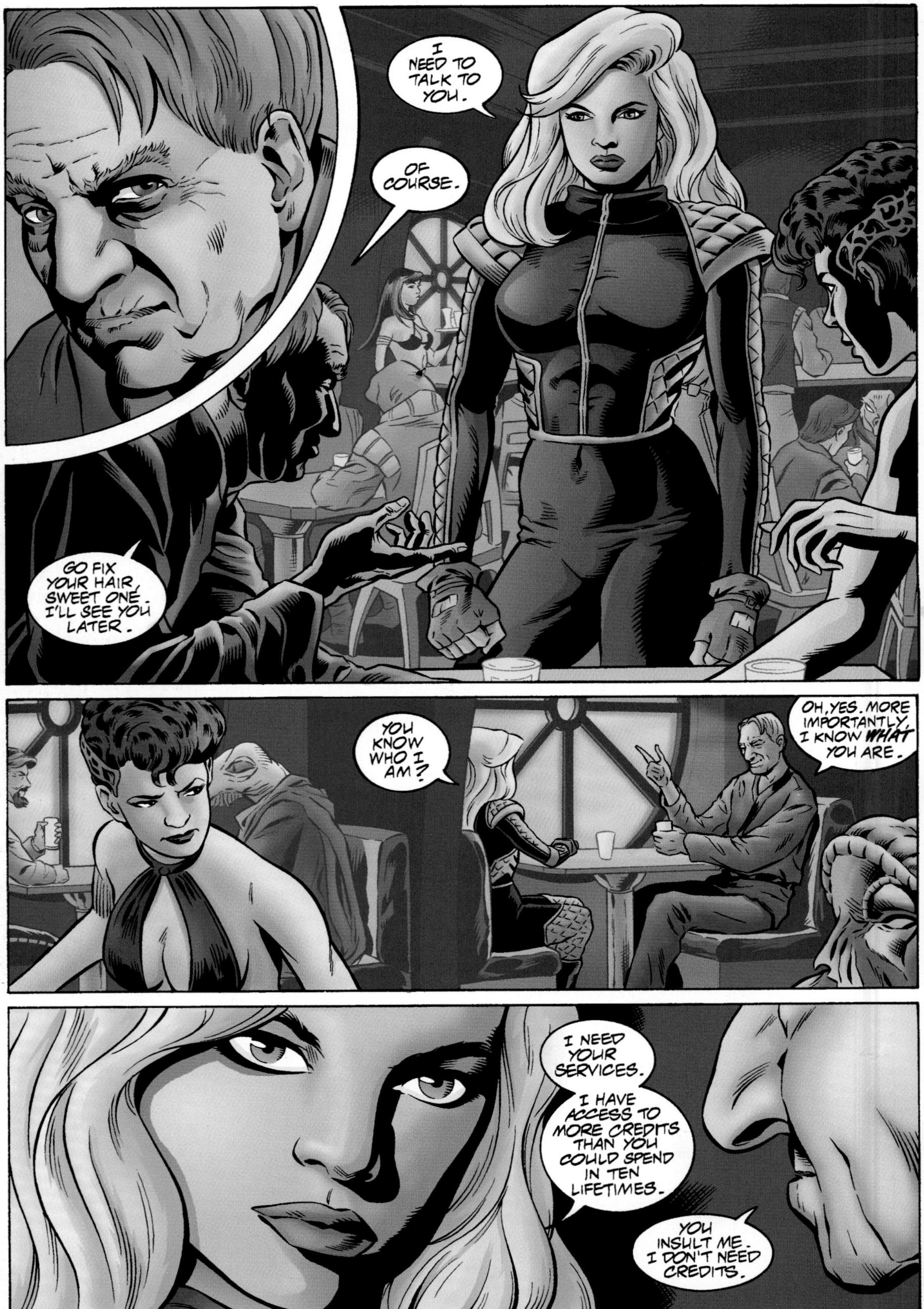
I NEED TO TALK TO YOU.
OF COURSE.
GO FIX YOUR HAIR, SWEET ONE. I'LL SEE YOU LATER.
YOU KNOW WHO I AM?
OH, YES. MORE IMPORTANTLY, I KNOW *WHAT* YOU ARE.
I NEED YOUR SERVICES.
I HAVE ACCESS TO MORE CREDITS THAN YOU COULD SPEND IN TEN LIFETIMES.
YOU INSULT ME. I DON'T NEED CREDITS.

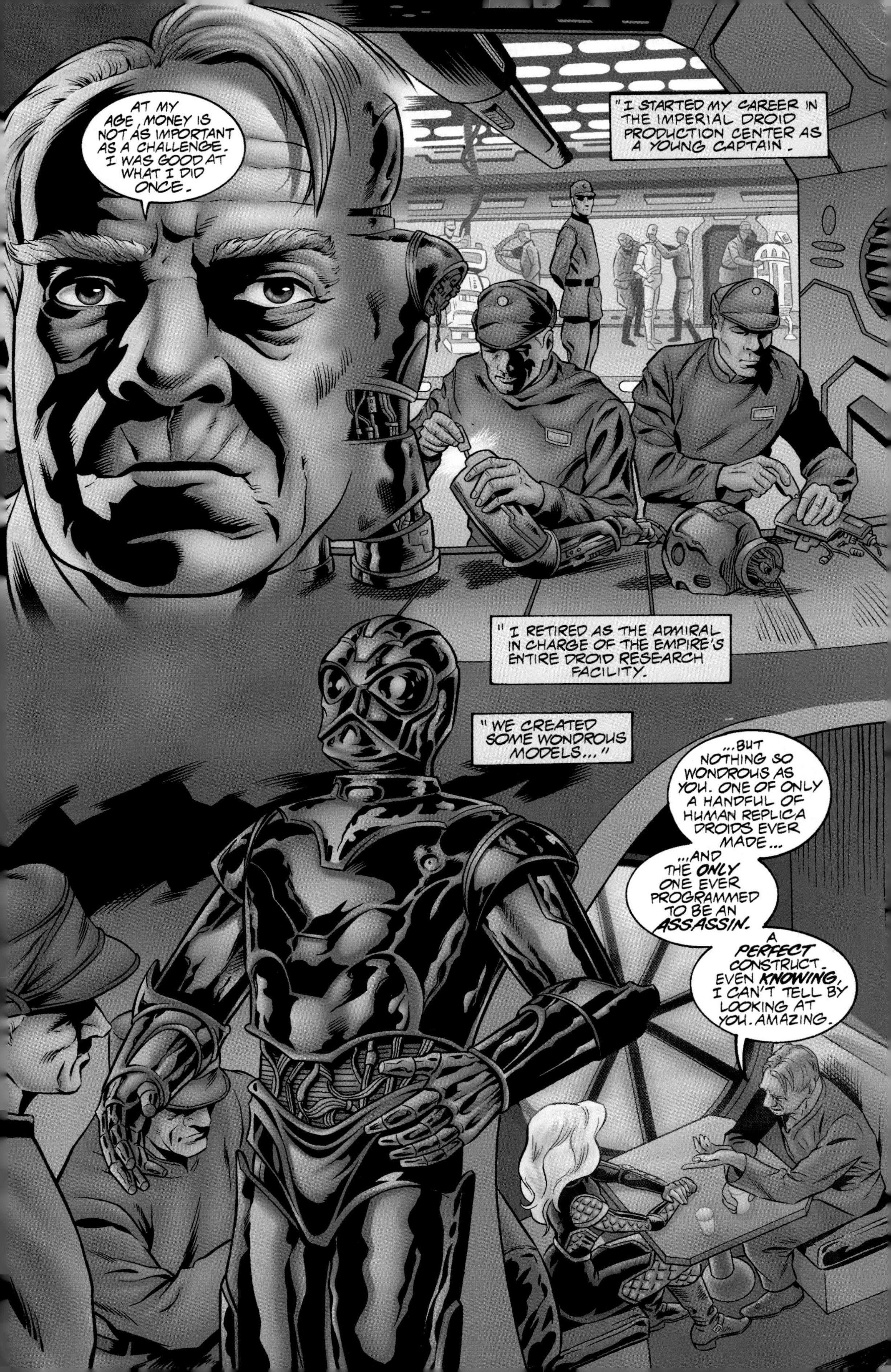
AT MY AGE, MONEY IS NOT AS IMPORTANT AS A CHALLENGE. I WAS GOOD AT WHAT I DID ONCE.
"I STARTED MY CAREER IN THE IMPERIAL DROID PRODUCTION CENTER AS A YOUNG CAPTAIN.
"I RETIRED AS THE ADMIRAL IN CHARGE OF THE EMPIRE'S ENTIRE DROID RESEARCH FACILITY.
"WE CREATED SOME WONDROUS MODELS..."
...BUT NOTHING SO WONDROUS AS YOU. ONE OF ONLY A HANDFUL OF HUMAN REPLICA DROIDS EVER MADE...
...AND THE ONLY ONE EVER PROGRAMMED TO BE AN ASSASSIN.
A PERFECT CONSTRUCT. EVEN KNOWING, I CAN'T TELL BY LOOKING AT YOU. AMAZING.

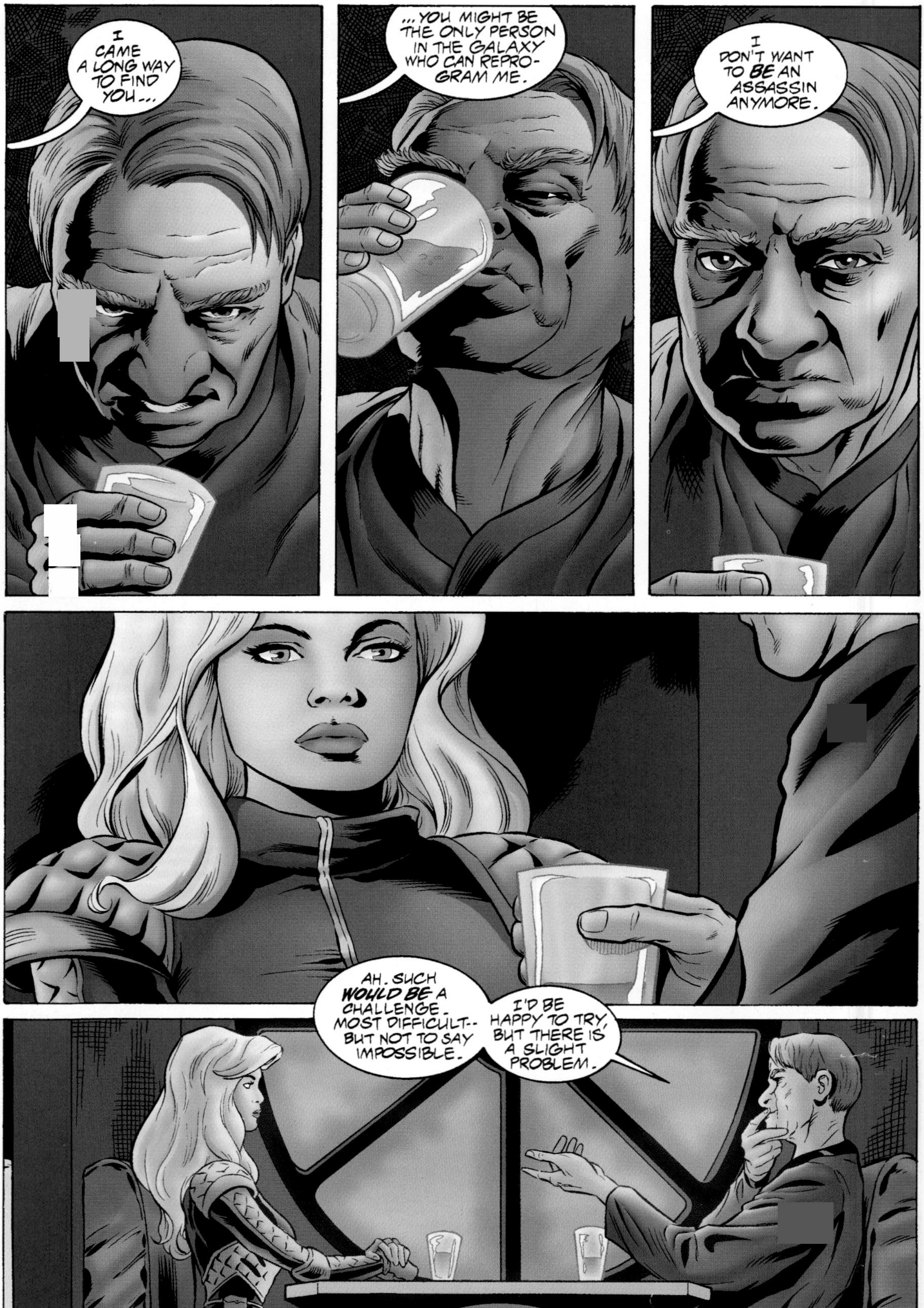
I CAME A LONG WAY TO FIND YOU...
...YOU MIGHT BE THE ONLY PERSON IN THE GALAXY WHO CAN REPROGRAM ME.
I DON'T WANT TO **BE** AN ASSASSIN ANYMORE.
AH. SUCH **WOULD BE** A CHALLENGE. MOST DIFFICULT-- BUT NOT TO SAY IMPOSSIBLE.
I'D BE HAPPY TO TRY, BUT THERE IS A SLIGHT PROBLEM.

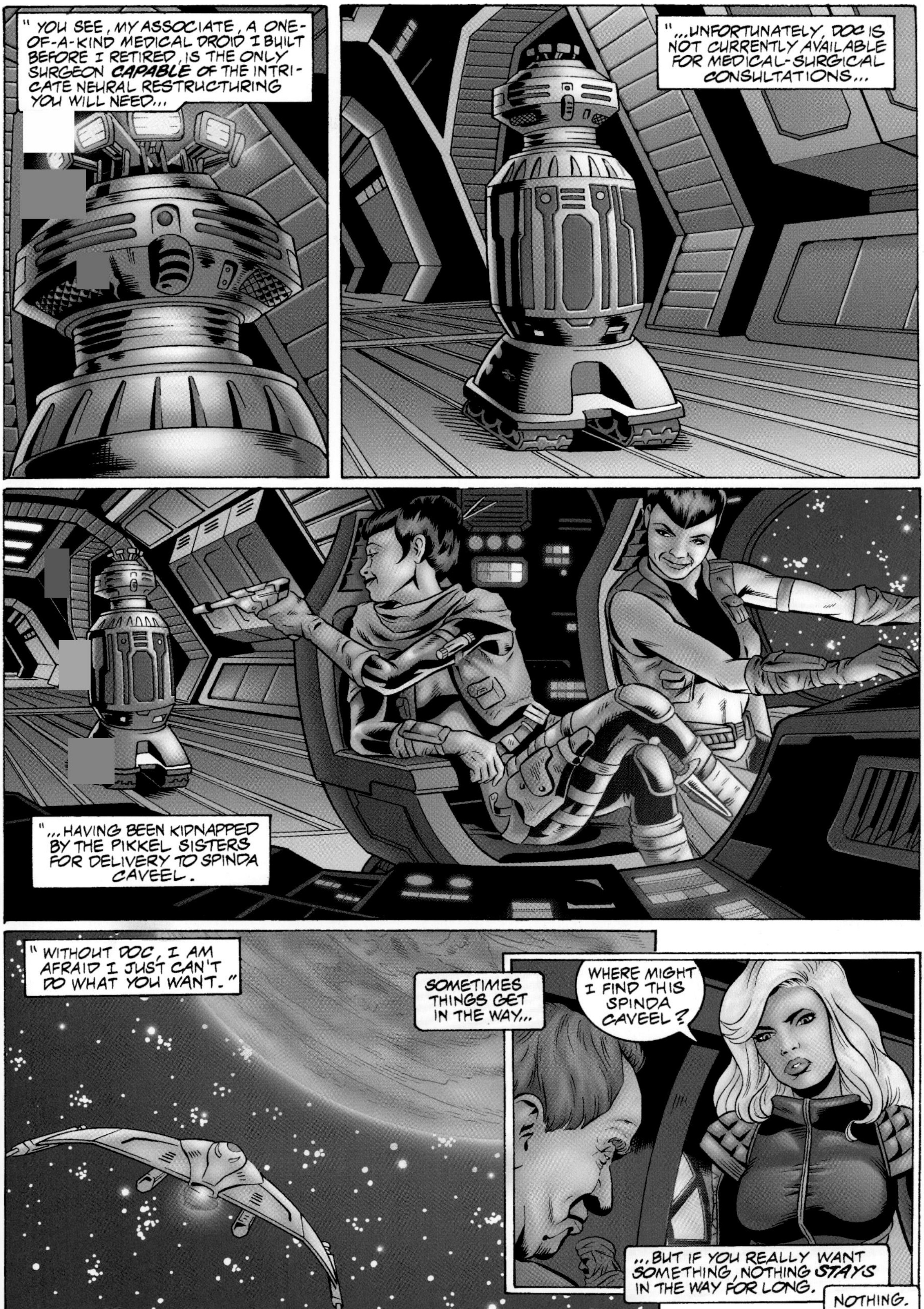
"YOU SEE, MY ASSOCIATE, A ONE-OF-A-KIND MEDICAL DROID I BUILT BEFORE I RETIRED, IS THE ONLY SURGEON CAPABLE OF THE INTRICATE NEURAL RESTRUCTURING YOU WILL NEED...
"...UNFORTUNATELY, DOC IS NOT CURRENTLY AVAILABLE FOR MEDICAL-SURGICAL CONSULTATIONS...
"...HAVING BEEN KIDNAPPED BY THE PIKKEL SISTERS FOR DELIVERY TO SPINDA CAVEEL.
"WITHOUT DOC, I AM AFRAID I JUST CAN'T DO WHAT YOU WANT."
SOMETIMES THINGS GET IN THE WAY...
WHERE MIGHT I FIND THIS SPINDA CAVEEL?
...BUT IF YOU REALLY WANT SOMETHING, NOTHING STAYS IN THE WAY FOR LONG.
NOTHING.

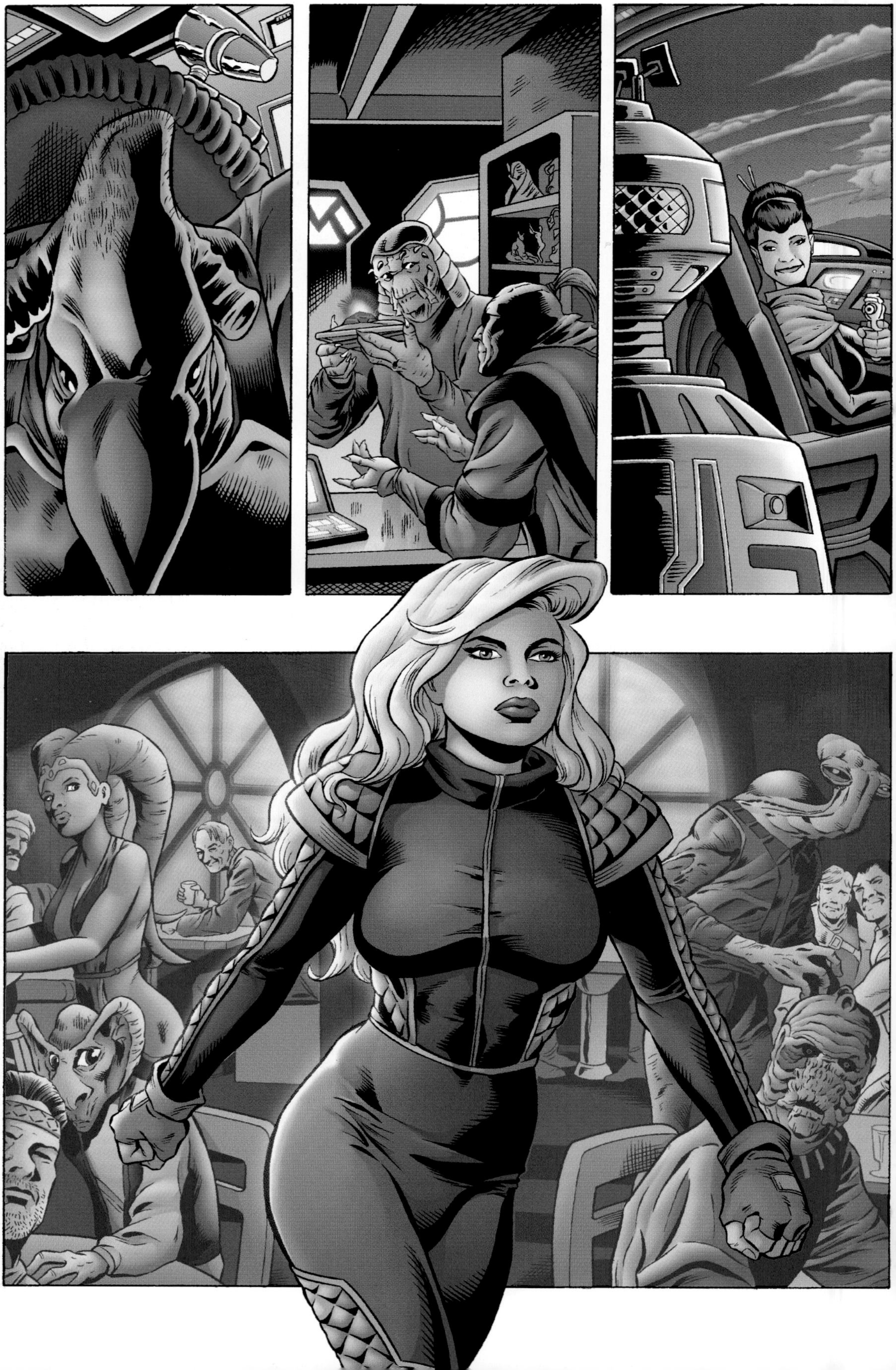

MURNINKAM, A SPARSELY-SETTLED TROPICAL WORLD FAR FROM MOST SPACE LANES.

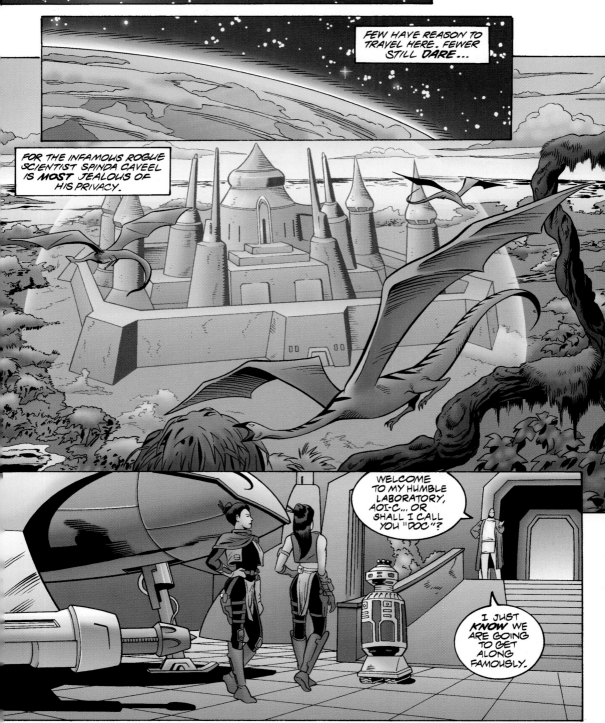

FEW HAVE REASON TO TRAVEL HERE. FEWER STILL *DARE*...

FOR THE INFAMOUS ROGUE SCIENTIST SPINDA CAVEEL IS *MOST* JEALOUS OF HIS PRIVACY.

WELCOME TO MY HUMBLE LABORATORY, AOI-C... OR SHALL I CALL YOU "DOC"?

I JUST *KNOW* WE ARE GOING TO GET ALONG FAMOUSLY.

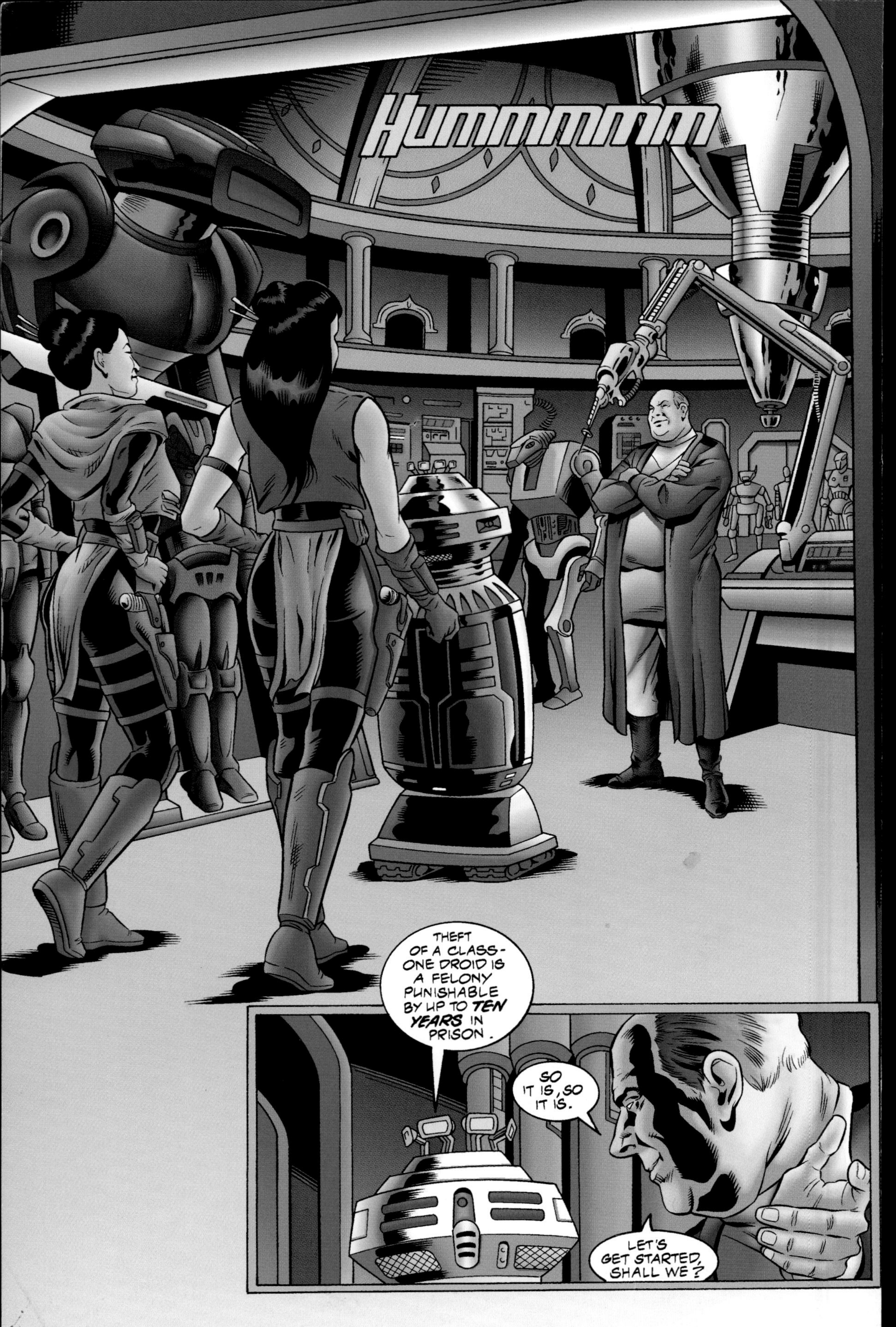
HUMMMMMM
THEFT OF A CLASS-ONE DROID IS A FELONY PUNISHABLE BY UP TO TEN YEARS IN PRISON.
SO IT IS, SO IT IS.
LET'S GET STARTED, SHALL WE?

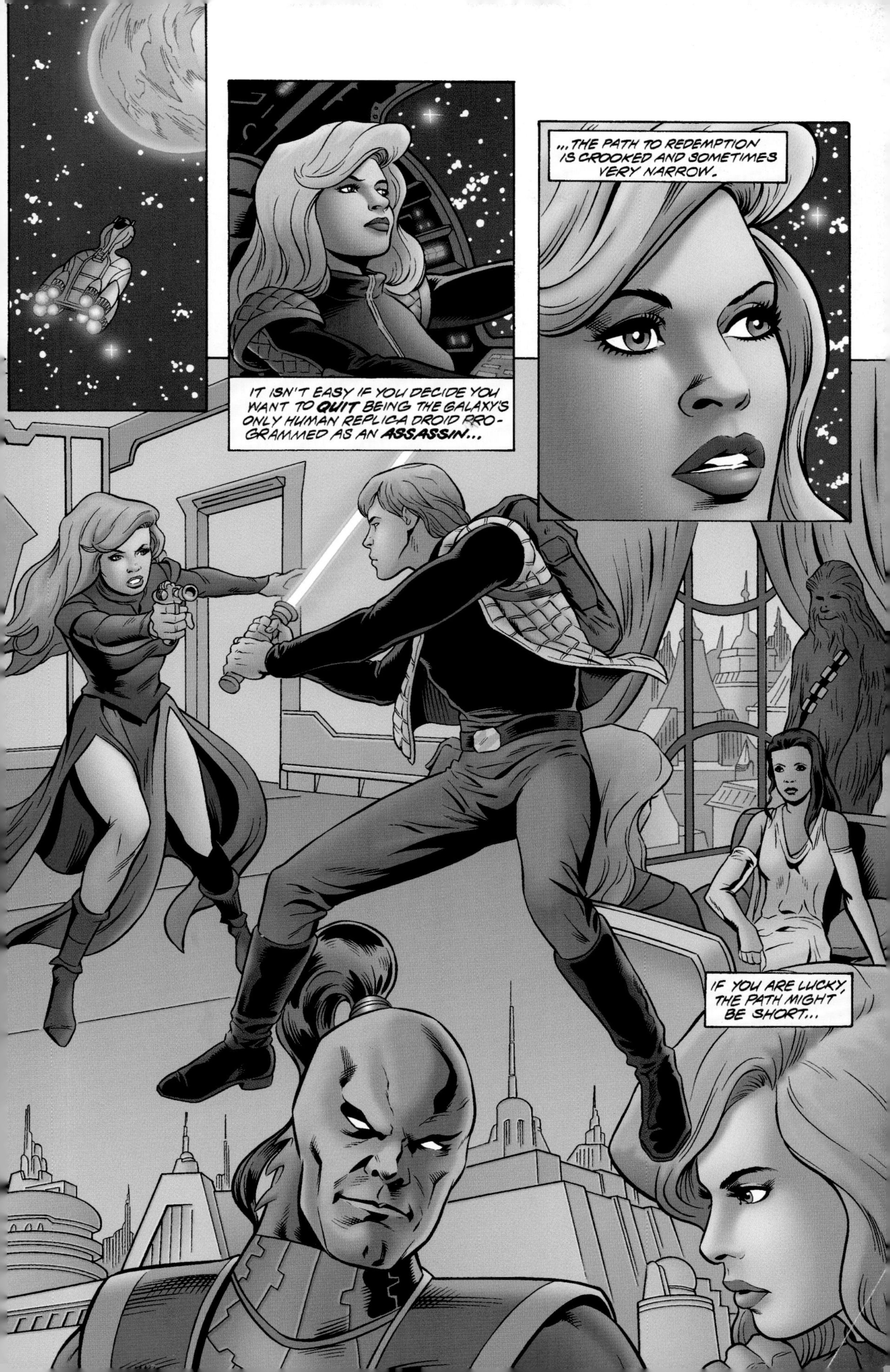
IT ISN'T EASY IF YOU DECIDE YOU WANT TO QUIT BEING THE GALAXY'S ONLY HUMAN REPLICA DROID PRO-GRAMMED AS AN ASSASSIN...
...THE PATH TO REDEMPTION IS CROOKED AND SOMETIMES VERY NARROW.
IF YOU ARE LUCKY, THE PATH MIGHT BE SHORT...

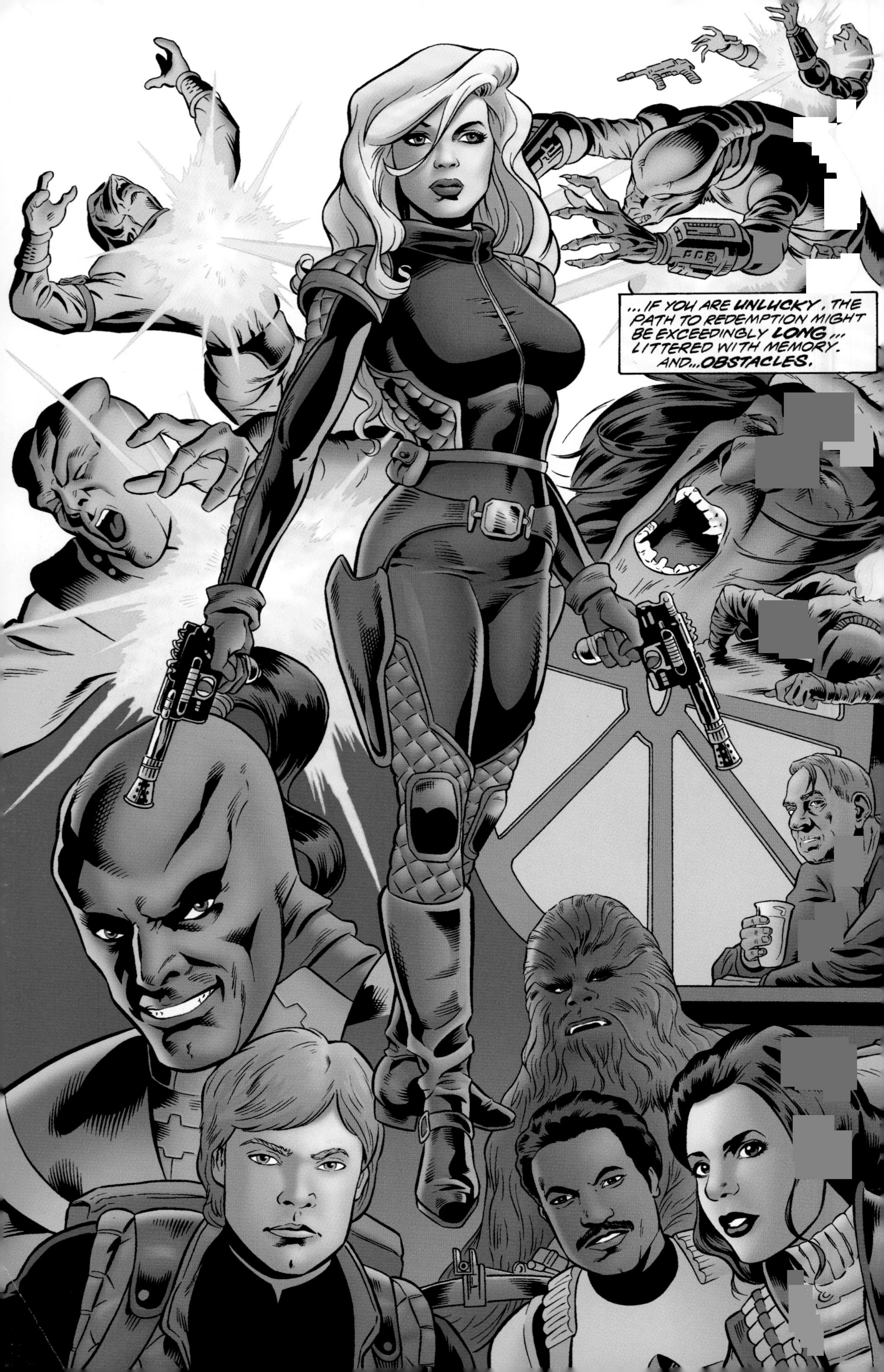
...IF YOU ARE UNLUCKY, THE PATH TO REDEMPTION MIGHT BE EXCEEDINGLY LONG... LITTERED WITH MEMORY. AND...OBSTACLES.

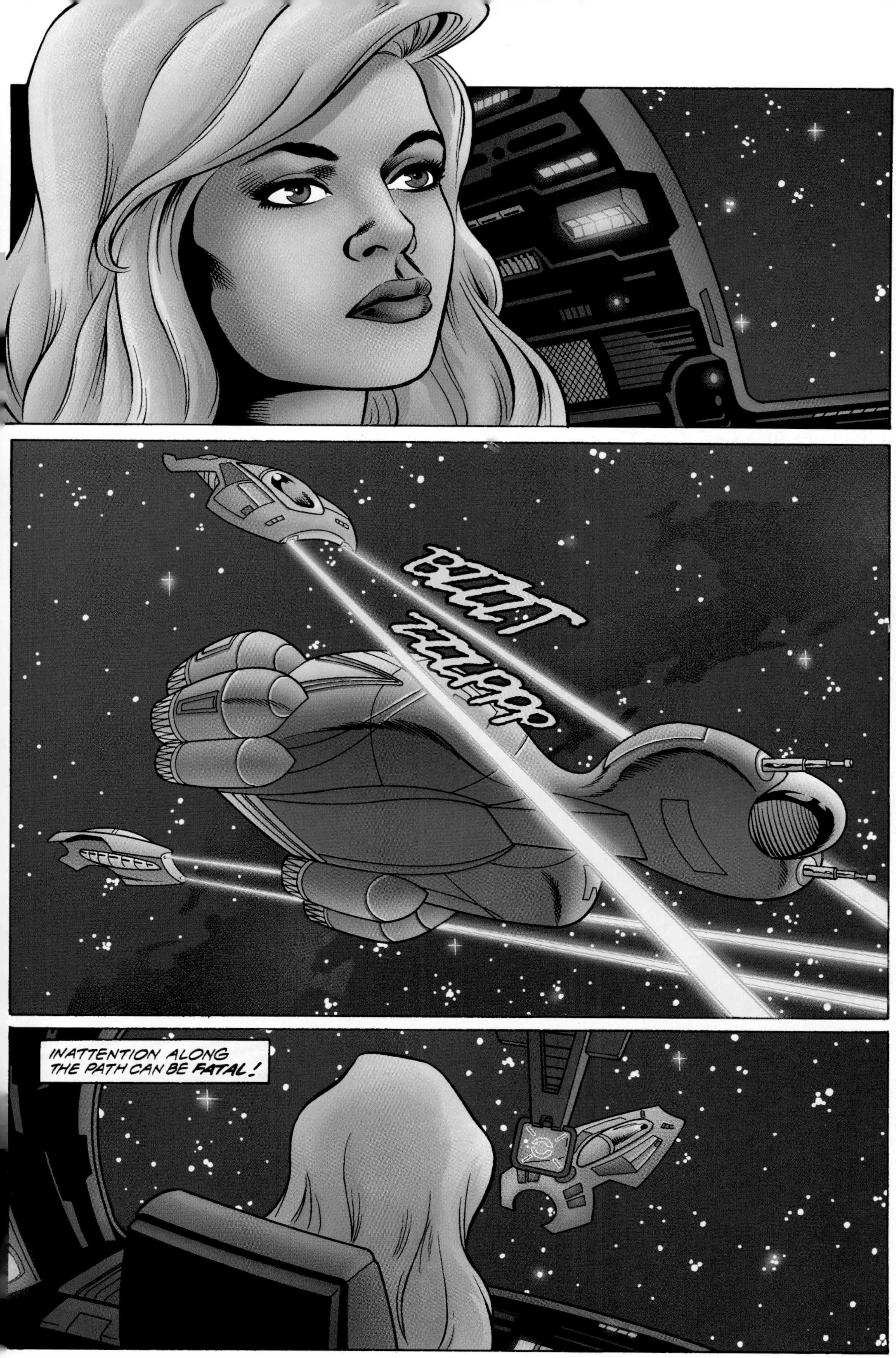
INATTENTION ALONG THE PATH CAN BE FATAL!

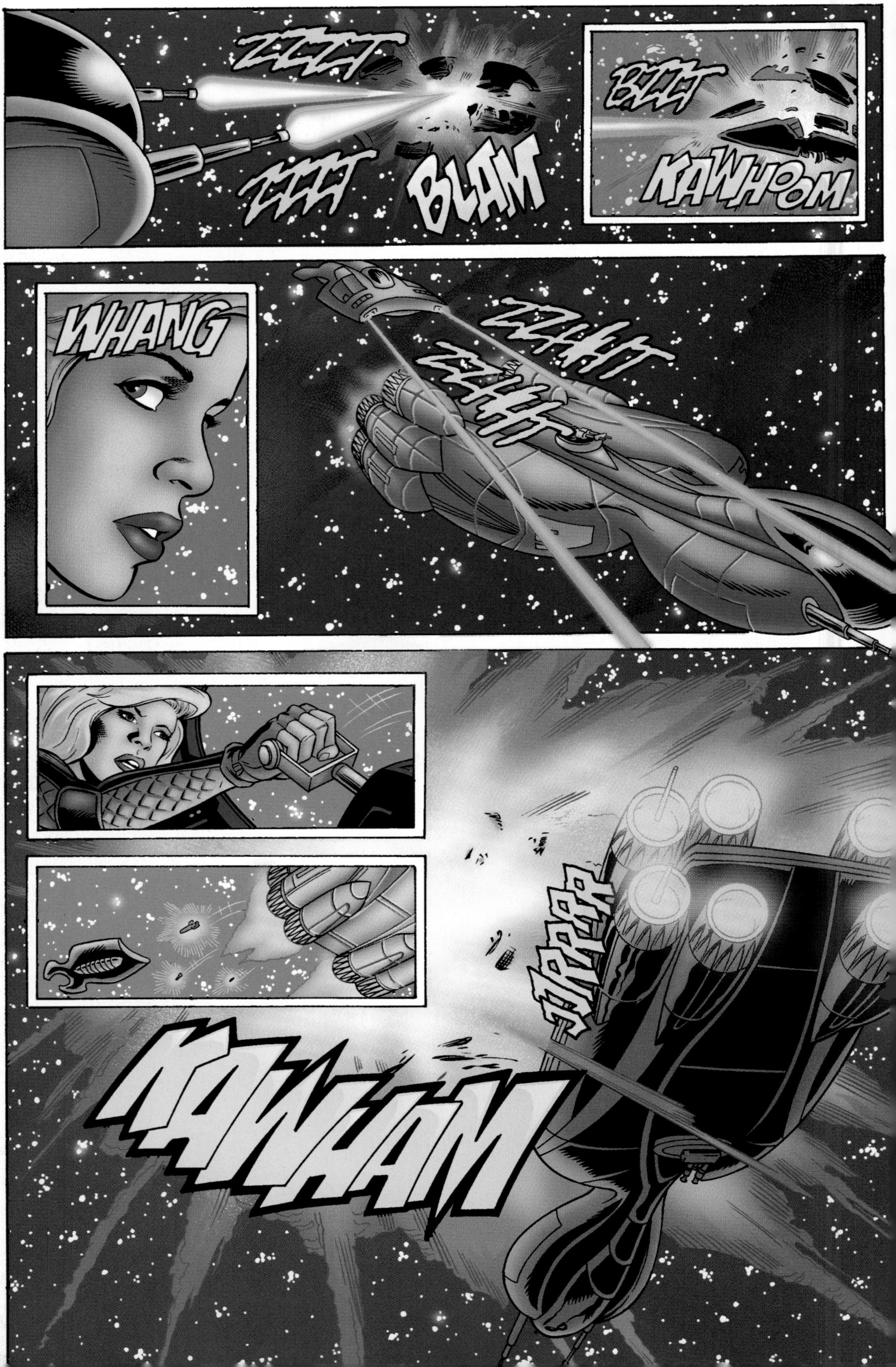
ZZZZT
ZZZT
BLAM
BZZZT
KAWHOOM
WHANG
ZZHHT
ZZHHT
BRRRR
KAWHAM

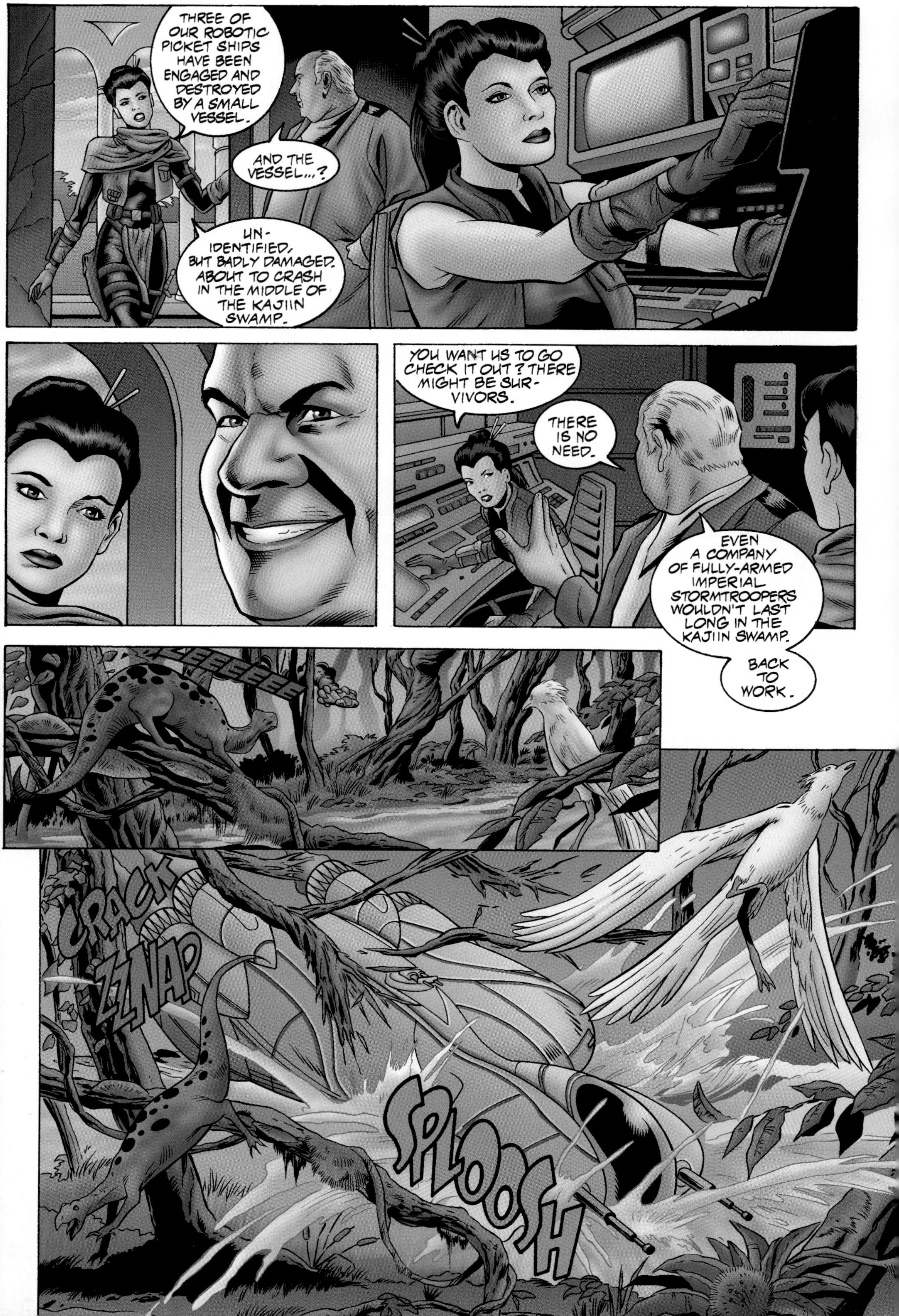
THREE OF OUR ROBOTIC PICKET SHIPS HAVE BEEN ENGAGED AND DESTROYED BY A SMALL VESSEL.
AND THE VESSEL...?
UN-IDENTIFIED, BUT BADLY DAMAGED. ABOUT TO CRASH IN THE MIDDLE OF THE KAJIIN SWAMP.
YOU WANT US TO GO CHECK IT OUT? THERE MIGHT BE SUR-VIVORS.
THERE IS NO NEED.
EVEN A COMPANY OF FULLY-ARMED IMPERIAL STORMTROOPERS WOULDN'T LAST LONG IN THE KAJIIN SWAMP.
BACK TO WORK.
CRACK
ZZNAP
SPLOOSH

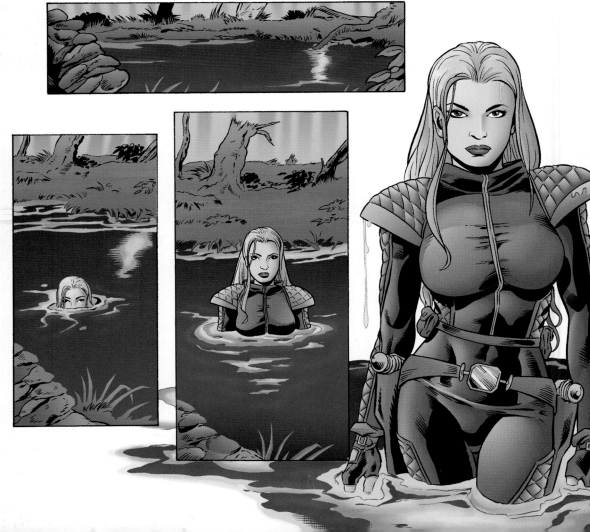

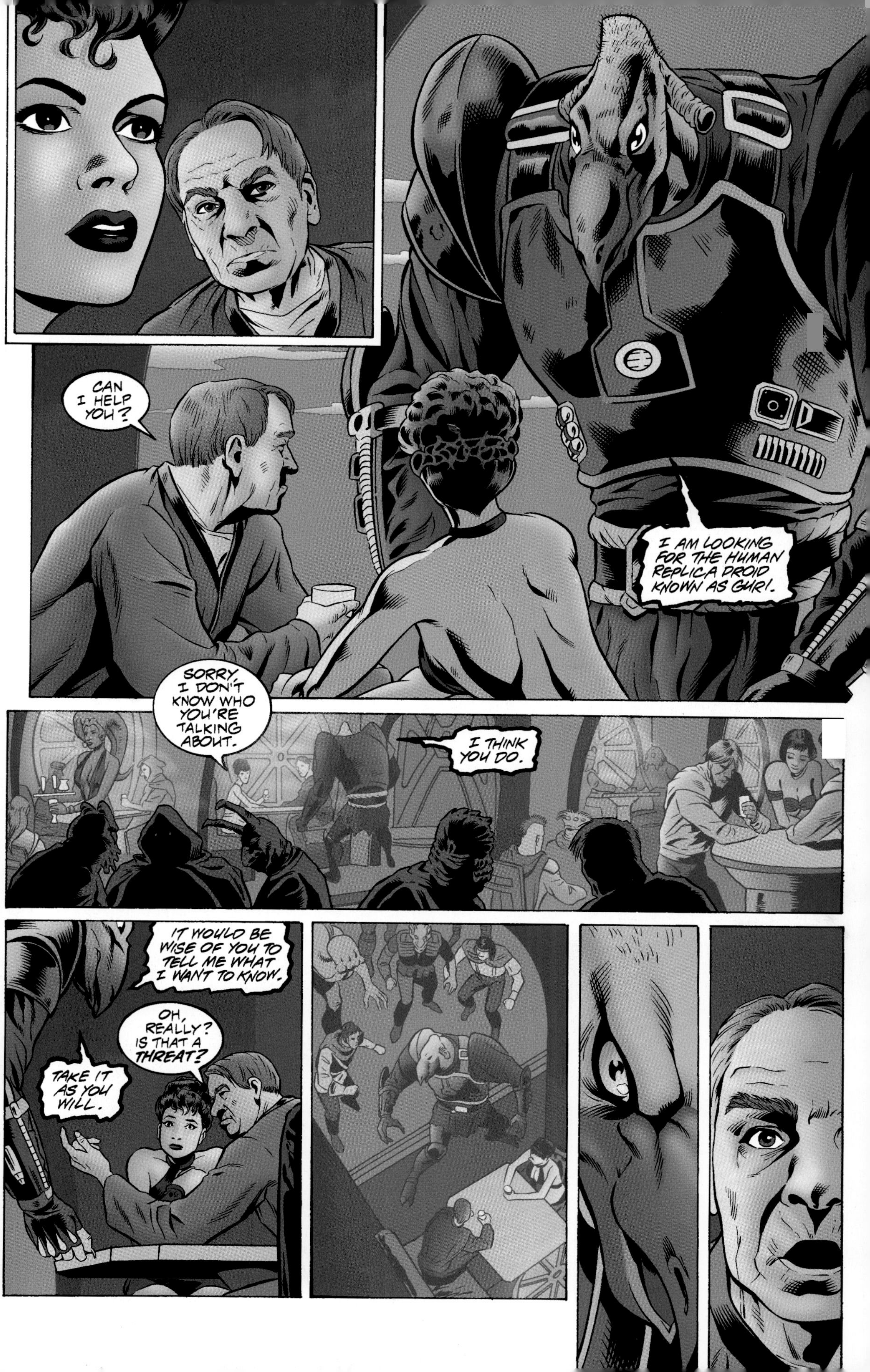
CAN I HELP YOU?
I AM LOOKING FOR THE HUMAN REPLICA DROID KNOWN AS GURI.
SORRY, I DON'T KNOW WHO YOU'RE TALKING ABOUT.
I THINK YOU DO.
IT WOULD BE WISE OF YOU TO TELL ME WHAT I WANT TO KNOW.
OH, REALLY? IS THAT A THREAT?
TAKE IT AS YOU WILL.

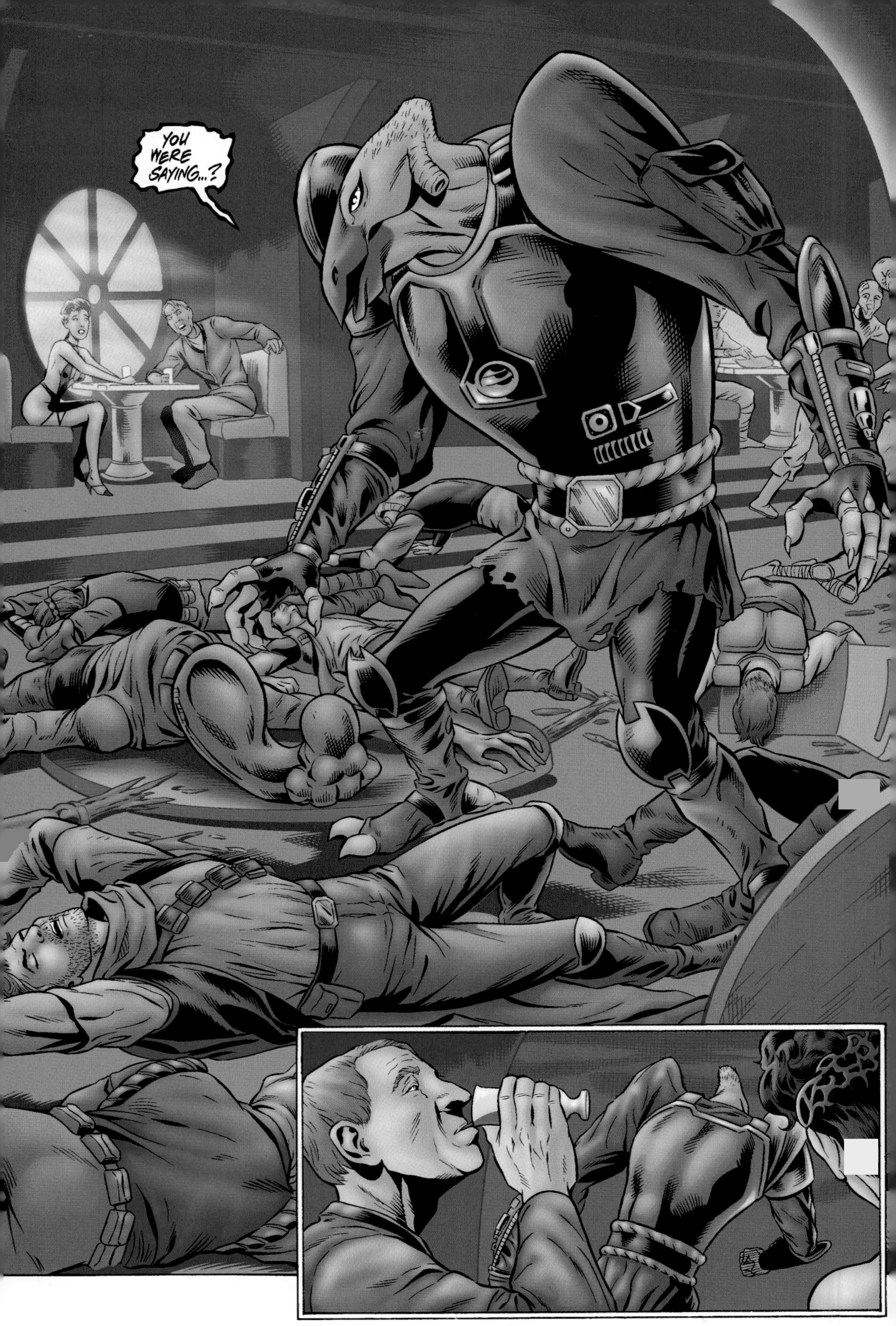
YOU WERE SAYING...?

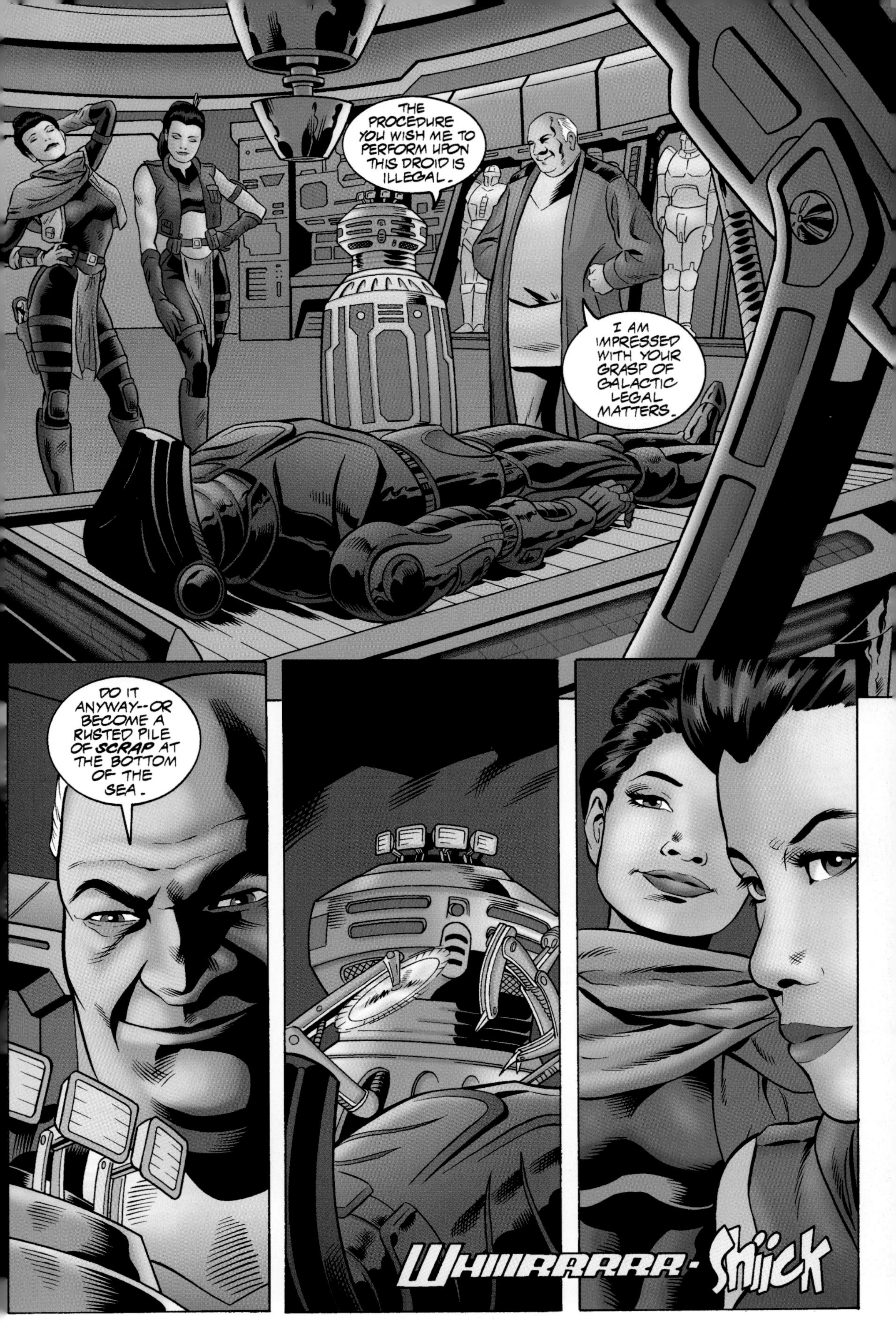
THE PROCEDURE YOU WISH ME TO PERFORM UPON THIS DROID IS ILLEGAL.
I AM IMPRESSED WITH YOUR GRASP OF GALACTIC LEGAL MATTERS.
DO IT ANYWAY--OR BECOME A RUSTED PILE OF SCRAP AT THE BOTTOM OF THE SEA.
WHIIIRRRRRR-SHIICK

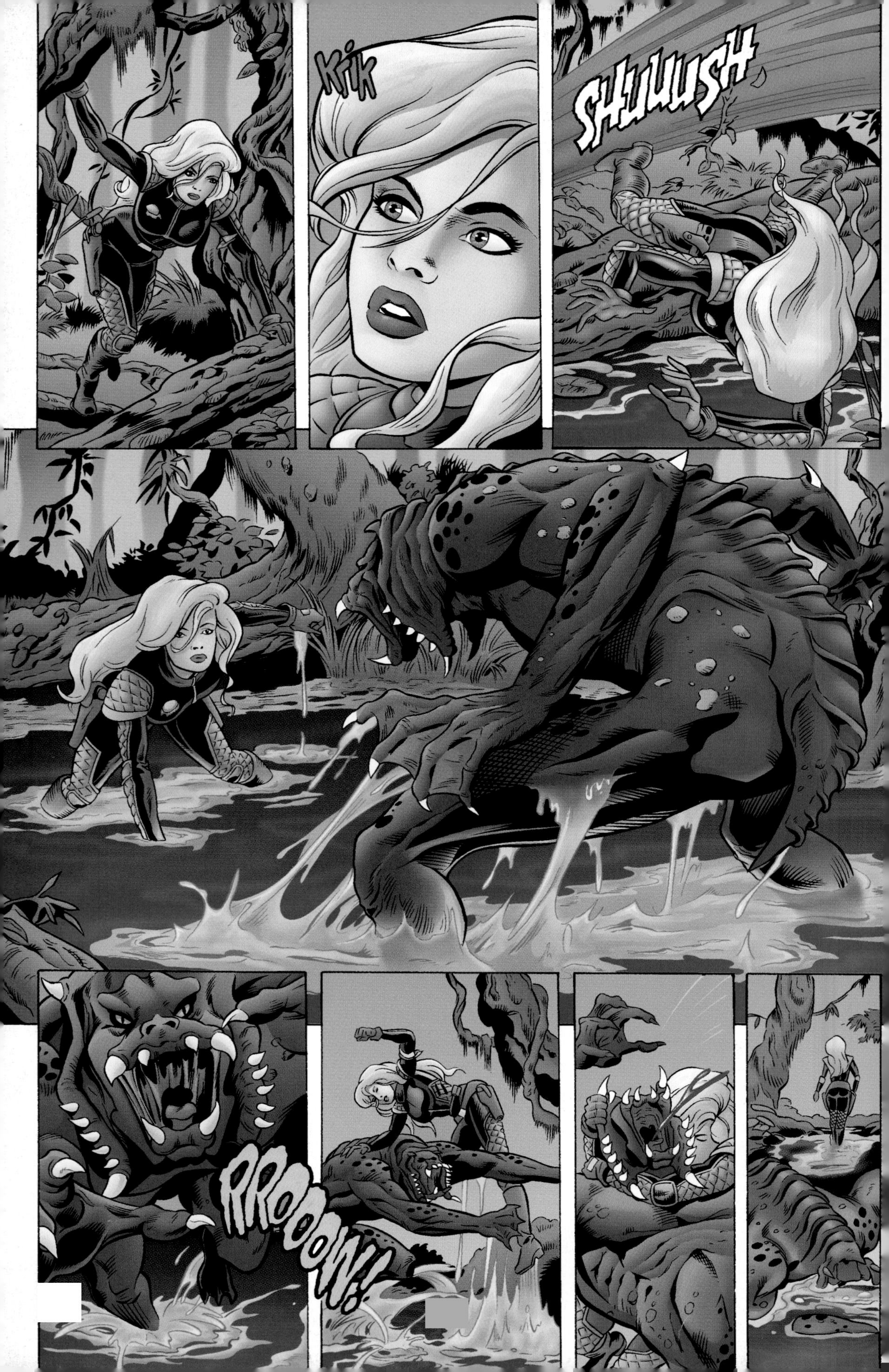
KRIK
SHUUUSH
RROOOOW!!

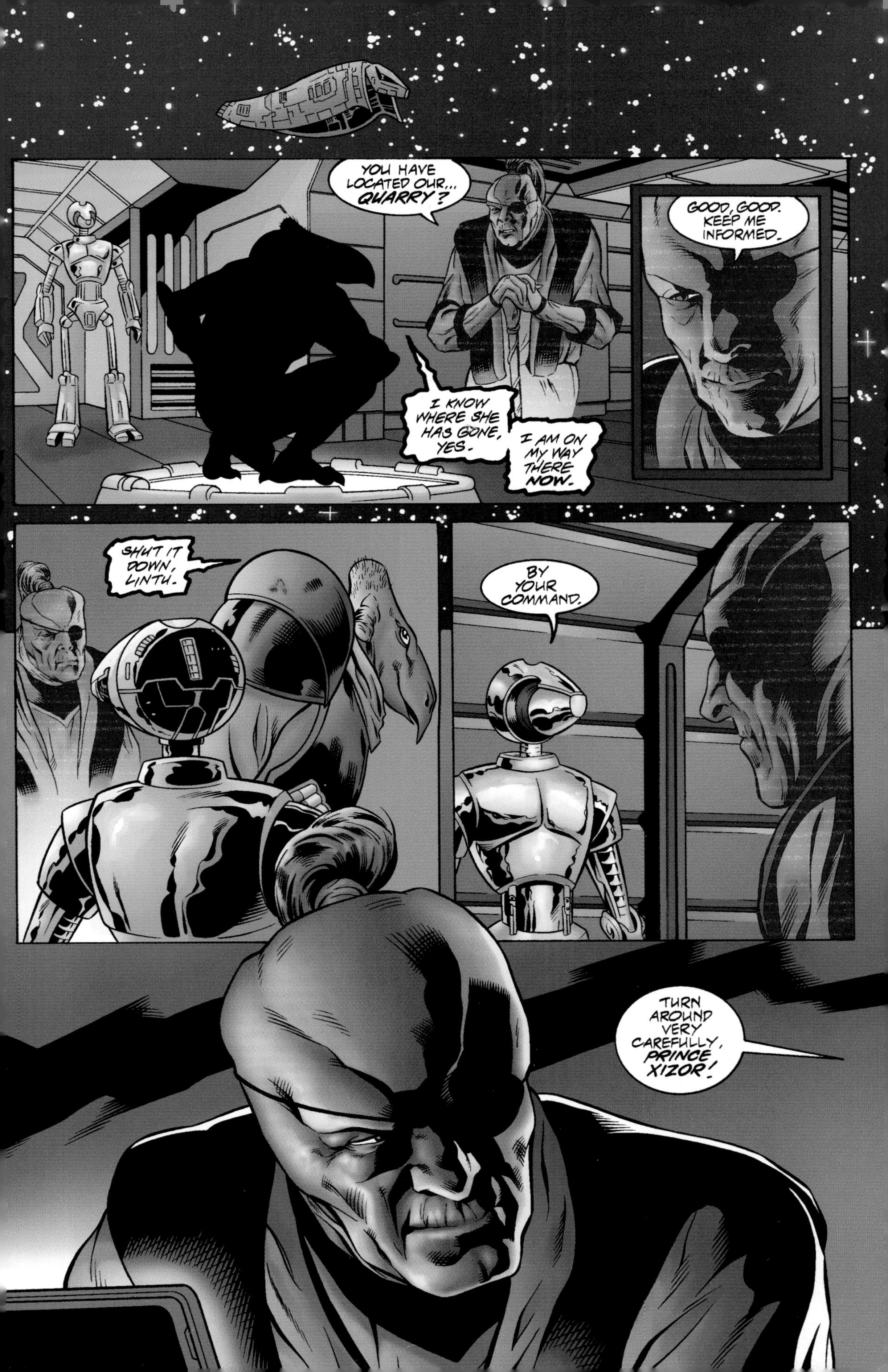
YOU HAVE LOCATED OUR... QUARRY?
I KNOW WHERE SHE HAS GONE, YES.
I AM ON MY WAY THERE NOW.
GOOD, GOOD. KEEP ME INFORMED.
SHUT IT DOWN, LINTU.
BY YOUR COMMAND.
TURN AROUND VERY CAREFULLY, PRINCE XIZOR!

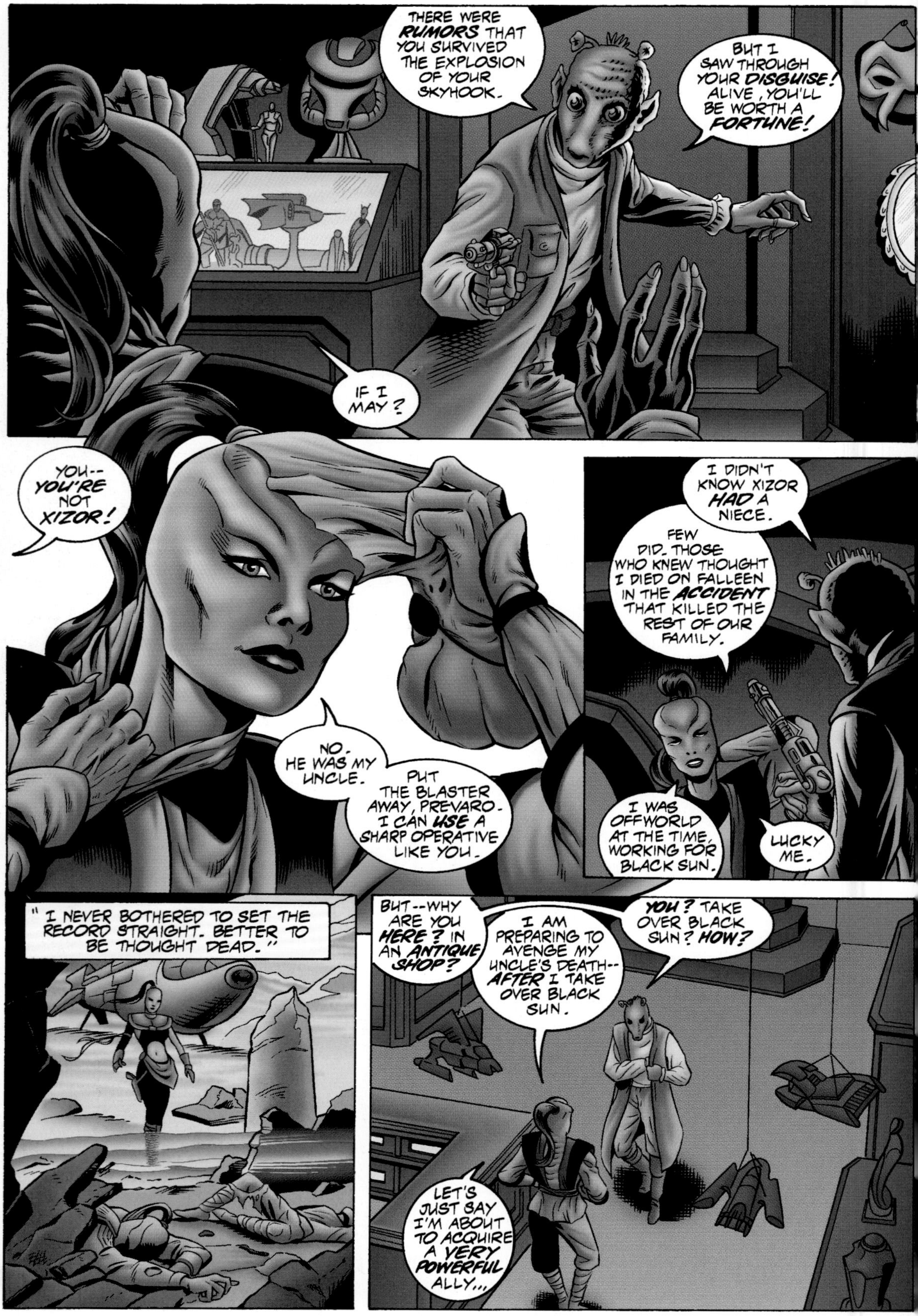
THERE WERE RUMORS THAT YOU SURVIVED THE EXPLOSION OF YOUR SKYHOOK.
BUT I SAW THROUGH YOUR DISGUISE! ALIVE, YOU'LL BE WORTH A FORTUNE!
IF I MAY?
YOU-- YOU'RE NOT XIZOR!
NO. HE WAS MY UNCLE.
PUT THE BLASTER AWAY, PREVARO. I CAN USE A SHARP OPERATIVE LIKE YOU.
I DIDN'T KNOW XIZOR HAD A NIECE.
FEW DID. THOSE WHO KNEW THOUGHT I DIED ON FALLEEN IN THE ACCIDENT THAT KILLED THE REST OF OUR FAMILY.
I WAS OFFWORLD AT THE TIME, WORKING FOR BLACK SUN.
LUCKY ME.
"I NEVER BOTHERED TO SET THE RECORD STRAIGHT. BETTER TO BE THOUGHT DEAD."
BUT--WHY ARE YOU HERE? IN AN ANTIQUE SHOP?
I AM PREPARING TO AVENGE MY UNCLE'S DEATH-- AFTER I TAKE OVER BLACK SUN.
YOU? TAKE OVER BLACK SUN? HOW?
LET'S JUST SAY I'M ABOUT TO ACQUIRE A VERY POWERFUL ALLY...

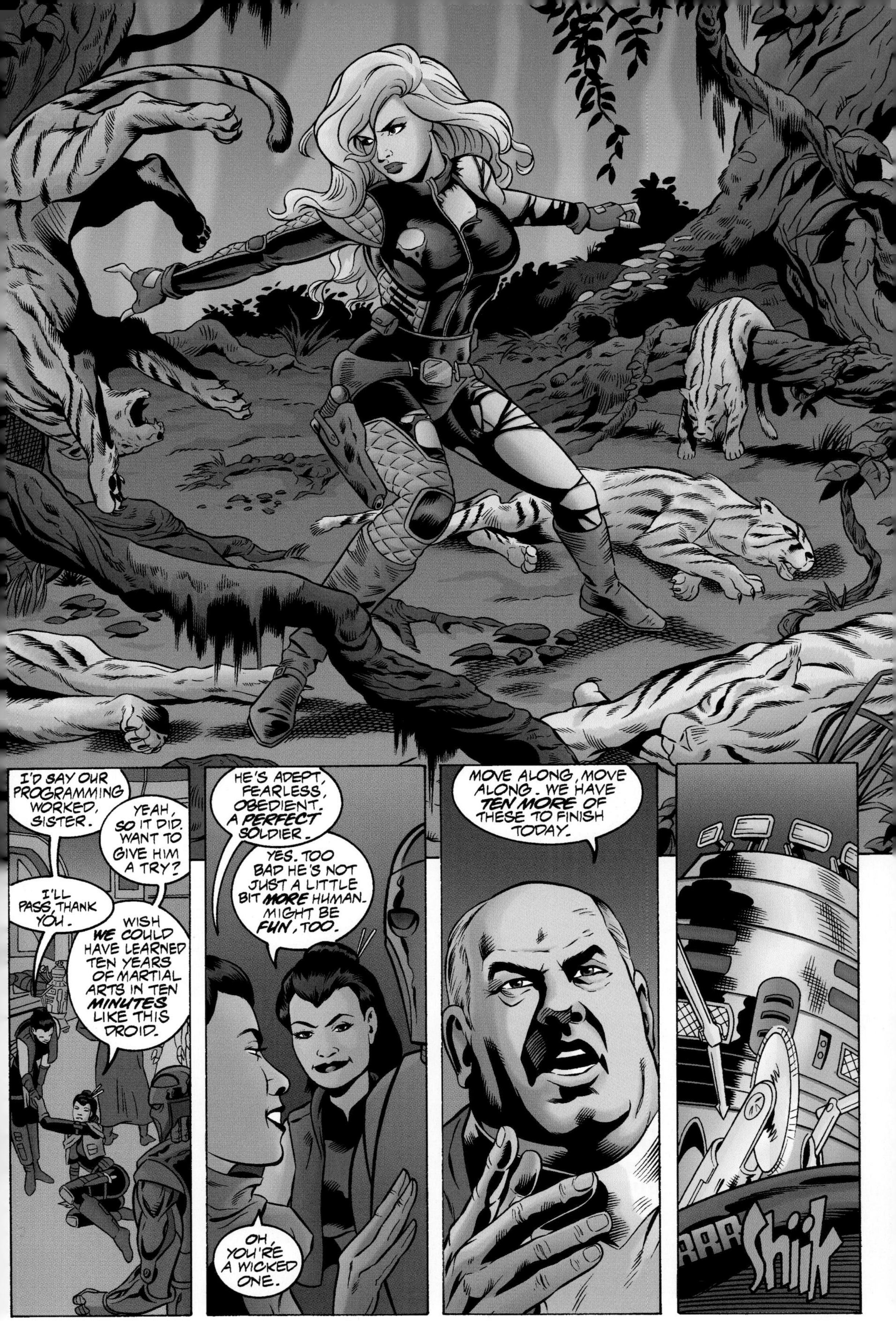
I'D SAY OUR PROGRAMMING WORKED, SISTER.
YEAH, SO IT DID. WANT TO GIVE HIM A TRY?
I'LL PASS, THANK YOU.
WISH WE COULD HAVE LEARNED TEN YEARS OF MARTIAL ARTS IN TEN MINUTES LIKE THIS DROID.
HE'S ADEPT, FEARLESS, OBEDIENT. A PERFECT SOLDIER.
YES. TOO BAD HE'S NOT JUST A LITTLE BIT MORE HUMAN. MIGHT BE FUN, TOO.
OH, YOU'RE A WICKED ONE.
MOVE ALONG, MOVE ALONG. WE HAVE TEN MORE OF THESE TO FINISH TODAY.
RRRR SHIIK

BZZT

BZZT

ZZWP

LOCK ON TARGETS.

LOCK CONFIRMED.

FIRE!

ZZZTT

SSZZTT

ZZWIP

KABLAM

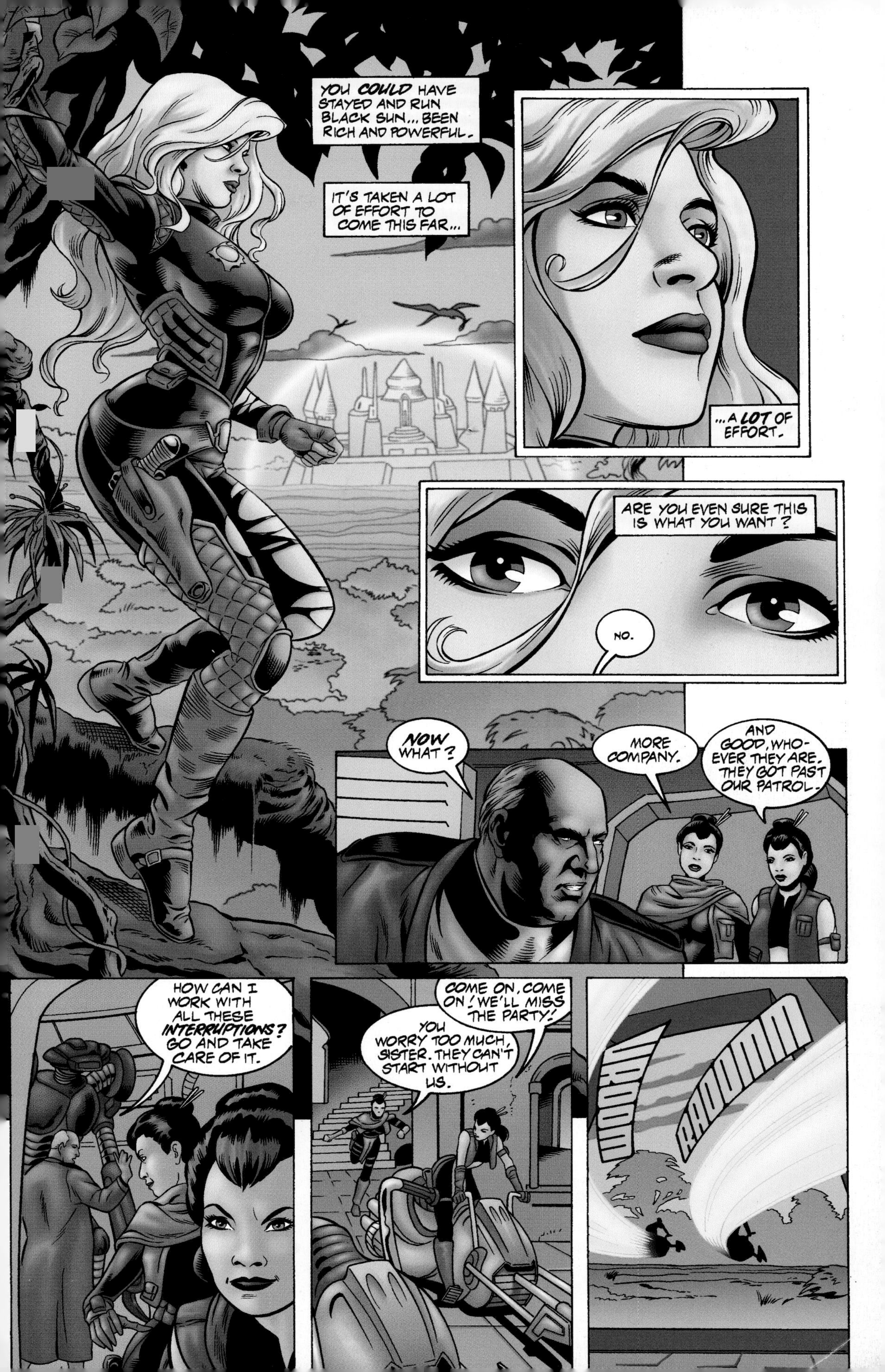
YOU COULD HAVE STAYED AND RUN BLACK SUN... BEEN RICH AND POWERFUL.
IT'S TAKEN A LOT OF EFFORT TO COME THIS FAR...
...A LOT OF EFFORT.
ARE YOU EVEN SURE THIS IS WHAT YOU WANT?
NO.
NOW WHAT?
MORE COMPANY.
AND GOOD, WHO-EVER THEY ARE. THEY GOT PAST OUR PATROL.
HOW CAN I WORK WITH ALL THESE INTERRUPTIONS? GO AND TAKE CARE OF IT.
COME ON, COME ON! WE'LL MISS THE PARTY!
YOU WORRY TOO MUCH, SISTER. THEY CAN'T START WITHOUT US.
VROOM
RRRUMMM

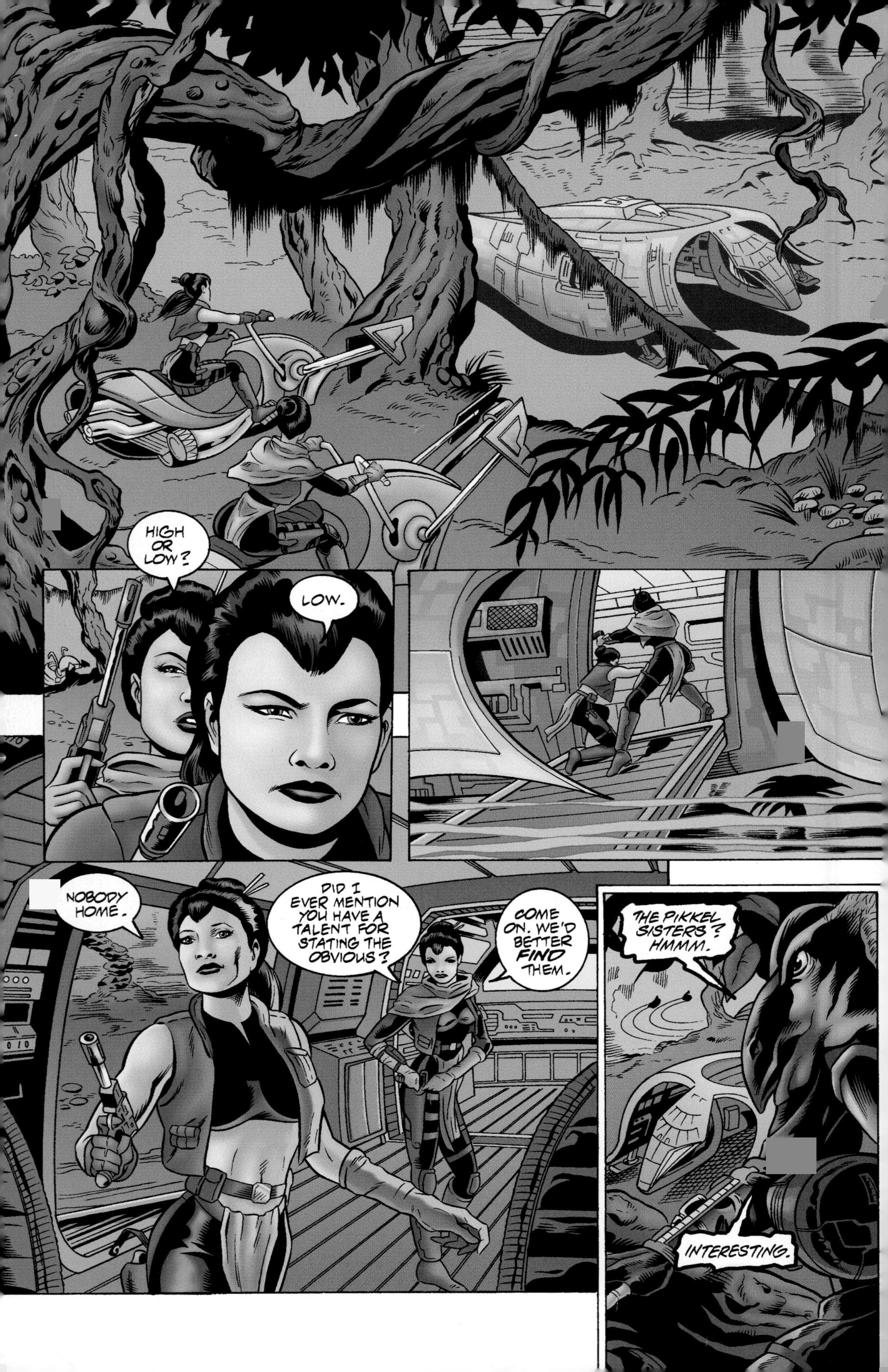
HIGH OR LOW?
LOW.
NOBODY HOME.
DID I EVER MENTION YOU HAVE A TALENT FOR STATING THE OBVIOUS?
COME ON. WE'D BETTER FIND THEM.
THE PIKKEL SISTERS? HMMM.
INTERESTING.

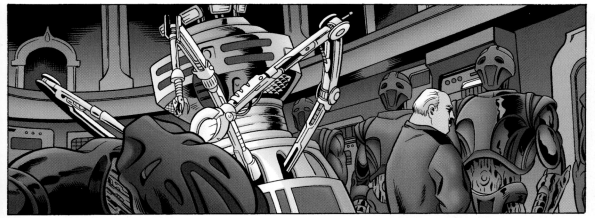

WHAT ARE YOU DOING?

JUST CHECKING THE MAIN SERVO. ALL DONE.

click

"I WONDER WHAT IS TAKING THE SISTERS SO LONG?"

BRUUMM

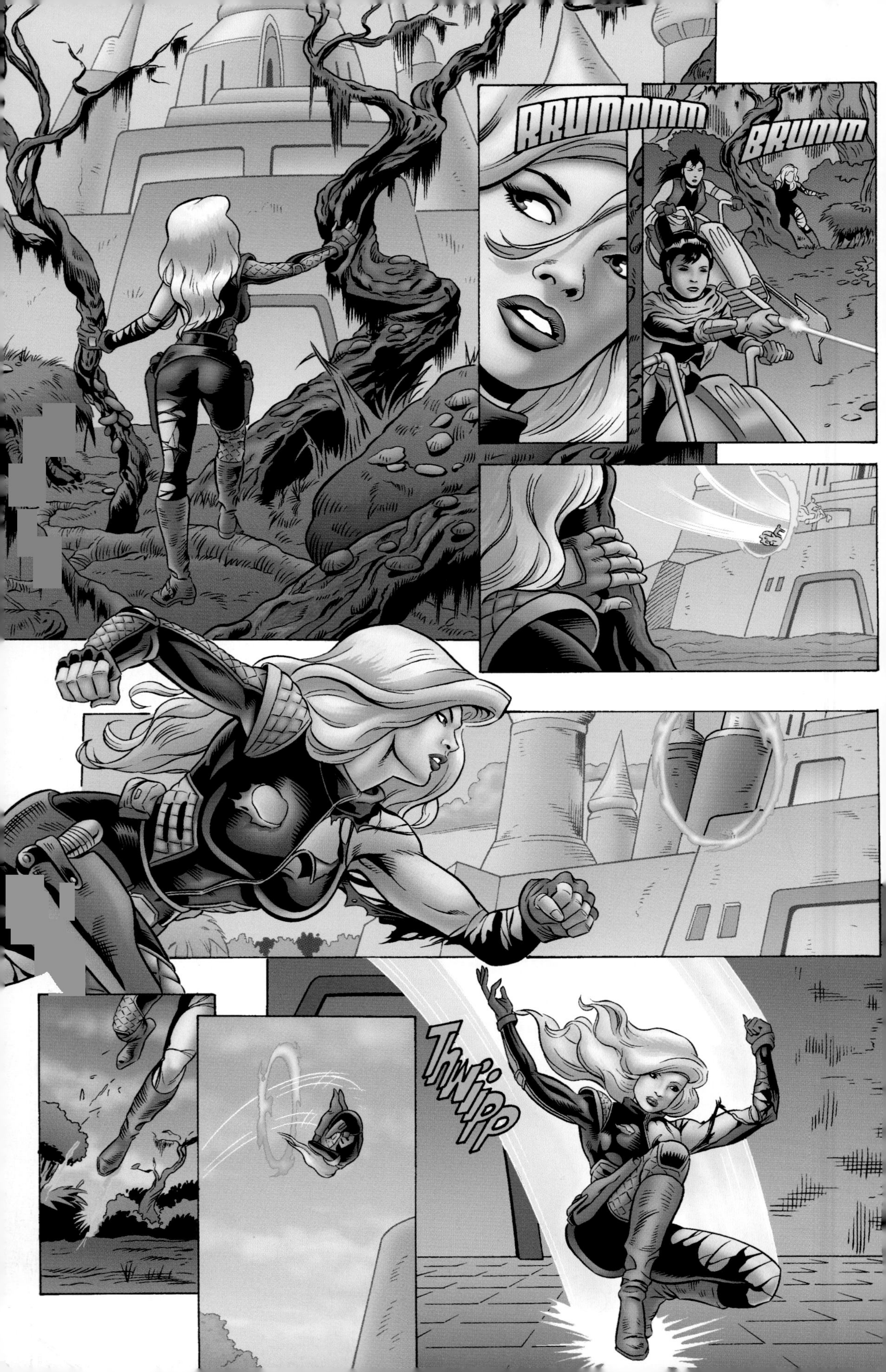
BRUMMMMM
BRUMM
THWIPP

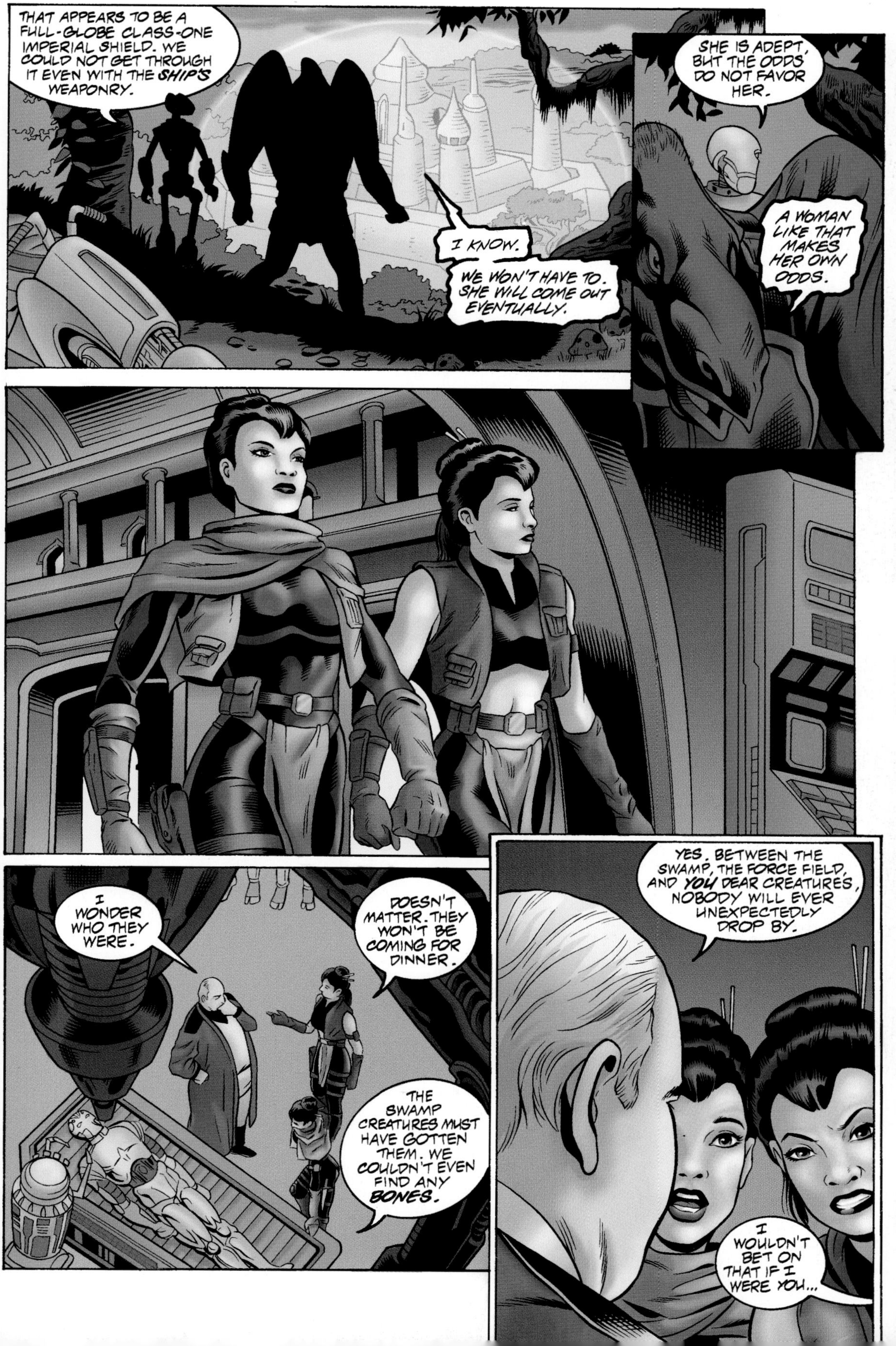
THAT APPEARS TO BE A FULL-GLOBE CLASS-ONE IMPERIAL SHIELD. WE COULD NOT GET THROUGH IT EVEN WITH THE SHIP'S WEAPONRY.
I KNOW.
WE WON'T HAVE TO. SHE WILL COME OUT EVENTUALLY.
SHE IS ADEPT, BUT THE ODDS DO NOT FAVOR HER.
A WOMAN LIKE THAT MAKES HER OWN ODDS.
I WONDER WHO THEY WERE.
DOESN'T MATTER. THEY WON'T BE COMING FOR DINNER.
THE SWAMP CREATURES MUST HAVE GOTTEN THEM. WE COULDN'T EVEN FIND ANY BONES.
YES. BETWEEN THE SWAMP, THE FORCE FIELD, AND YOU DEAR CREATURES, NOBODY WILL EVER UNEXPECTEDLY DROP BY.
I WOULDN'T BET ON THAT IF I WERE YOU...

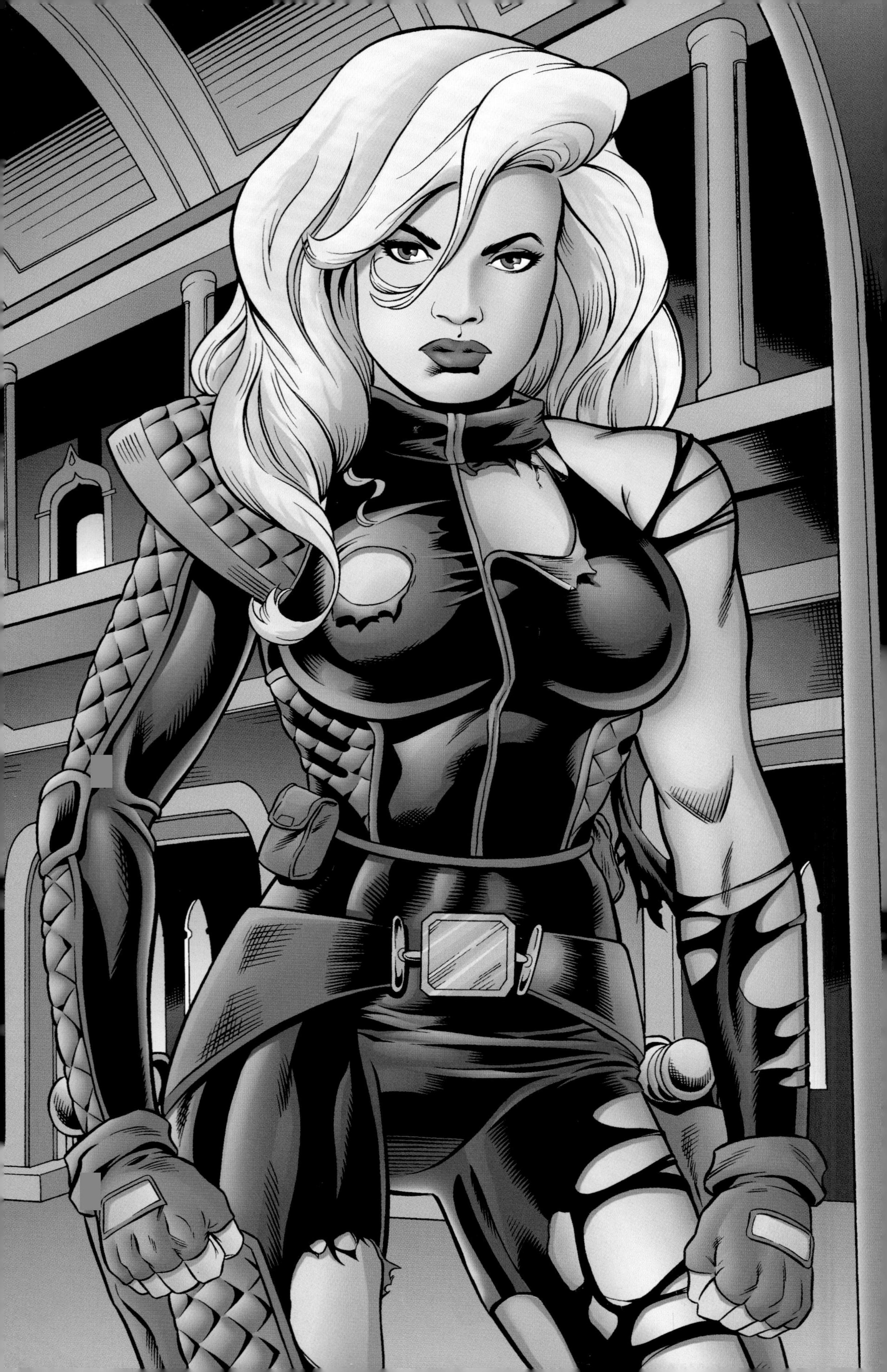

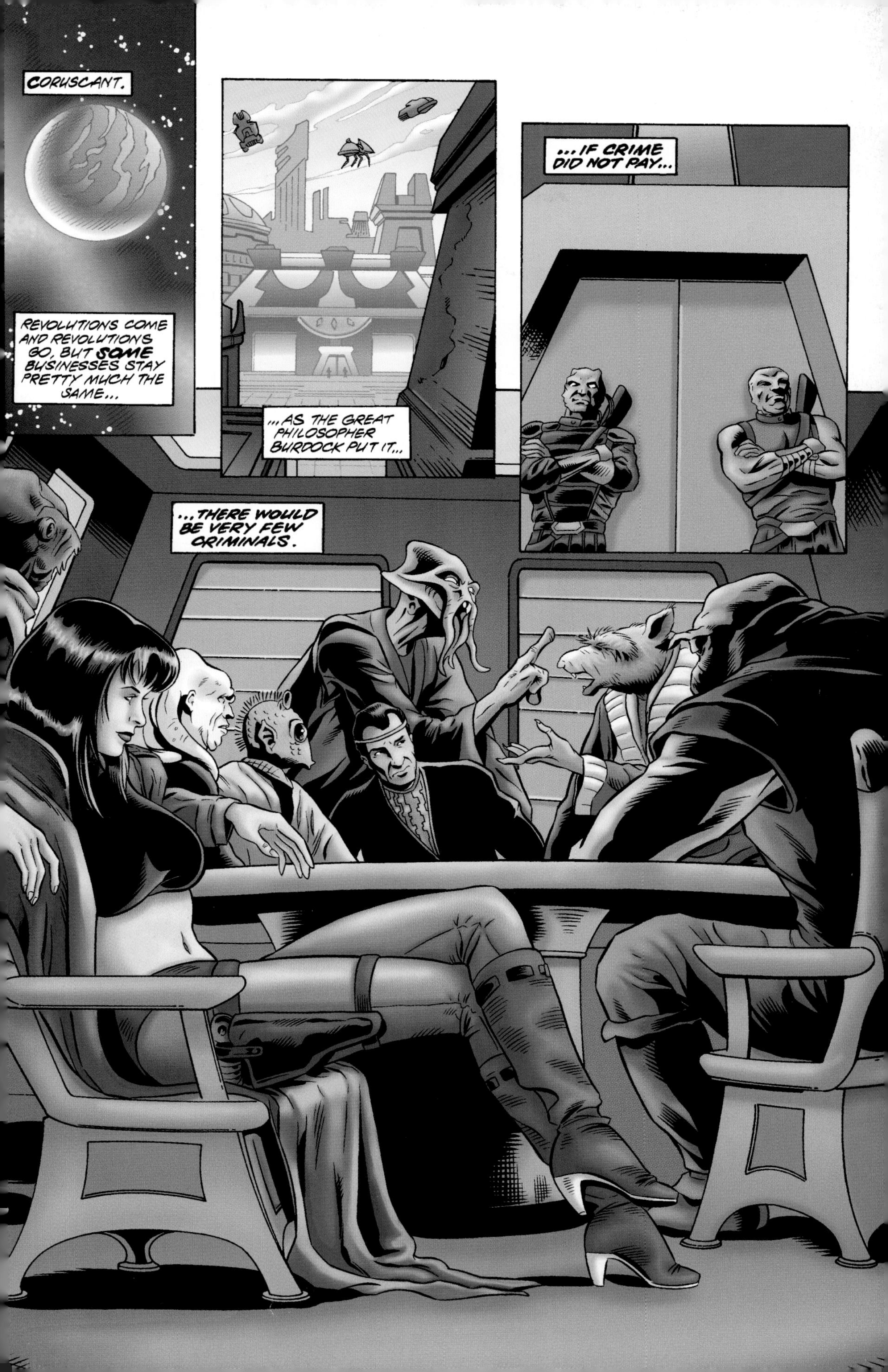
CORUSCANT.
REVOLUTIONS COME AND REVOLUTIONS GO, BUT SOME BUSINESSES STAY PRETTY MUCH THE SAME...
...AS THE GREAT PHILOSOPHER BURDOCK PUT IT...
...IF CRIME DID NOT PAY...
...THERE WOULD BE VERY FEW CRIMINALS.

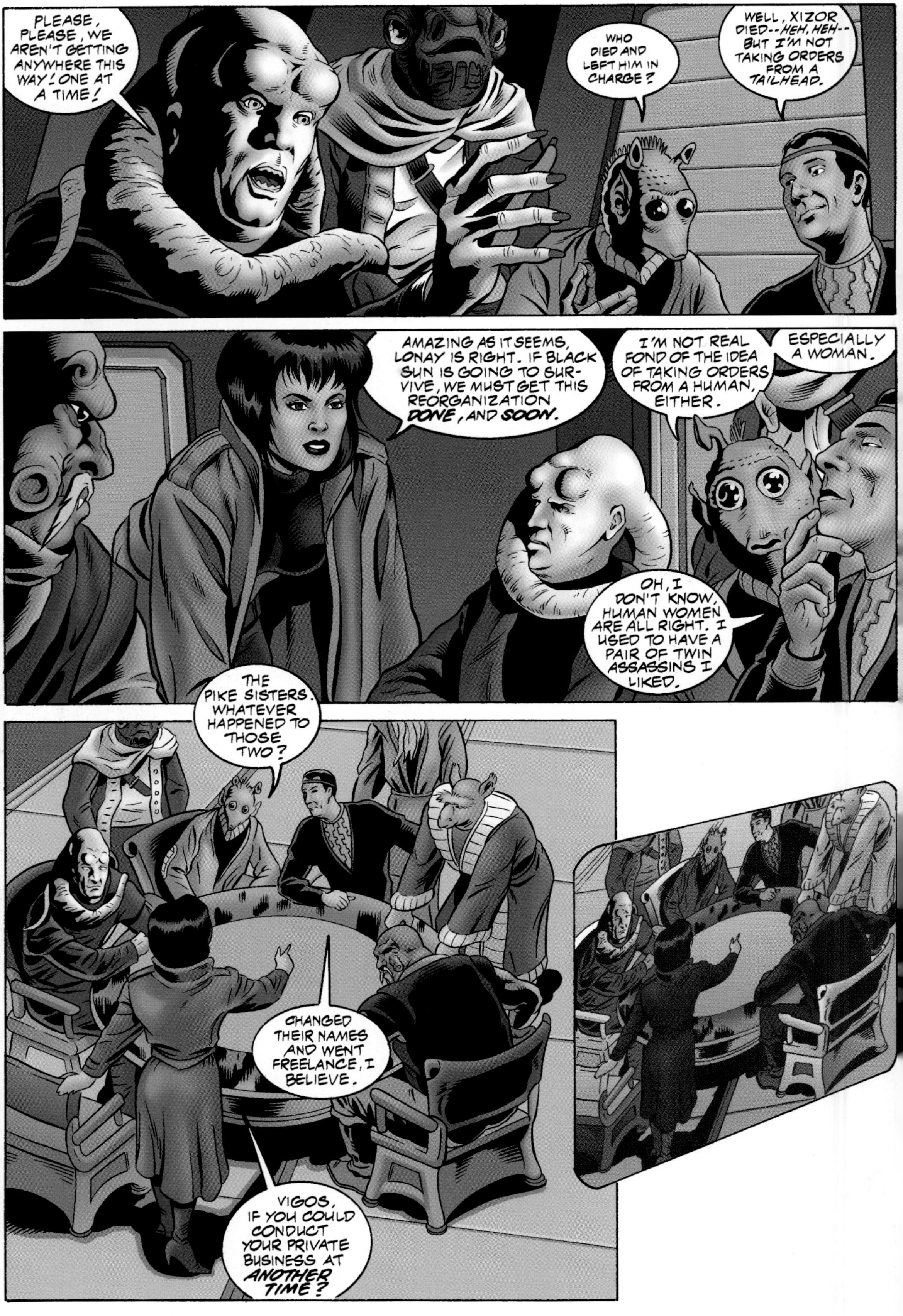
PLEASE, PLEASE, WE AREN'T GETTING ANYWHERE THIS WAY! ONE AT A TIME!
WHO DIED AND LEFT HIM IN CHARGE?
WELL, XIZOR DIED--*HEH, HEH*--BUT I'M NOT TAKING ORDERS FROM A *TAILHEAD*.
AMAZING AS IT SEEMS, LONAY IS RIGHT. IF BLACK SUN IS GOING TO SURVIVE, WE MUST GET THIS REORGANIZATION ***DONE***, AND ***SOON***.
I'M NOT REAL FOND OF THE IDEA OF TAKING ORDERS FROM A HUMAN, EITHER.
ESPECIALLY A WOMAN.
OH, I DON'T KNOW. HUMAN WOMEN ARE ALL RIGHT. I USED TO HAVE A PAIR OF TWIN ASSASSINS I LIKED.
THE PIKE SISTERS. WHATEVER HAPPENED TO THOSE TWO?
CHANGED THEIR NAMES AND WENT FREELANCE, I BELIEVE.
VIGOS, IF YOU COULD CONDUCT YOUR PRIVATE BUSINESS AT ***ANOTHER TIME***?

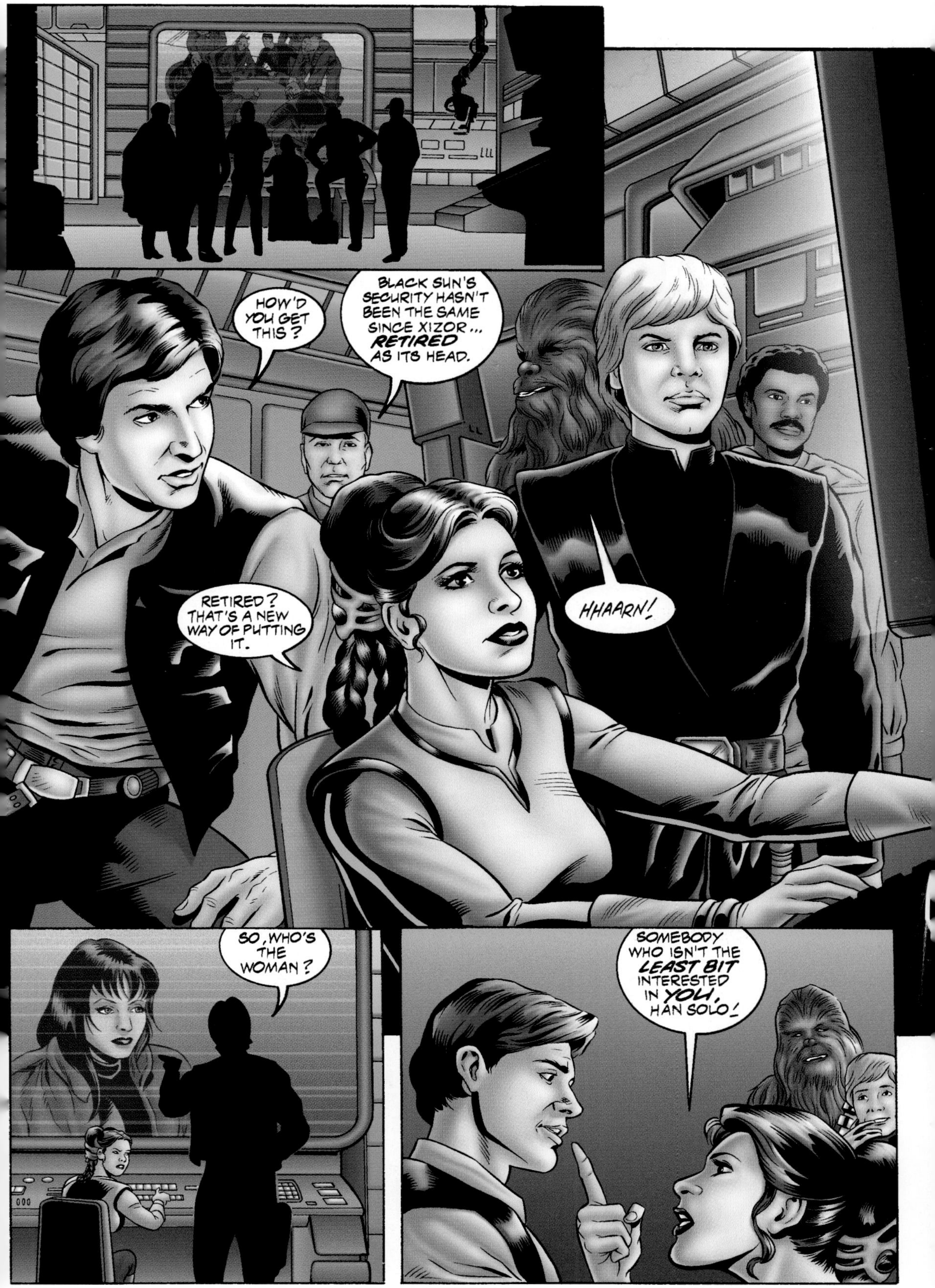
HOW'D YOU GET THIS?
BLACK SUN'S SECURITY HASN'T BEEN THE SAME SINCE XIZOR... RETIRED AS ITS HEAD.
RETIRED? THAT'S A NEW WAY OF PUTTING IT.
HHAARN!
SO, WHO'S THE WOMAN?
SOMEBODY WHO ISN'T THE LEAST BIT INTERESTED IN YOU, HAN SOLO!

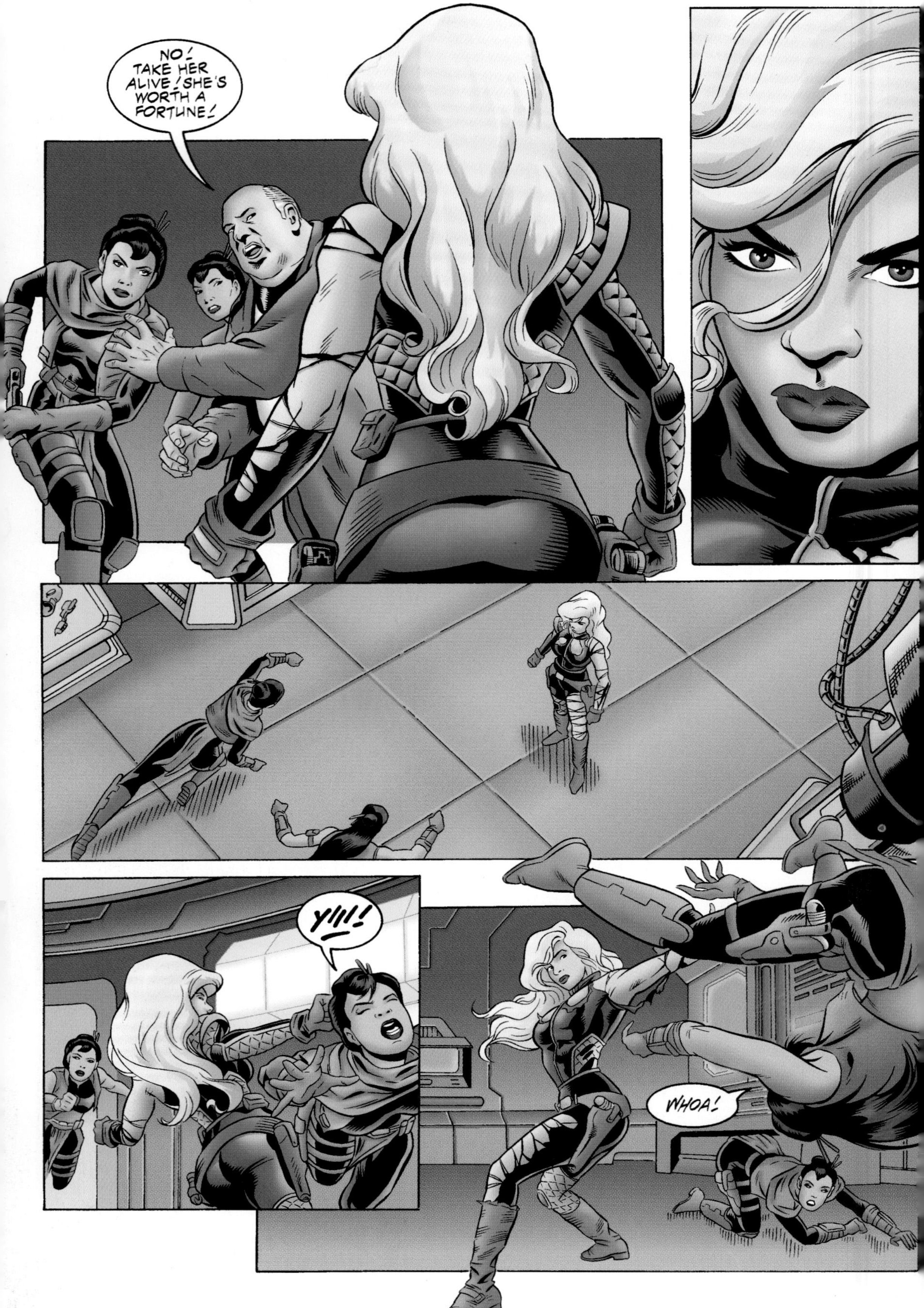
NO! TAKE HER ALIVE! SHE'S WORTH A FORTUNE!
YII!
WHOA!

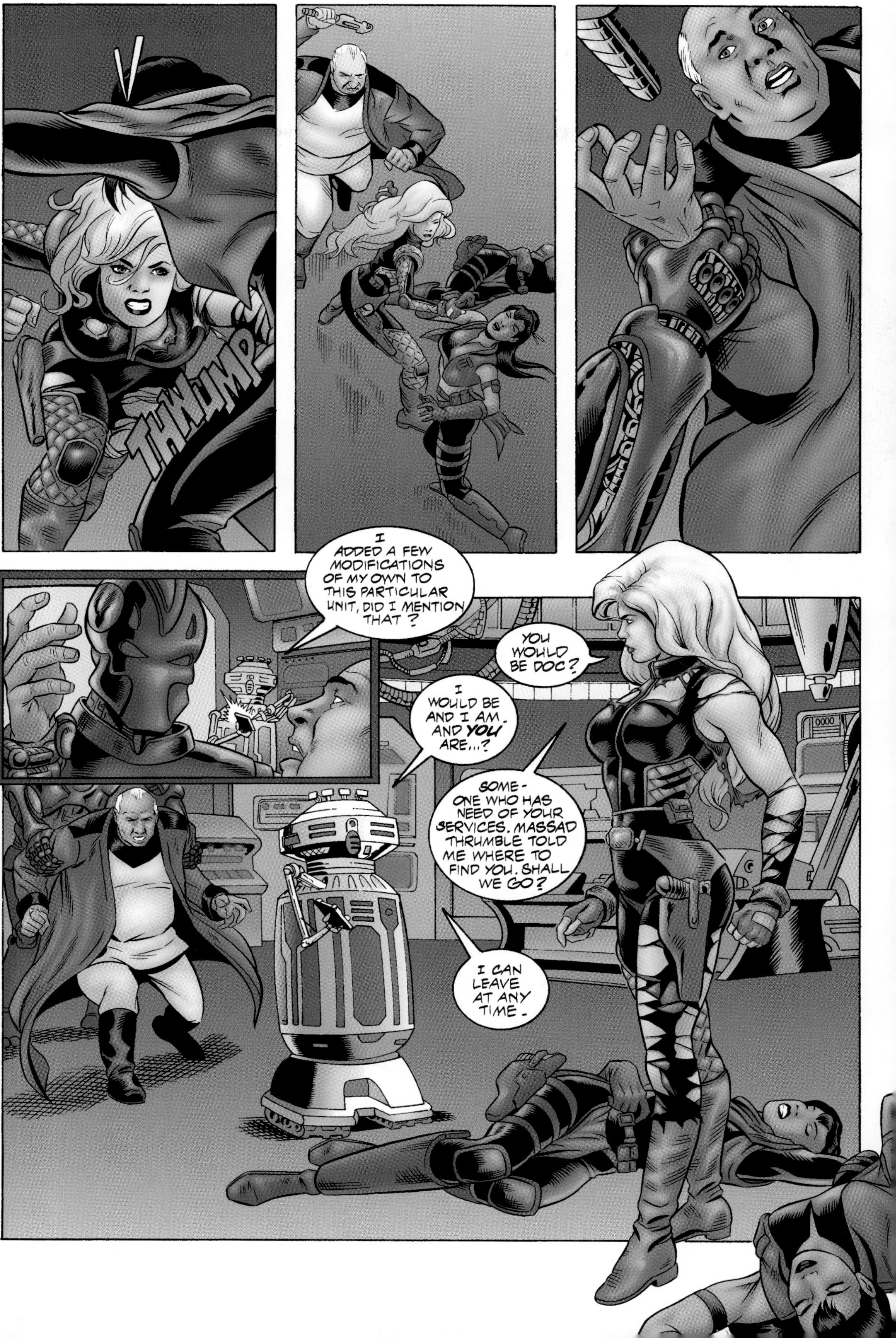
THUMP
I ADDED A FEW MODIFICATIONS OF MY OWN TO THIS PARTICULAR UNIT, DID I MENTION THAT ?
YOU WOULD BE DOC ?
I WOULD BE AND I AM. AND YOU ARE...?
SOME-ONE WHO HAS NEED OF YOUR SERVICES. MASSAD THRUMBLE TOLD ME WHERE TO FIND YOU. SHALL WE GO ?
I CAN LEAVE AT ANY TIME.

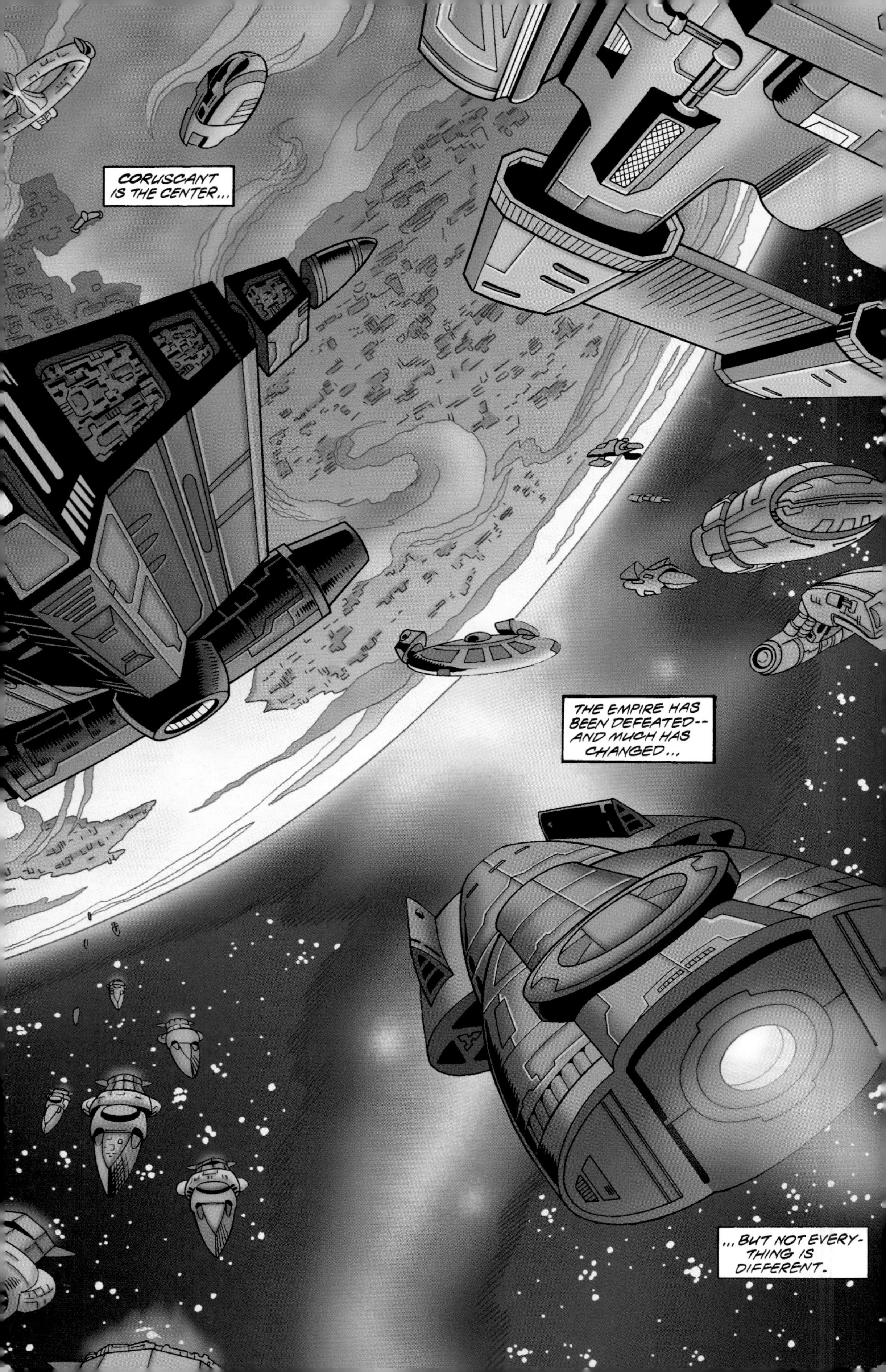
CORUSCANT IS THE CENTER...
THE EMPIRE HAS BEEN DEFEATED--AND MUCH HAS CHANGED...
...BUT NOT EVERY-THING IS DIFFERENT.

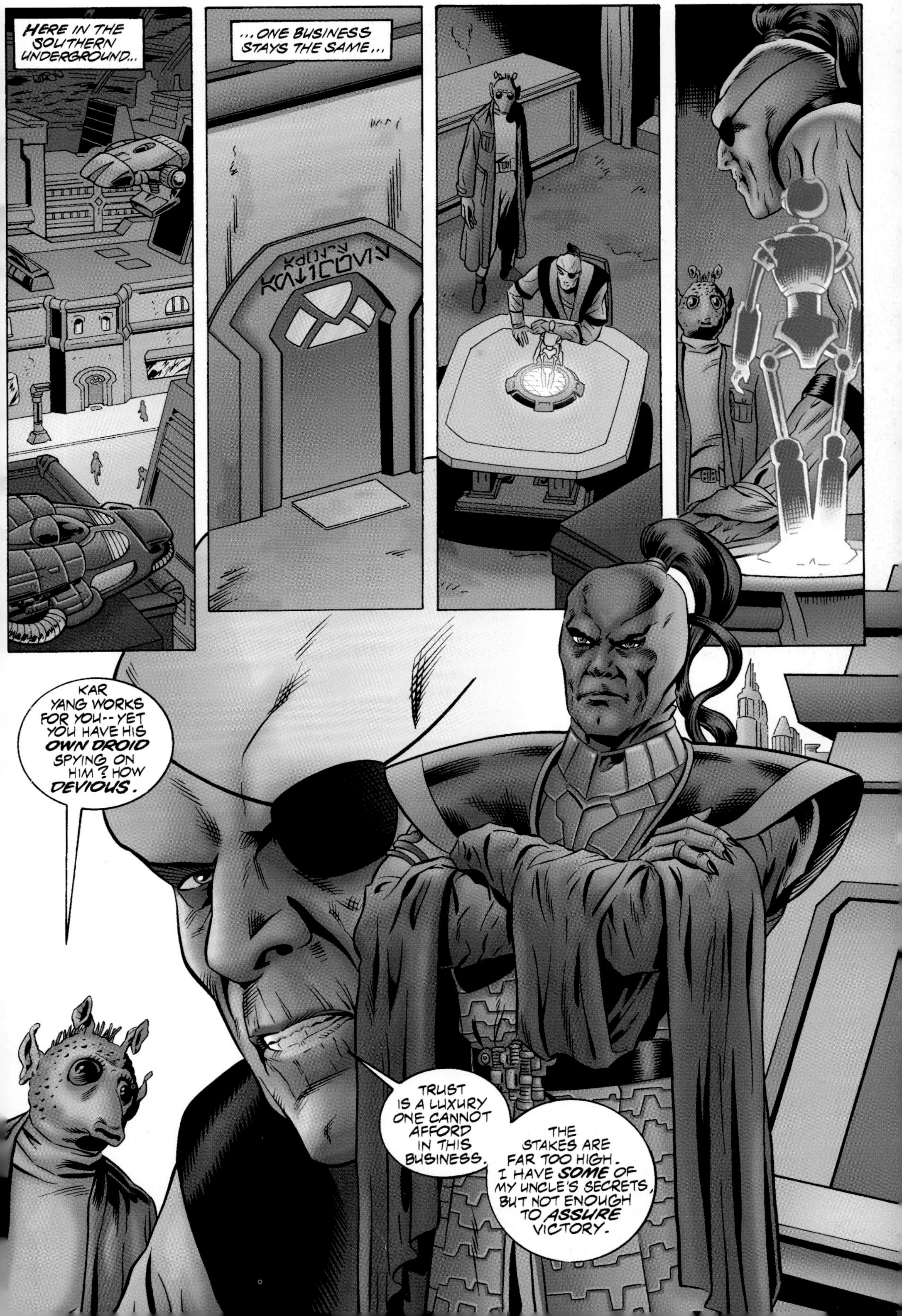
HERE IN THE SOUTHERN UNDERGROUND...
...ONE BUSINESS STAYS THE SAME...
KAR YANG WORKS FOR YOU--YET YOU HAVE HIS OWN DROID SPYING ON HIM? HOW DEVIOUS.
TRUST IS A LUXURY ONE CANNOT AFFORD IN THIS BUSINESS.
THE STAKES ARE FAR TOO HIGH. I HAVE SOME OF MY UNCLE'S SECRETS, BUT NOT ENOUGH TO ASSURE VICTORY.

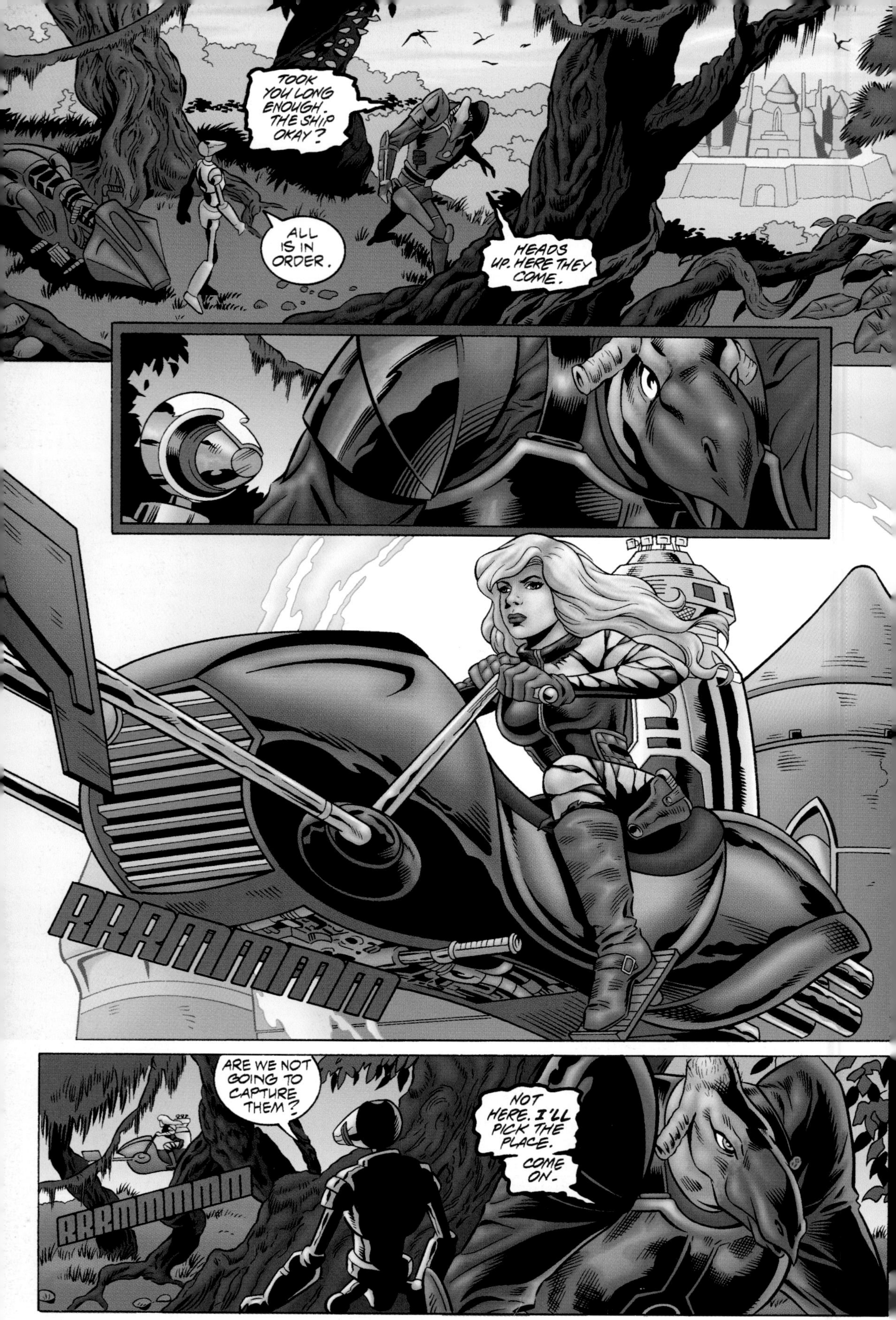
TOOK YOU LONG ENOUGH. THE SHIP OKAY?
ALL IS IN ORDER.
HEADS UP. HERE THEY COME.
RRRMMMMM
ARE WE NOT GOING TO CAPTURE THEM?
NOT HERE. I'LL PICK THE PLACE.
COME ON.
RRRMMMMM

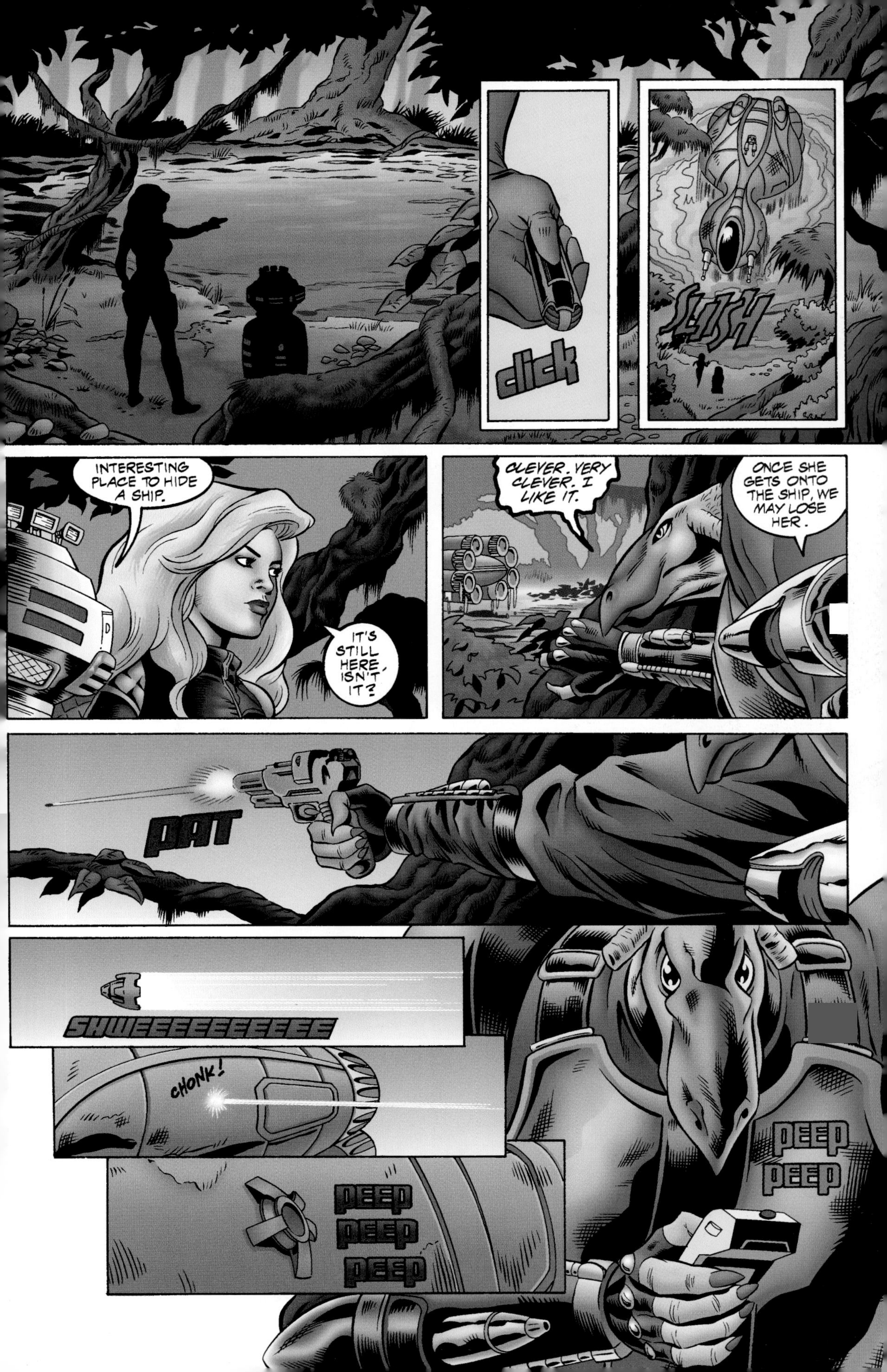
click
SHSH
INTERESTING PLACE TO HIDE A SHIP.
IT'S STILL HERE, ISN'T IT?
CLEVER. VERY CLEVER. I LIKE IT.
ONCE SHE GETS ONTO THE SHIP, WE MAY LOSE HER.
PAT
SHWEEEEEEEEEE
CHONK!
PEEP PEEP PEEP
PEEP PEEP

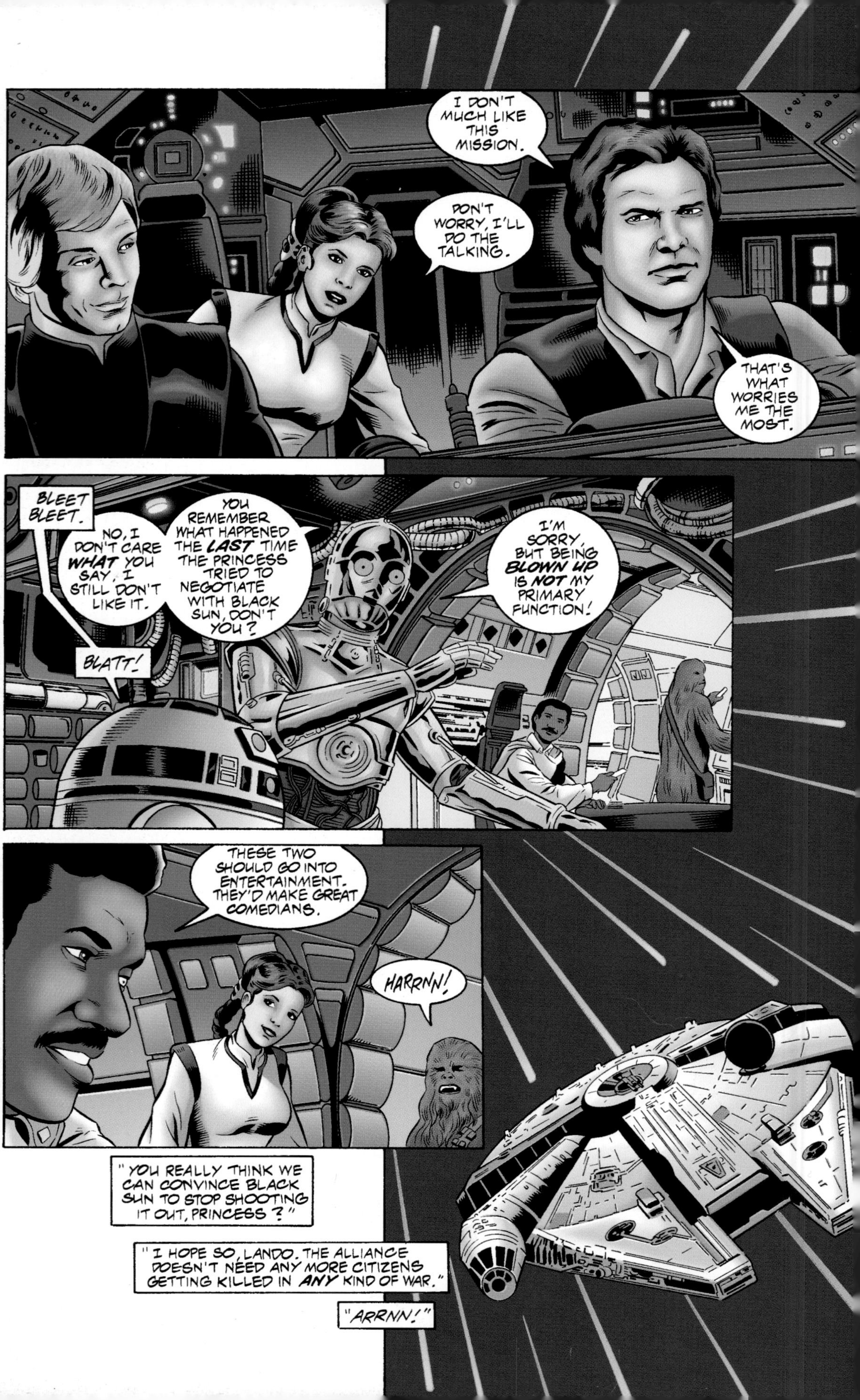
I DON'T MUCH LIKE THIS MISSION.
DON'T WORRY, I'LL DO THE TALKING.
THAT'S WHAT WORRIES ME THE MOST.
BLEET BLEET.
NO, I DON'T CARE WHAT YOU SAY. I STILL DON'T LIKE IT.
YOU REMEMBER WHAT HAPPENED THE LAST TIME THE PRINCESS TRIED TO NEGOTIATE WITH BLACK SUN, DON'T YOU?
BLATT!
I'M SORRY, BUT BEING BLOWN UP IS NOT MY PRIMARY FUNCTION!
THESE TWO SHOULD GO INTO ENTERTAINMENT. THEY'D MAKE GREAT COMEDIANS.
HARRNN!
"YOU REALLY THINK WE CAN CONVINCE BLACK SUN TO STOP SHOOTING IT OUT, PRINCESS?"
"I HOPE SO, LANDO. THE ALLIANCE DOESN'T NEED ANY MORE CITIZENS GETTING KILLED IN ANY KIND OF WAR."
"ARRNN!"

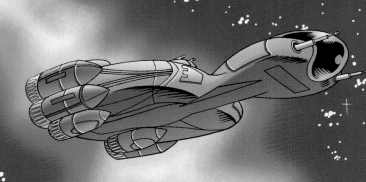

THE SIGNAL IS STILL STRONG. SHE APPEARS TO BE RETURNING TO HURD'S MOON.

OF COURSE. SHE MUST HAVE BEEN HIRED TO RETRIEVE THE MEDICAL DROID.

I WOULDN'T HAVE THOUGHT SUCH A THING TO BE *THAT* VALUABLE.

HOW VERY INTERESTING. AND YOU HAVE MASTER CAVEEL'S APPROVAL?

YES. THE PRICE FOR BRINGING YOU BACK.

HMM. IT SHOULD BE A WONDERFUL TECHNICAL CHALLENGE.

I HAVE HEARD OF THIS DROID. A *UNIQUE* MODEL. IT HAS TOP-OF-THE-LINE MEDICAL/SURGICAL SKILLS.

A TECHNICAL CHALLENGE? YES, IN HIS PLACE SHE WOULD THINK THE SAME THING.

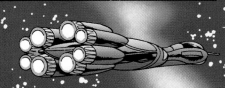

BUT SHE WASN'T IN HIS PLACE.

SHOULD WE NOT TAKE HER BEFORE SHE LANDS?

NO. YOU KNOW, SUCH A DEVICE AS SHE IS WOULD BE *MOST USEFUL* TO ME, IF SHE WAS PROPERLY *PROGRAMMED.*

WHAT ARE YOU SAYING?

I'M SAYING THAT THIS HUMAN REPLICA DROID IS WORTH A *LOT MORE* THAN THE FEE WE'D MAKE TURNING HER OVER TO OUR CLIENT.

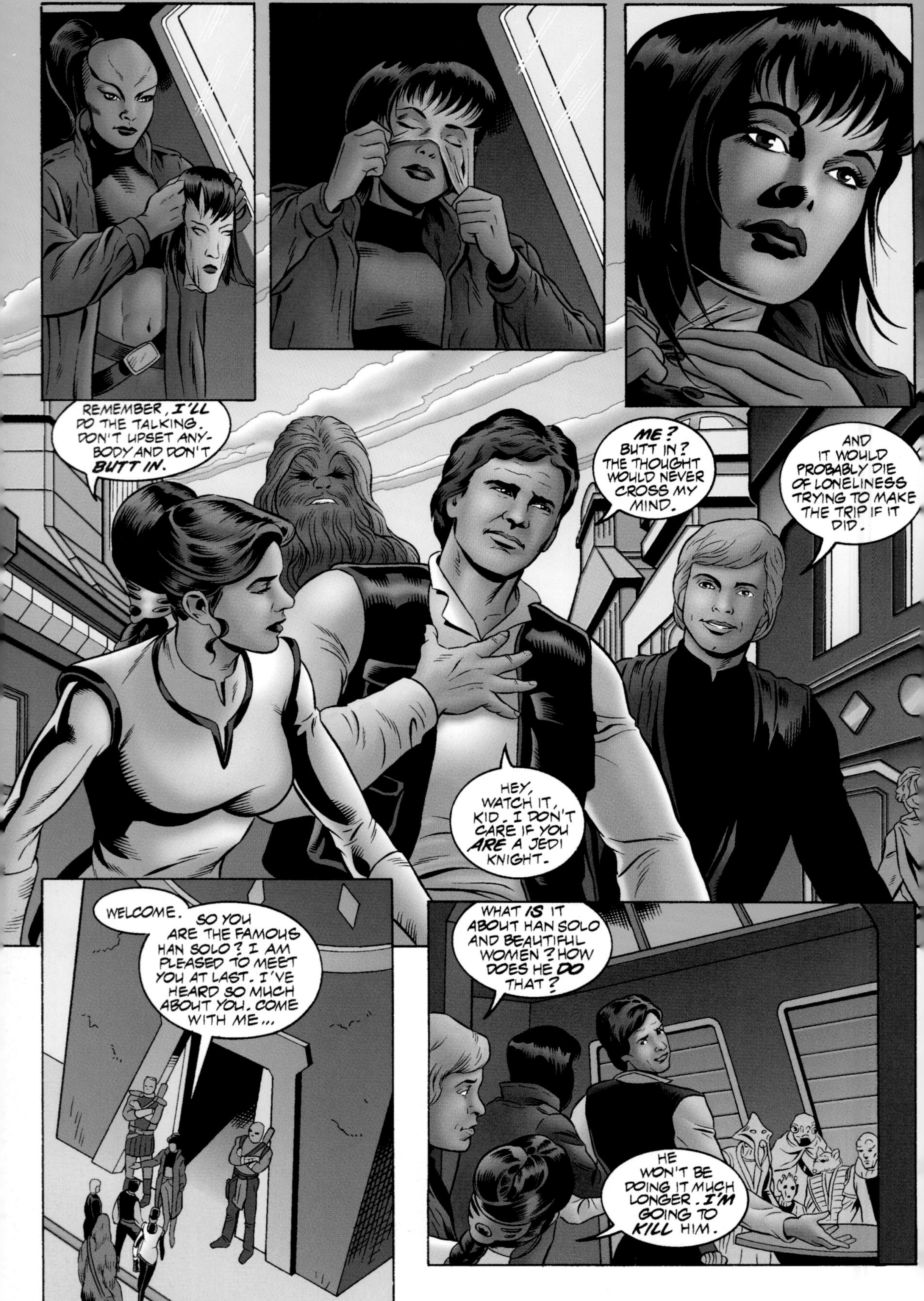
REMEMBER, I'LL DO THE TALKING. DON'T UPSET ANY-BODY AND DON'T BUTT IN.
ME? BUTT IN? THE THOUGHT WOULD NEVER CROSS MY MIND.
AND IT WOULD PROBABLY DIE OF LONELINESS TRYING TO MAKE THE TRIP IF IT DID.
HEY, WATCH IT, KID. I DON'T CARE IF YOU ARE A JEDI KNIGHT.
WELCOME. SO YOU ARE THE FAMOUS HAN SOLO? I AM PLEASED TO MEET YOU AT LAST. I'VE HEARD SO MUCH ABOUT YOU. COME WITH ME...
WHAT IS IT ABOUT HAN SOLO AND BEAUTIFUL WOMEN? HOW DOES HE DO THAT?
HE WON'T BE DOING IT MUCH LONGER. I'M GOING TO KILL HIM.

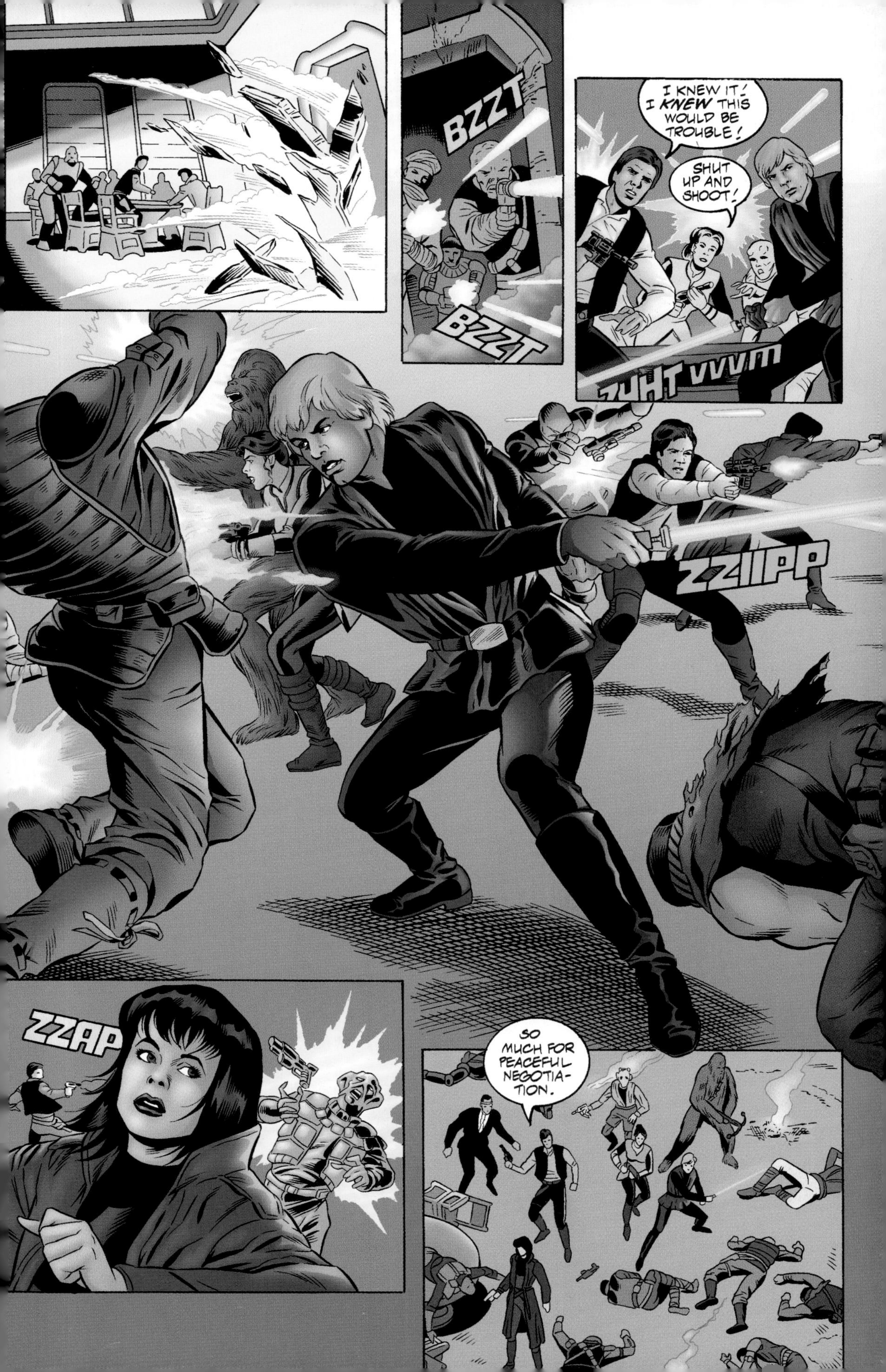
BZZT
BZZT
I KNEW IT! I KNEW THIS WOULD BE TROUBLE!
SHUT UP AND SHOOT!
ZUHT VVVM
ZZIIPP
ZZAP
SO MUCH FOR PEACEFUL NEGOTIATION.

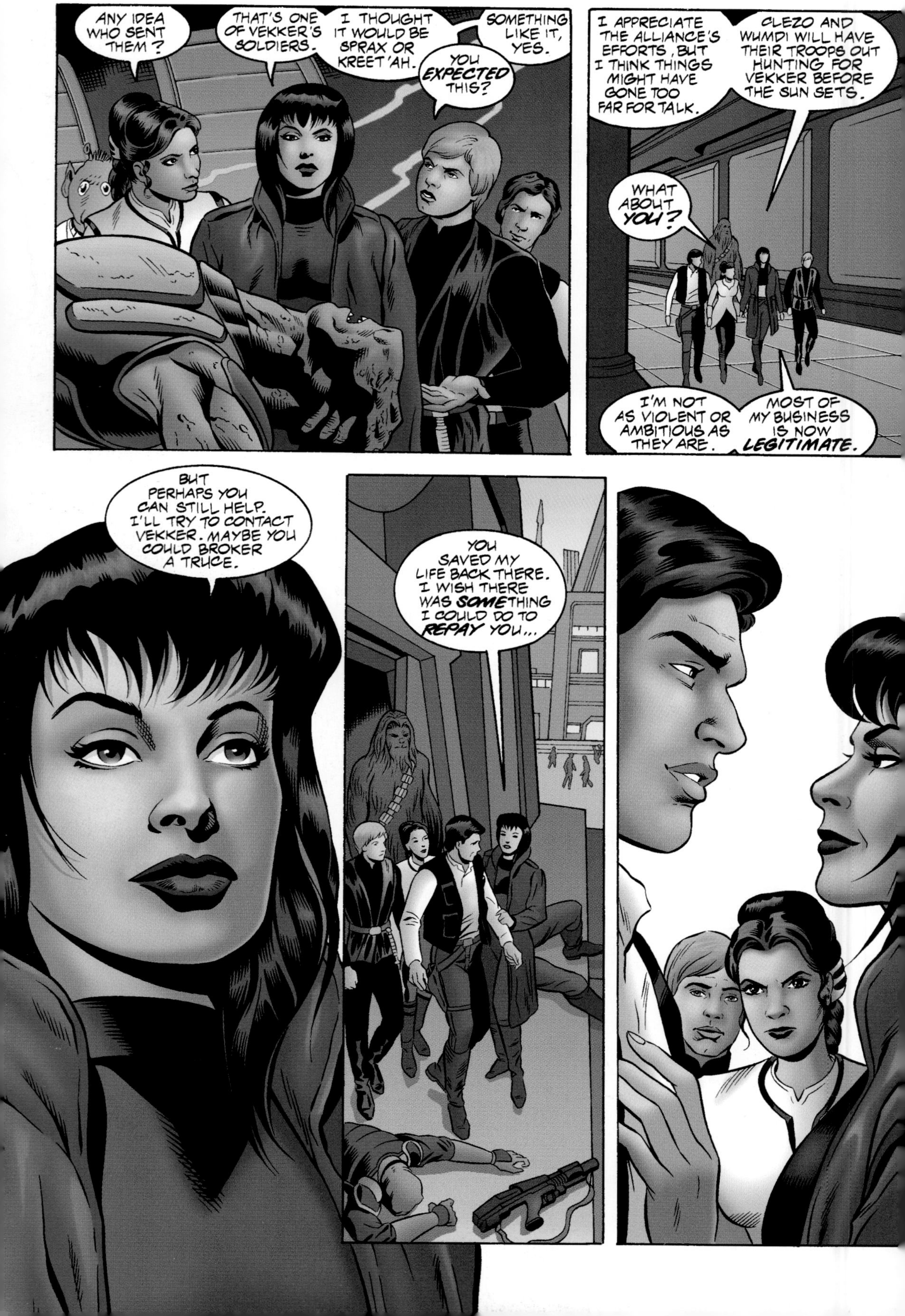
ANY IDEA WHO SENT THEM?
THAT'S ONE OF VEKKER'S SOLDIERS.
I THOUGHT IT WOULD BE SPRAX OR KREET'AH.
YOU EXPECTED THIS?
SOMETHING LIKE IT, YES.
I APPRECIATE THE ALLIANCE'S EFFORTS, BUT I THINK THINGS MIGHT HAVE GONE TOO FAR FOR TALK.
CLEZO AND WUMDI WILL HAVE THEIR TROOPS OUT HUNTING FOR VEKKER BEFORE THE SUN SETS.
WHAT ABOUT YOU?
I'M NOT AS VIOLENT OR AMBITIOUS AS THEY ARE.
MOST OF MY BUSINESS IS NOW LEGITIMATE.
BUT PERHAPS YOU CAN STILL HELP. I'LL TRY TO CONTACT VEKKER. MAYBE YOU COULD BROKER A TRUCE.
YOU SAVED MY LIFE BACK THERE. I WISH THERE WAS SOMETHING I COULD DO TO REPAY YOU...

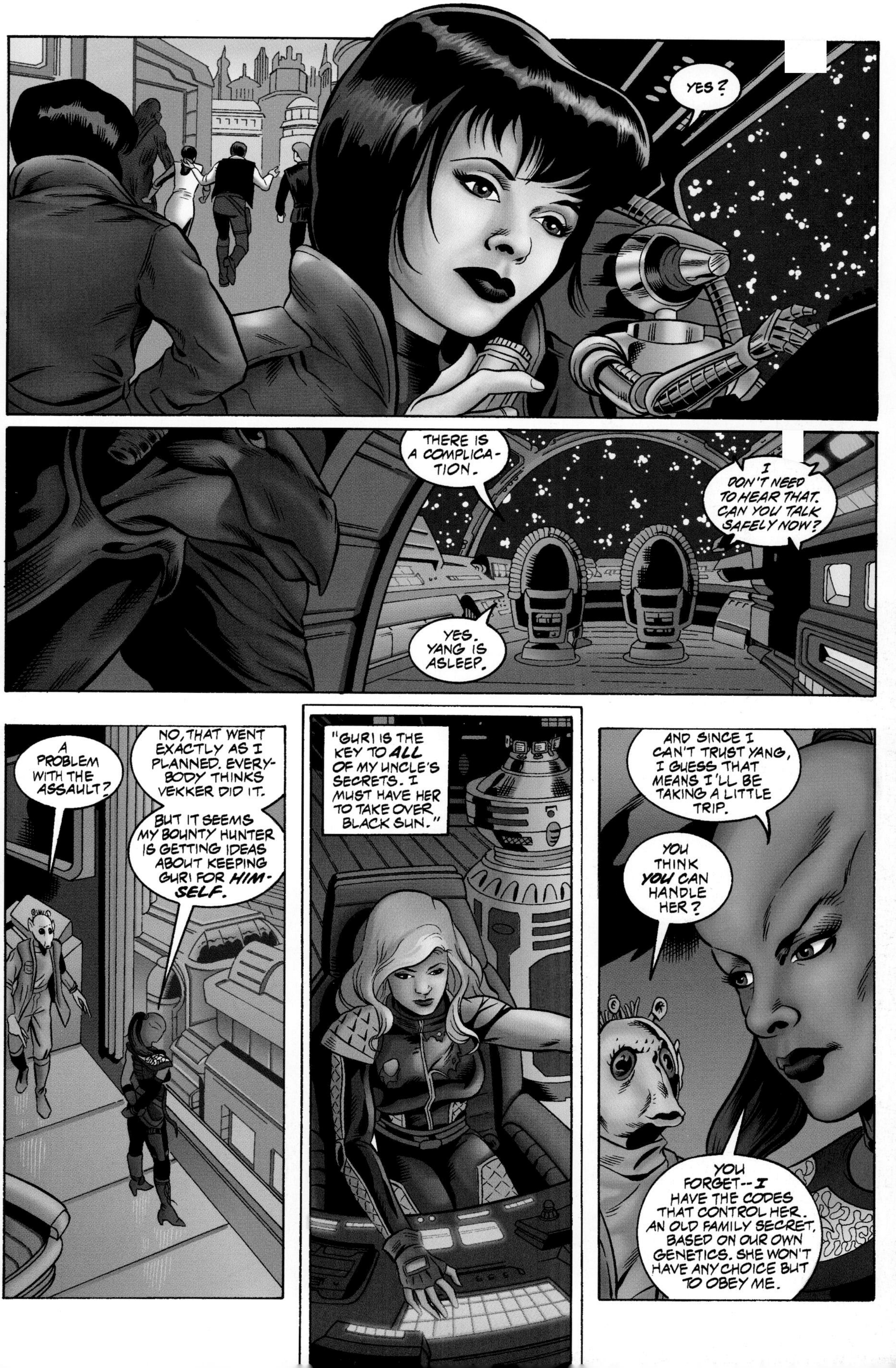
YES?
THERE IS A COMPLICATION.
I DON'T NEED TO HEAR THAT. CAN YOU TALK SAFELY NOW?
YES. YANG IS ASLEEP.
A PROBLEM WITH THE ASSAULT?
NO, THAT WENT EXACTLY AS I PLANNED. EVERYBODY THINKS VEKKER DID IT.
BUT IT SEEMS MY BOUNTY HUNTER IS GETTING IDEAS ABOUT KEEPING GURI FOR HIMSELF.
"GURI IS THE KEY TO ALL OF MY UNCLE'S SECRETS. I MUST HAVE HER TO TAKE OVER BLACK SUN."
AND SINCE I CAN'T TRUST YANG, I GUESS THAT MEANS I'LL BE TAKING A LITTLE TRIP.
YOU THINK YOU CAN HANDLE HER?
YOU FORGET-- I HAVE THE CODES THAT CONTROL HER. AN OLD FAMILY SECRET, BASED ON OUR OWN GENETICS. SHE WON'T HAVE ANY CHOICE BUT TO OBEY ME.

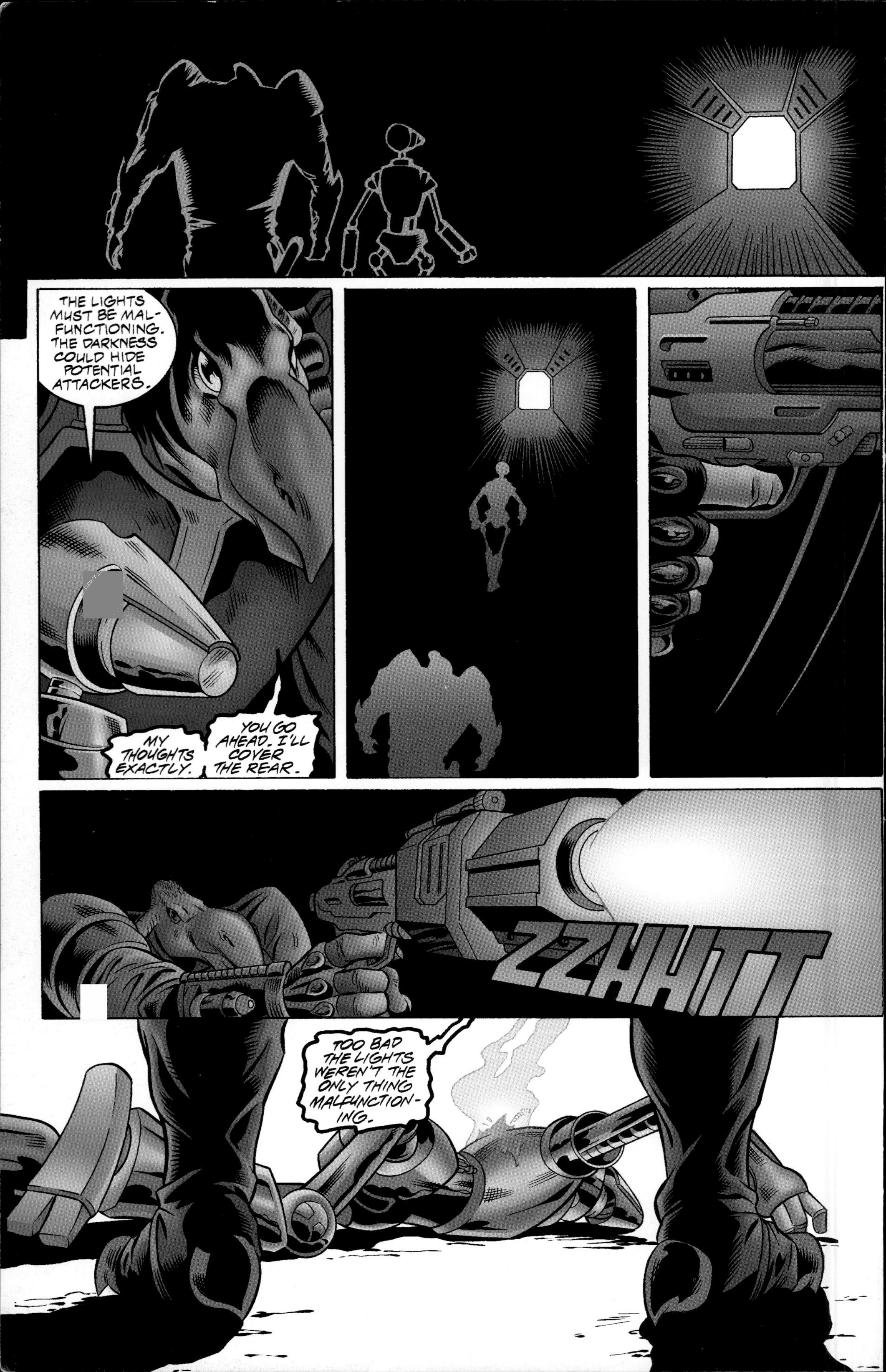
THE LIGHTS MUST BE MALFUNCTIONING. THE DARKNESS COULD HIDE POTENTIAL ATTACKERS.
MY THOUGHTS EXACTLY.
YOU GO AHEAD. I'LL COVER THE REAR.
ZZHHTT
TOO BAD THE LIGHTS WEREN'T THE ONLY THING MALFUNCTIONING.

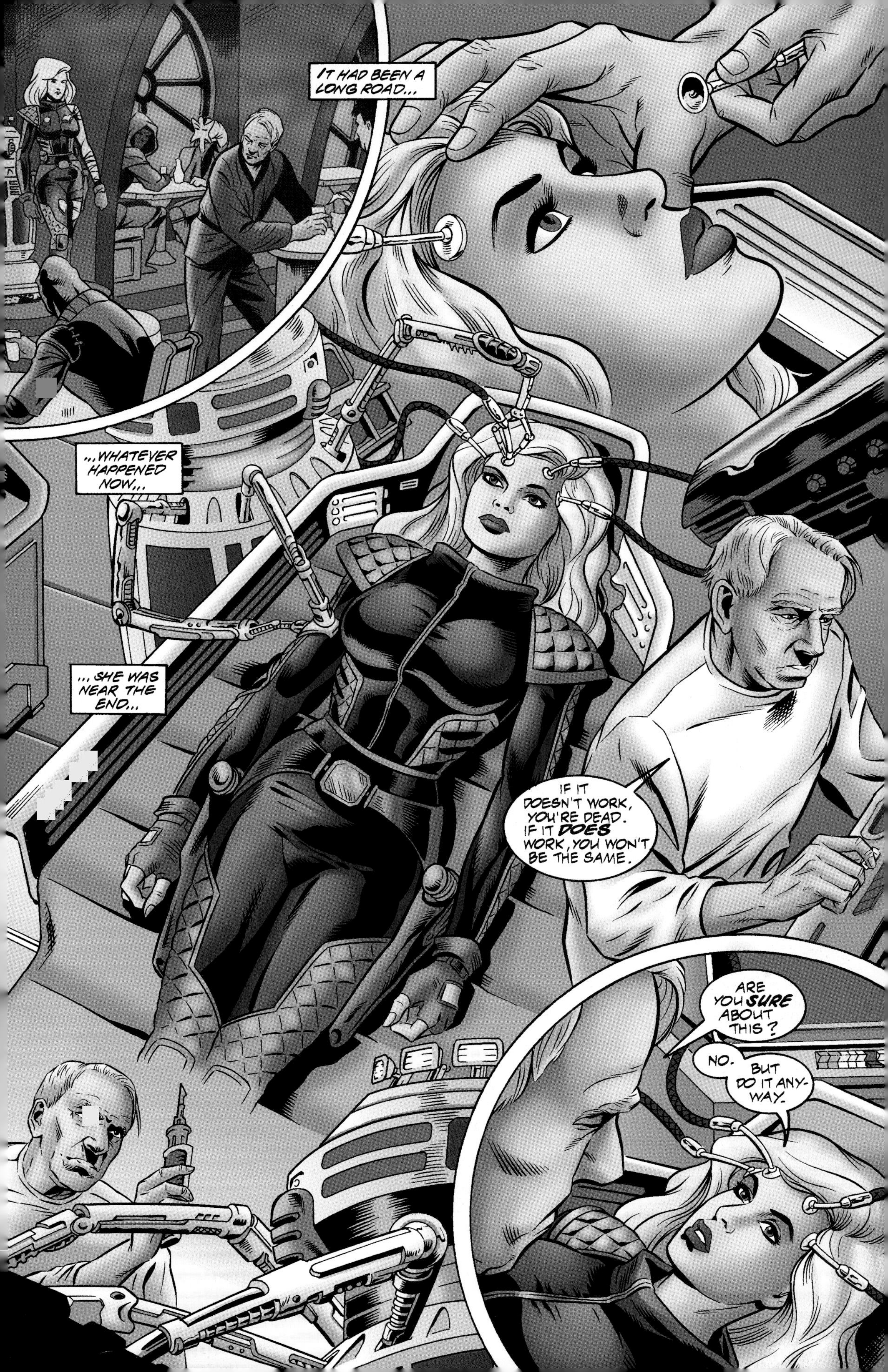
IT HAD BEEN A LONG ROAD...
...WHATEVER HAPPENED NOW...
...SHE WAS NEAR THE END...
IF IT DOESN'T WORK, YOU'RE DEAD. IF IT DOES WORK, YOU WON'T BE THE SAME.
ARE YOU SURE ABOUT THIS?
NO. BUT DO IT ANYWAY.

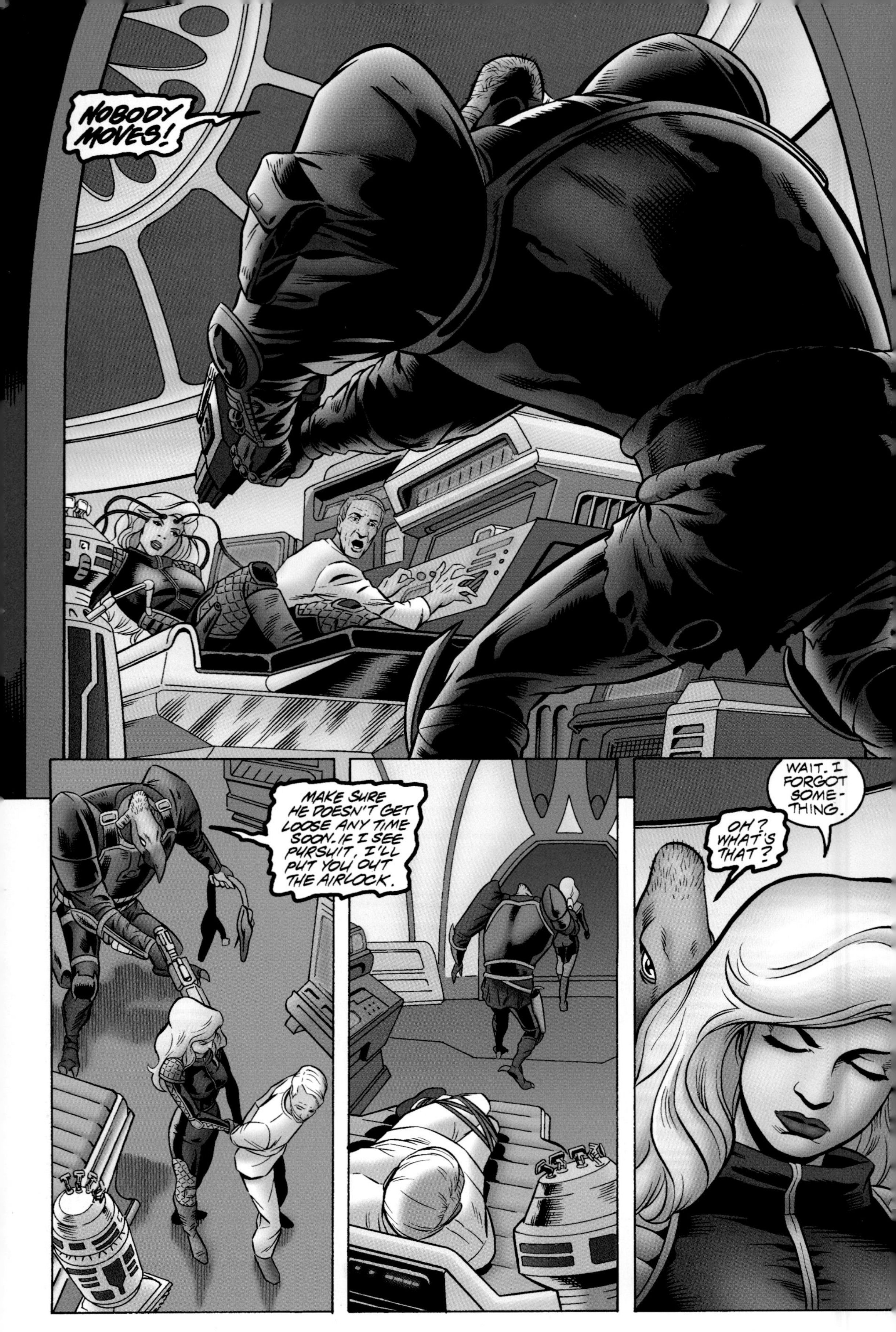
NOBODY MOVES!
MAKE SURE HE DOESN'T GET LOOSE ANY TIME SOON. IF I SEE PURSUIT, I'LL PUT YOU OUT THE AIRLOCK.
WAIT. I FORGOT SOME-THING.
OH? WHAT'S THAT?

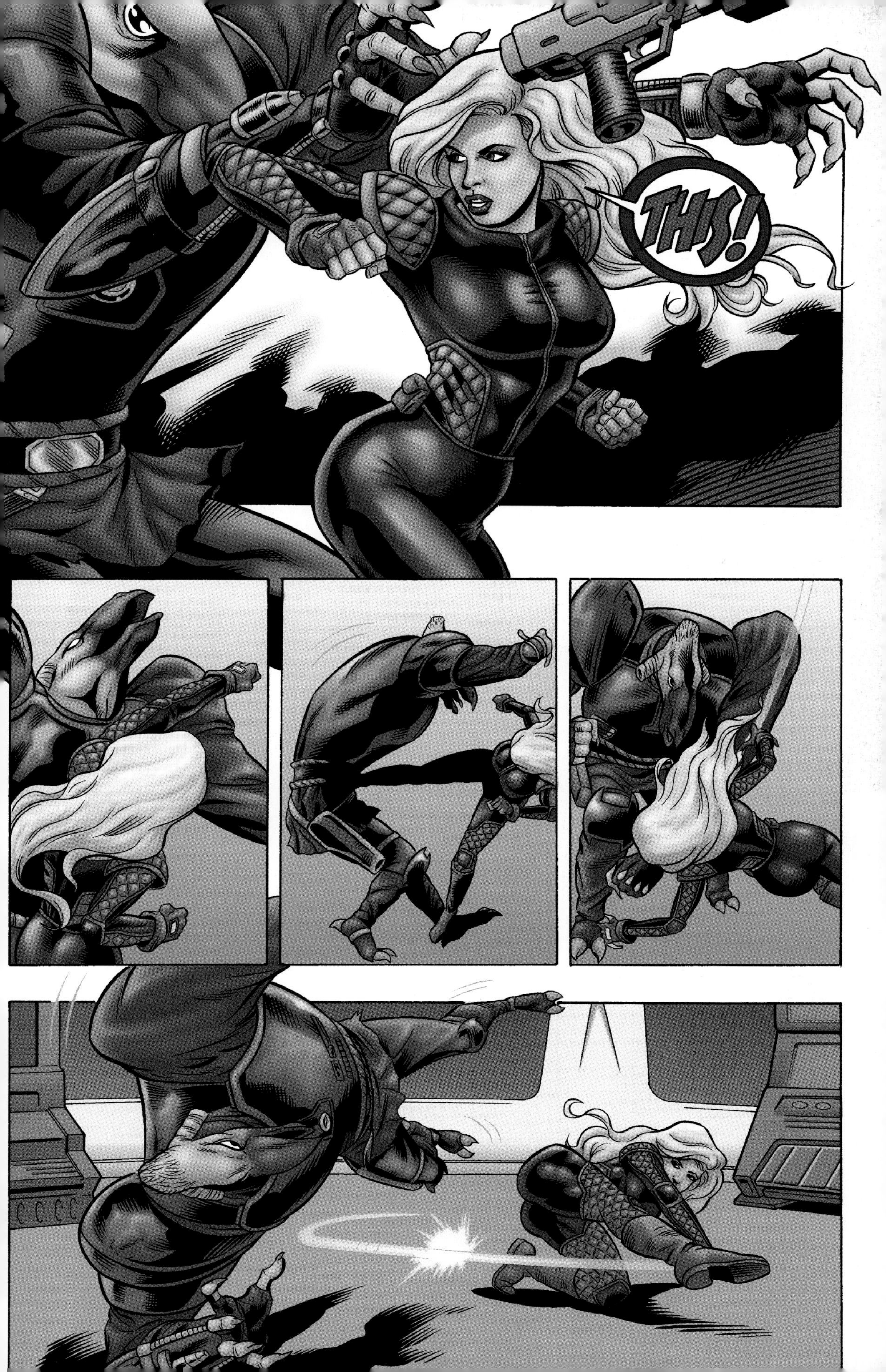
THIS!

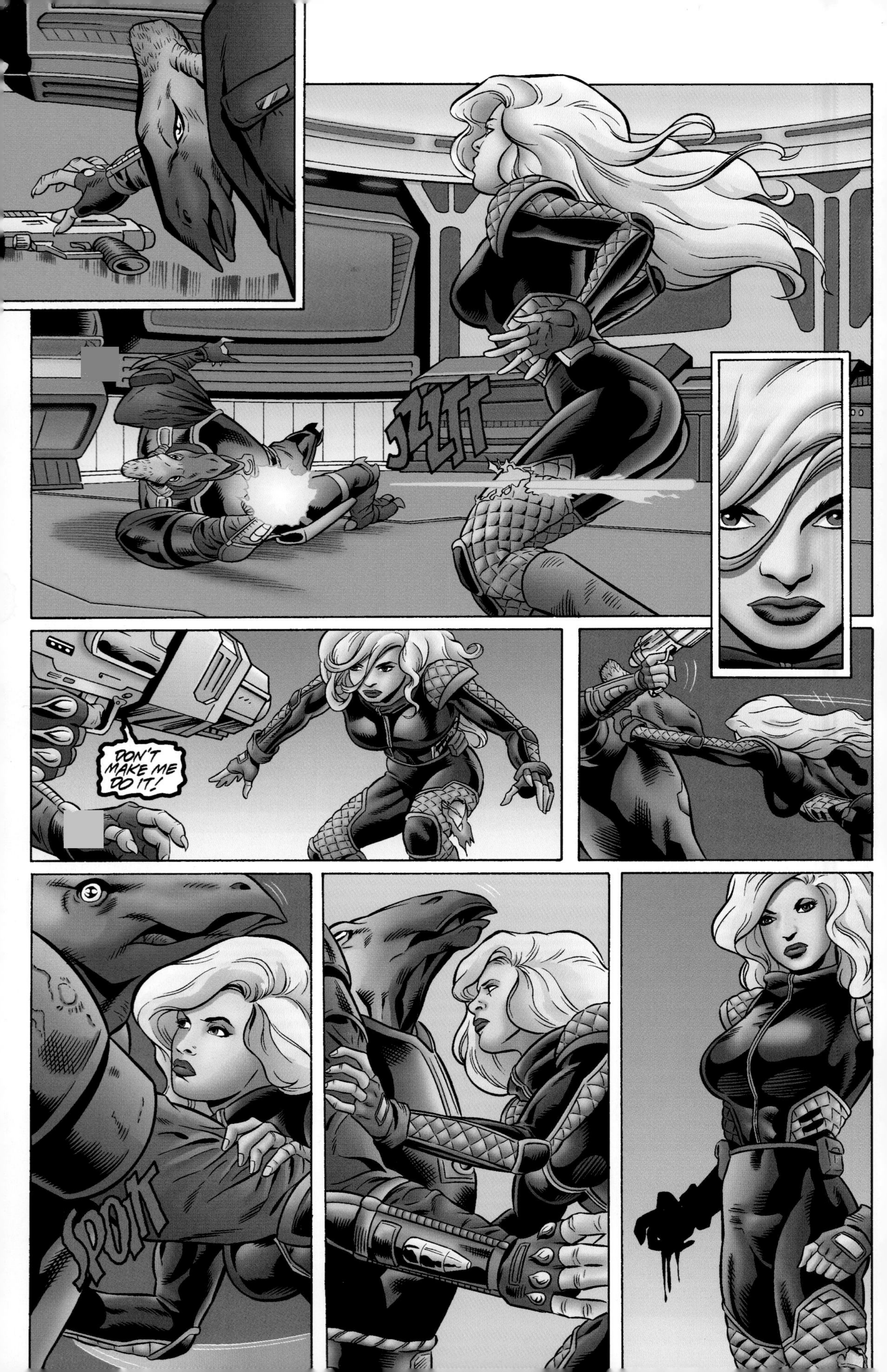
JZZTT
DON'T MAKE ME DO IT!
SPOIT

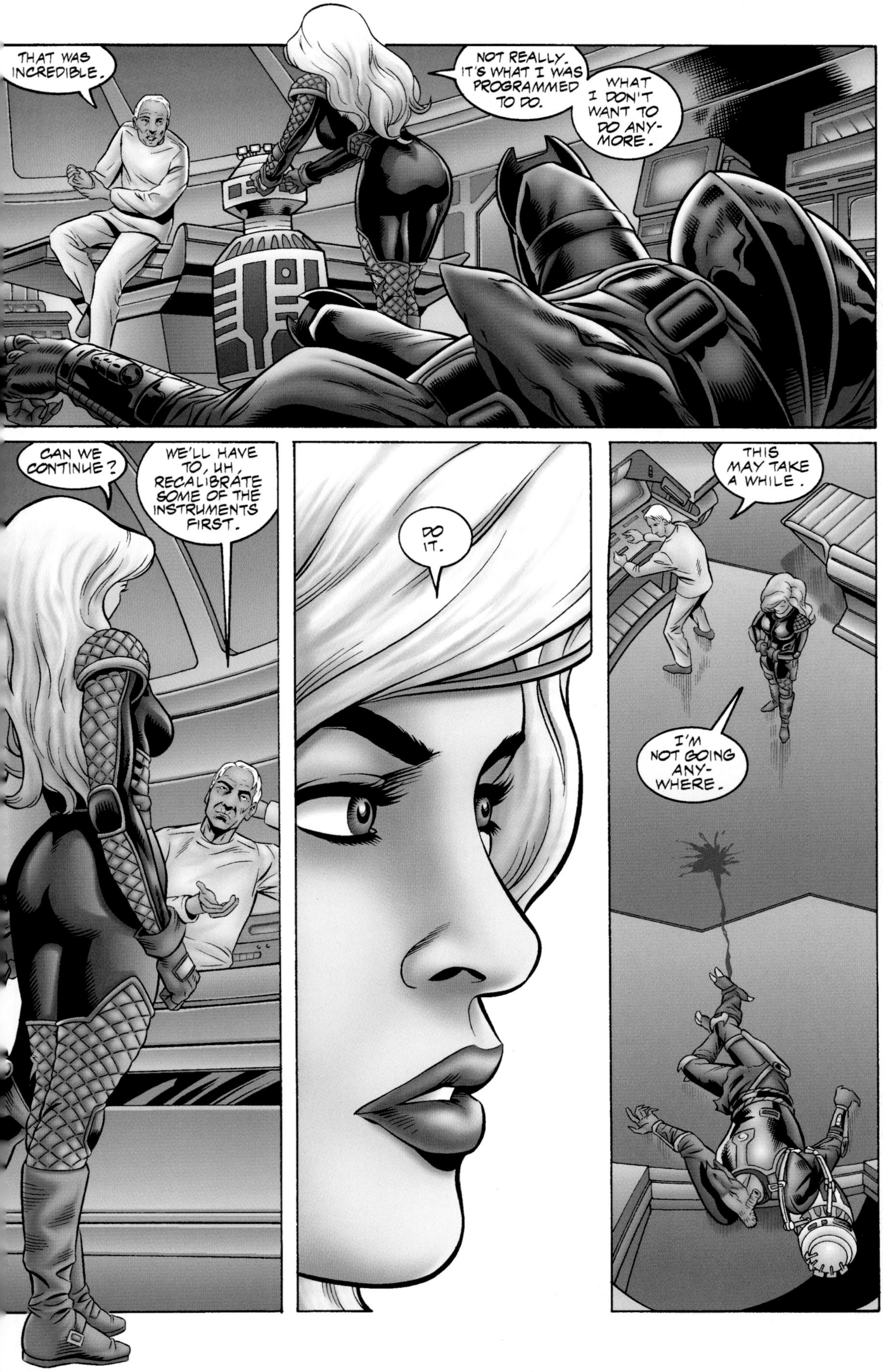
THAT WAS INCREDIBLE.
NOT REALLY. IT'S WHAT I WAS PROGRAMMED TO DO.
WHAT I DON'T WANT TO DO ANYMORE.
CAN WE CONTINUE?
WE'LL HAVE TO, UH, RECALIBRATE SOME OF THE INSTRUMENTS FIRST.
DO IT.
THIS MAY TAKE A WHILE.
I'M NOT GOING ANYWHERE.

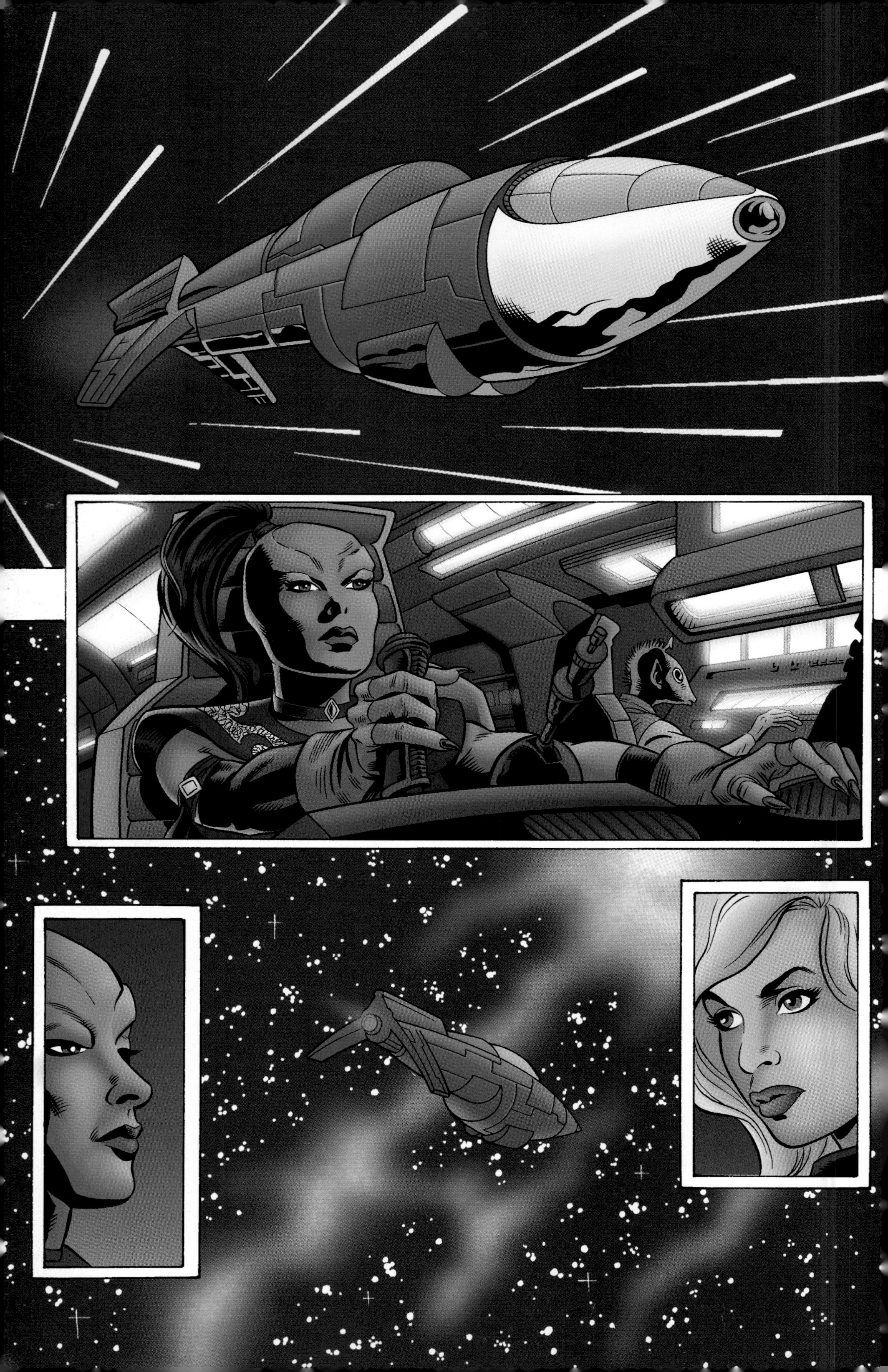

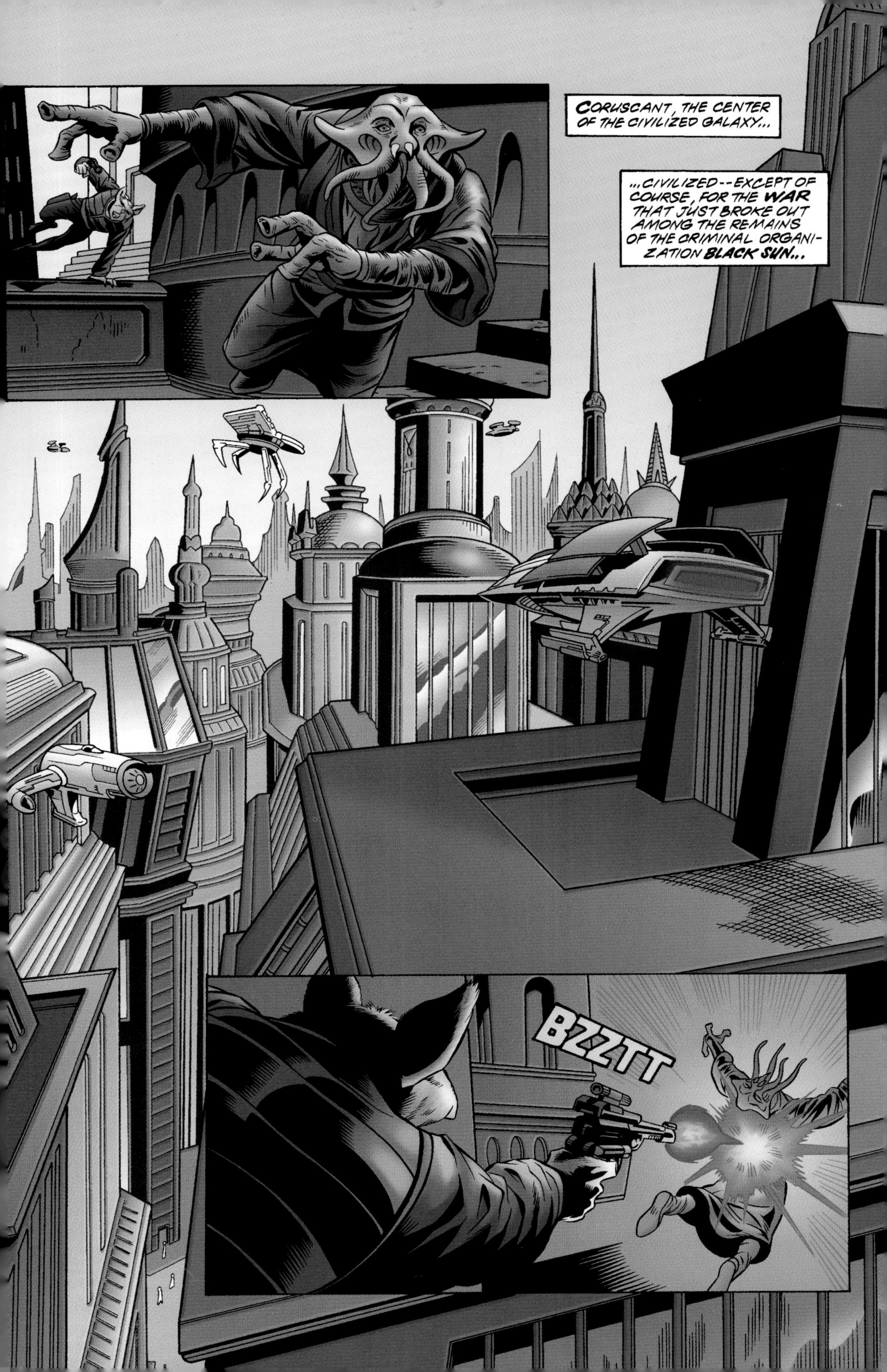
CORUSCANT, THE CENTER OF THE CIVILIZED GALAXY...
...CIVILIZED--EXCEPT OF COURSE, FOR THE WAR THAT JUST BROKE OUT AMONG THE REMAINS OF THE CRIMINAL ORGANIZATION BLACK SUN...
BZZTT

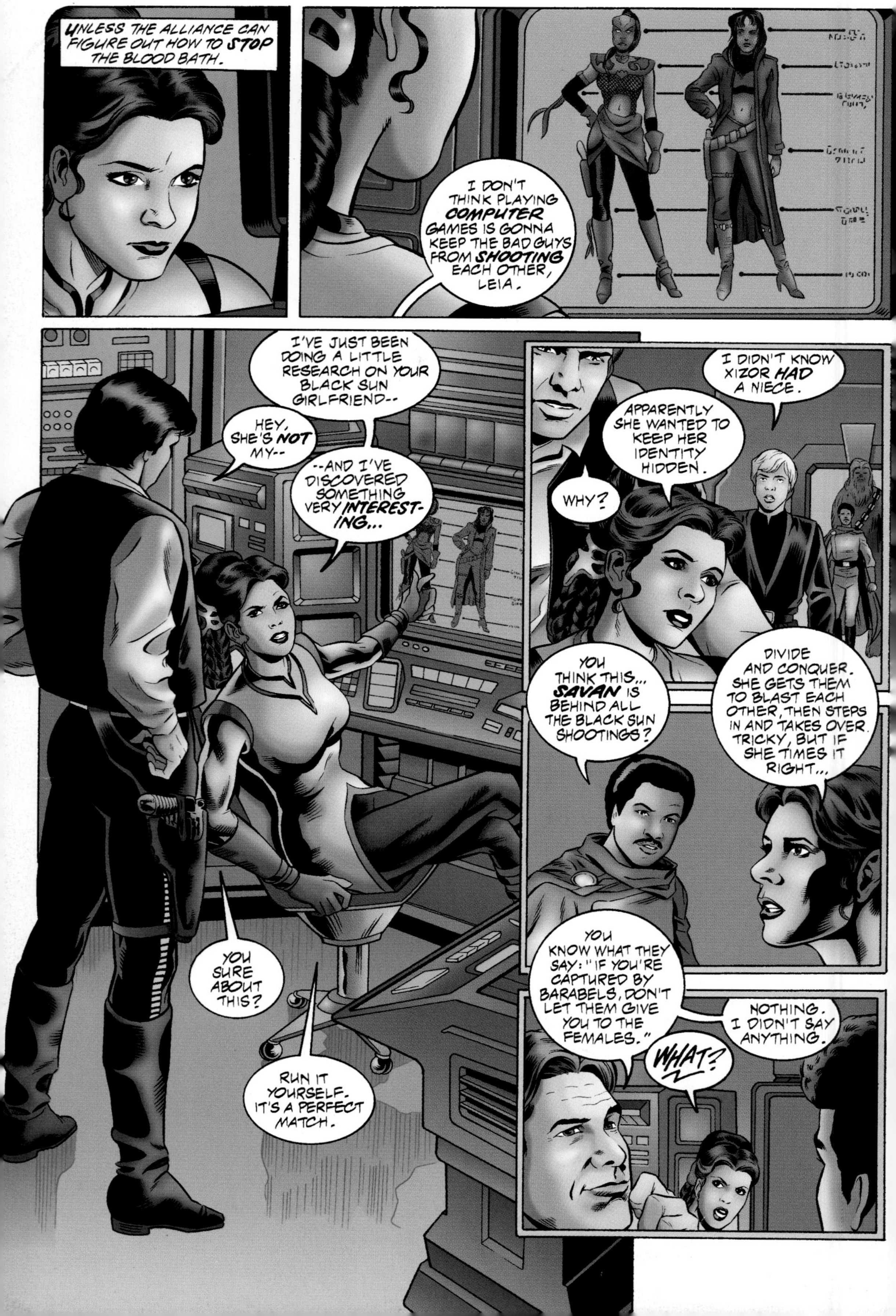
UNLESS THE ALLIANCE CAN FIGURE OUT HOW TO STOP THE BLOOD BATH.
I DON'T THINK PLAYING COMPUTER GAMES IS GONNA KEEP THE BAD GUYS FROM SHOOTING EACH OTHER, LEIA.
I'VE JUST BEEN DOING A LITTLE RESEARCH ON YOUR BLACK SUN GIRLFRIEND--
HEY, SHE'S NOT MY--
--AND I'VE DISCOVERED SOMETHING VERY INTERESTING...
YOU SURE ABOUT THIS?
RUN IT YOURSELF. IT'S A PERFECT MATCH.
I DIDN'T KNOW XIZOR HAD A NIECE.
APPARENTLY SHE WANTED TO KEEP HER IDENTITY HIDDEN.
WHY?
YOU THINK THIS... SAVAN IS BEHIND ALL THE BLACK SUN SHOOTINGS?
DIVIDE AND CONQUER. SHE GETS THEM TO BLAST EACH OTHER, THEN STEPS IN AND TAKES OVER. TRICKY, BUT IF SHE TIMES IT RIGHT...
YOU KNOW WHAT THEY SAY: "IF YOU'RE CAPTURED BY BARABELS, DON'T LET THEM GIVE YOU TO THE FEMALES."
WHAT?
NOTHING. I DIDN'T SAY ANYTHING.

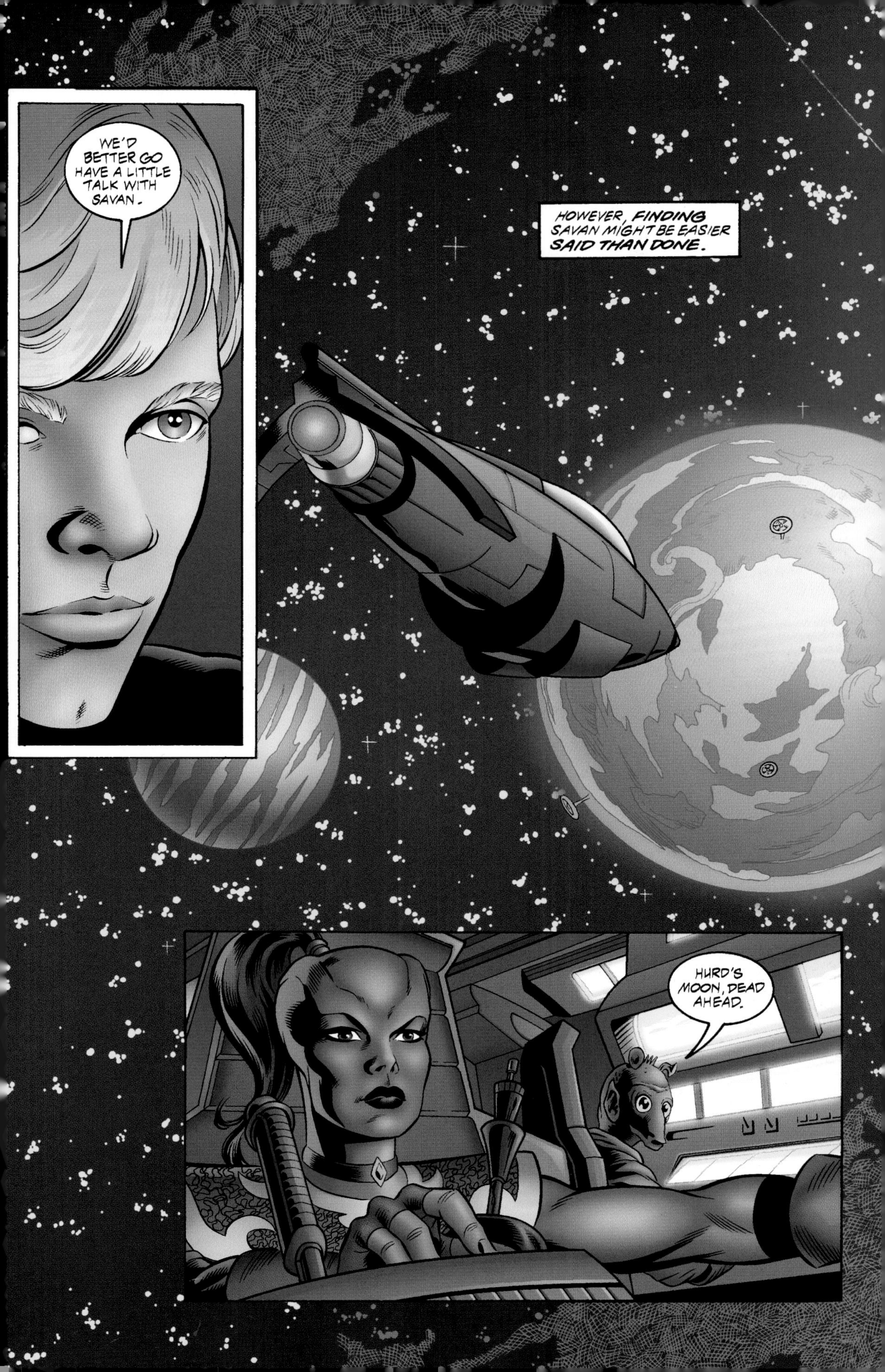
WE'D BETTER GO HAVE A LITTLE TALK WITH SAVAN.
HOWEVER, FINDING SAVAN MIGHT BE EASIER SAID THAN DONE.
HURD'S MOON, DEAD AHEAD.

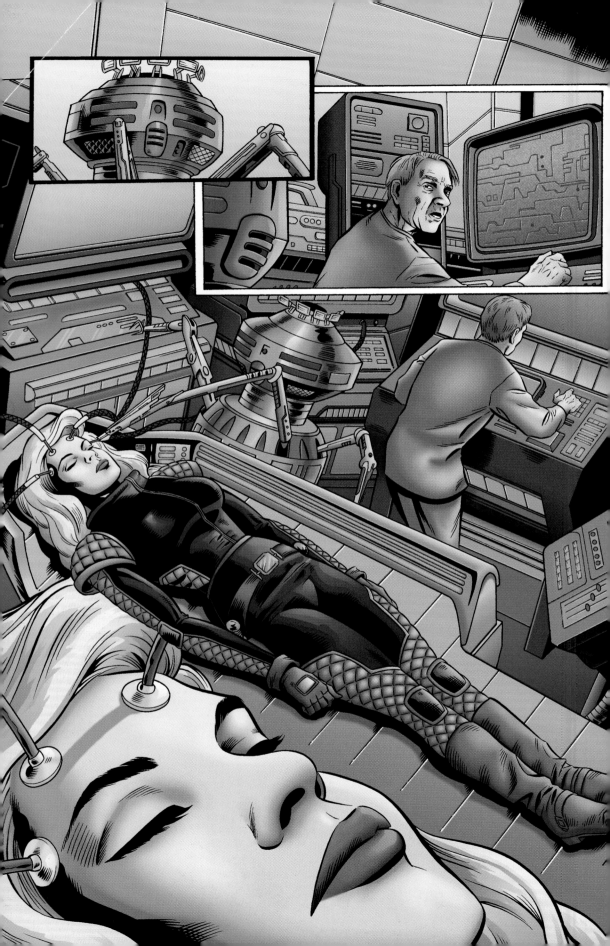

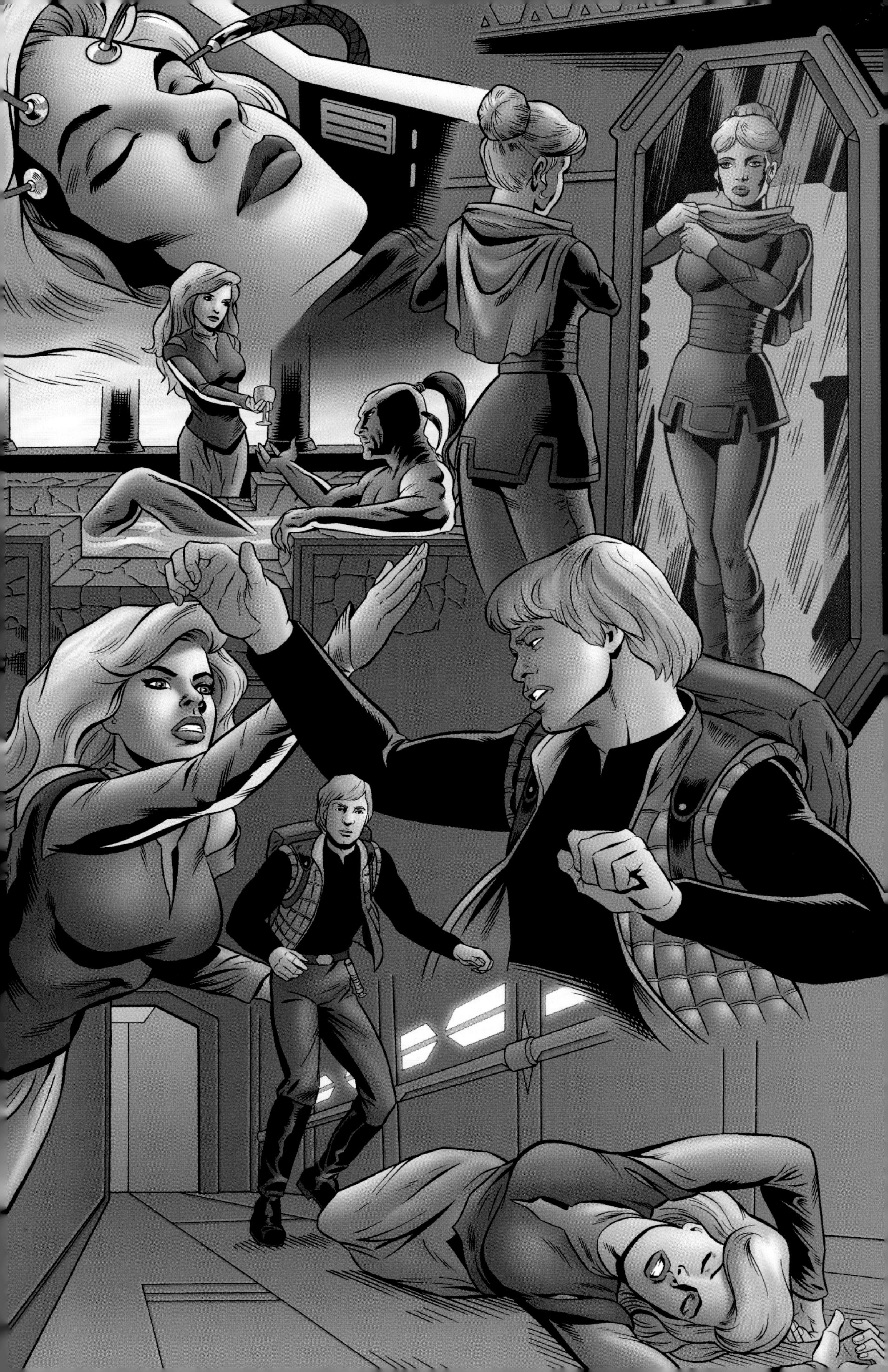

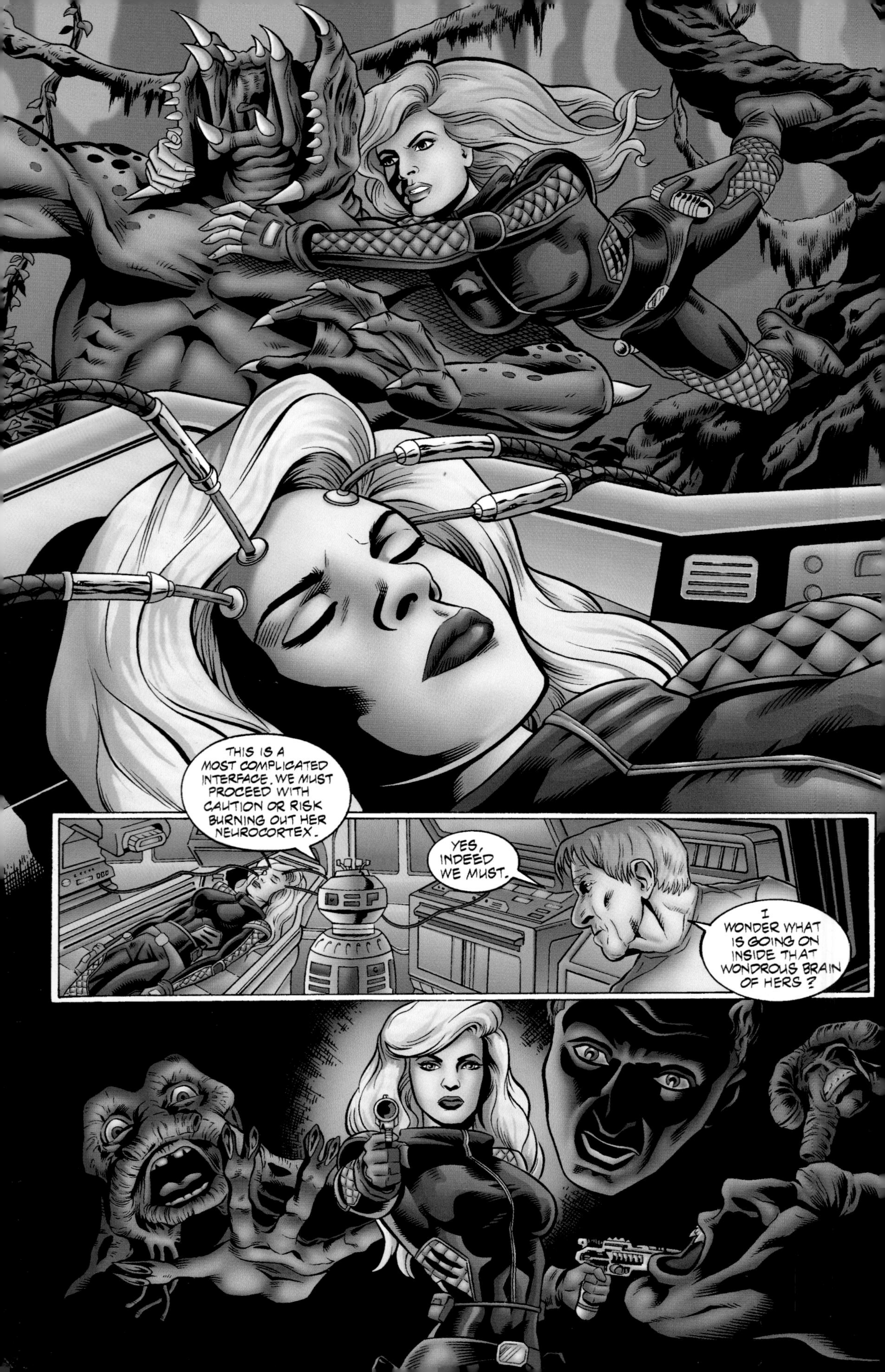
THIS IS A MOST COMPLICATED INTERFACE. WE MUST PROCEED WITH CAUTION OR RISK BURNING OUT HER NEUROCORTEX.
YES, INDEED WE MUST.
I WONDER WHAT IS GOING ON INSIDE THAT WONDROUS BRAIN OF HERS?

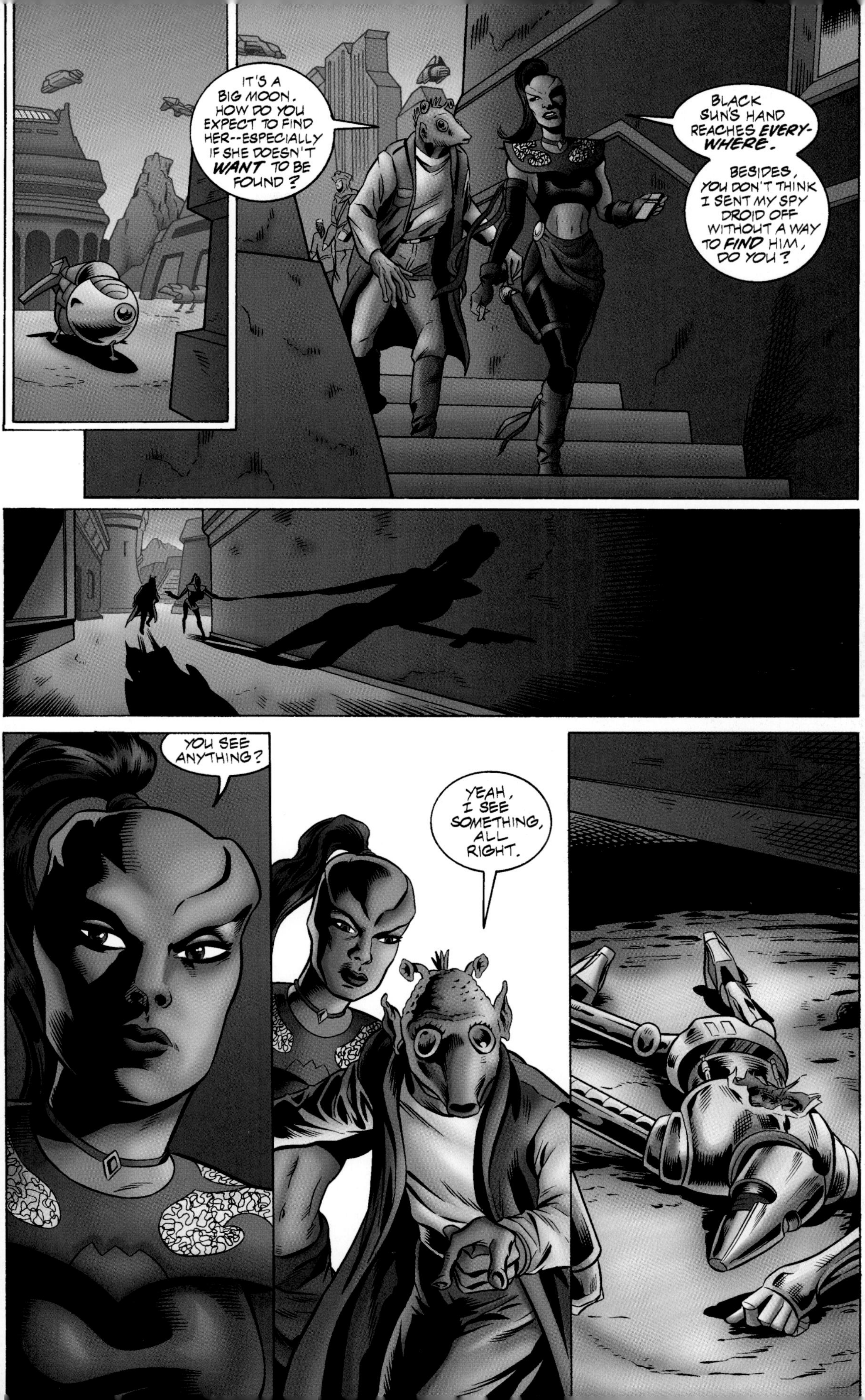
IT'S A BIG MOON. HOW DO YOU EXPECT TO FIND HER--ESPECIALLY IF SHE DOESN'T WANT TO BE FOUND?
BLACK SUN'S HAND REACHES EVERYWHERE.
BESIDES, YOU DON'T THINK I SENT MY SPY DROID OFF WITHOUT A WAY TO FIND HIM, DO YOU?
YOU SEE ANYTHING?
YEAH, I SEE SOMETHING, ALL RIGHT.

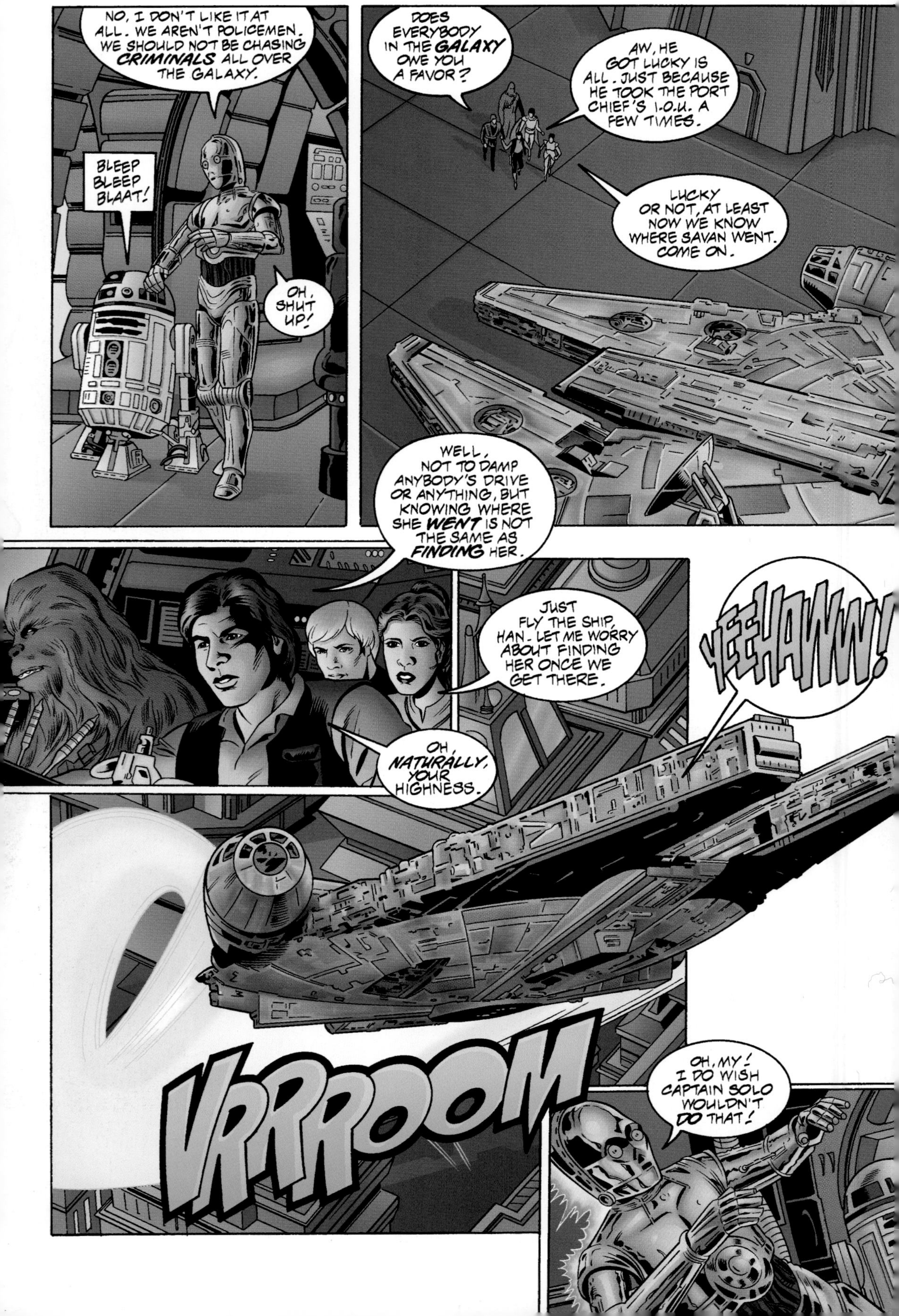
NO, I DON'T LIKE IT AT ALL. WE AREN'T POLICEMEN. WE SHOULD NOT BE CHASING *CRIMINALS* ALL OVER THE GALAXY.
BLEEP BLEEP BLAAT!
OH, SHUT UP!
DOES EVERYBODY IN THE *GALAXY* OWE YOU A FAVOR?
AW, HE GOT LUCKY IS ALL. JUST BECAUSE HE TOOK THE PORT CHIEF'S I.O.U. A FEW TIMES.
LUCKY OR NOT, AT LEAST NOW WE KNOW WHERE SAVAN WENT. COME ON.
WELL, NOT TO DAMP ANYBODY'S DRIVE OR ANYTHING, BUT KNOWING WHERE SHE *WENT* IS NOT THE SAME AS *FINDING* HER.
JUST FLY THE SHIP, HAN. LET ME WORRY ABOUT FINDING HER ONCE WE GET THERE.
OH, *NATURALLY,* YOUR HIGHNESS.
YEEHAWW!
VRRROOM
OH, MY! I DO WISH CAPTAIN SOLO WOULDN'T *DO* THAT!

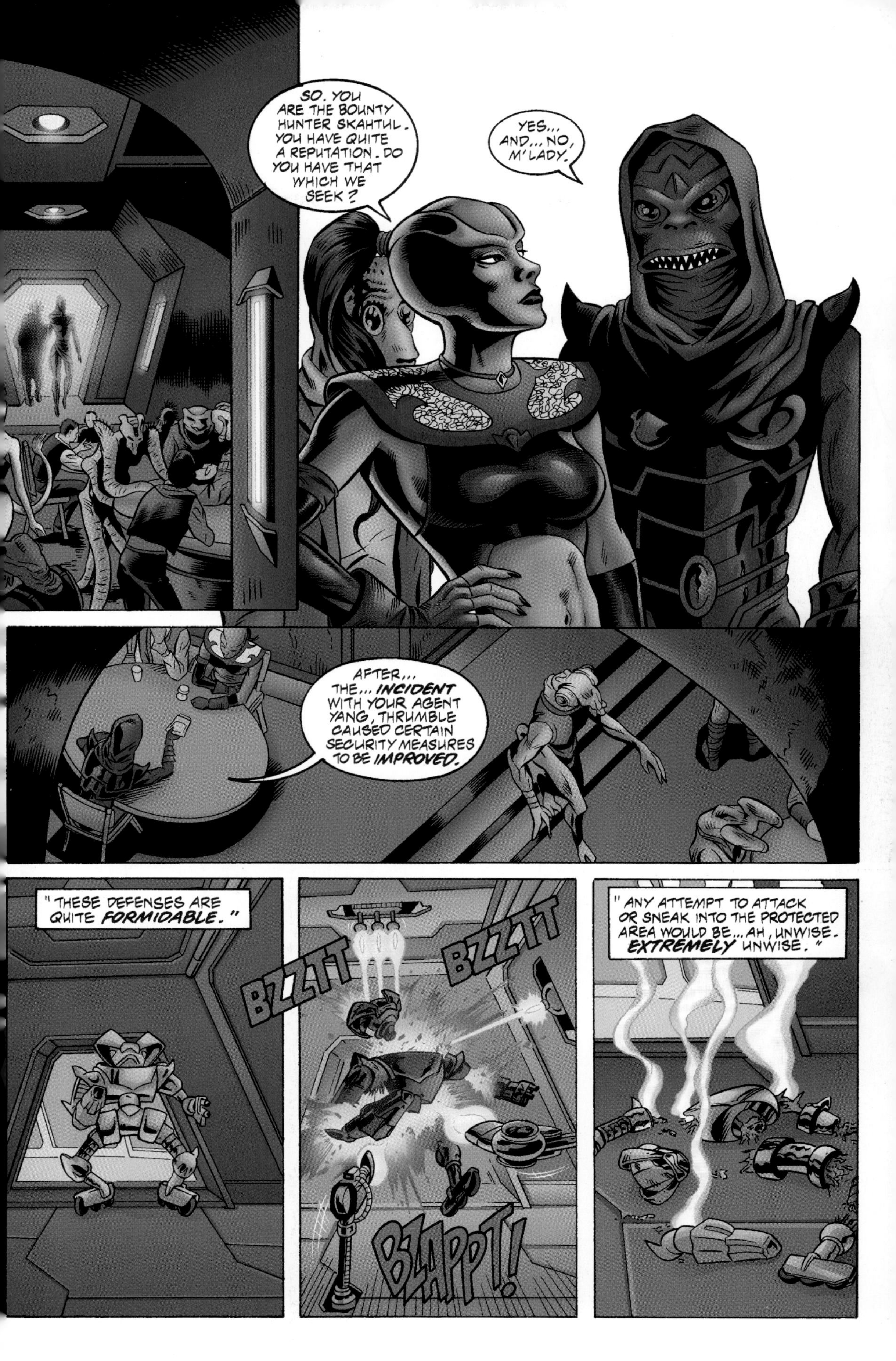
SO. YOU ARE THE BOUNTY HUNTER SKAHTUL. YOU HAVE QUITE A REPUTATION. DO YOU HAVE THAT WHICH WE SEEK?
YES... AND... NO, M'LADY.
AFTER... THE... INCIDENT WITH YOUR AGENT YANG, THRUMBLE CAUSED CERTAIN SECURITY MEASURES TO BE IMPROVED.
"THESE DEFENSES ARE QUITE FORMIDABLE."
BZZTT
BZZTT
BLAPPT!
"ANY ATTEMPT TO ATTACK OR SNEAK INTO THE PROTECTED AREA WOULD BE... AH, UNWISE. EXTREMELY UNWISE."

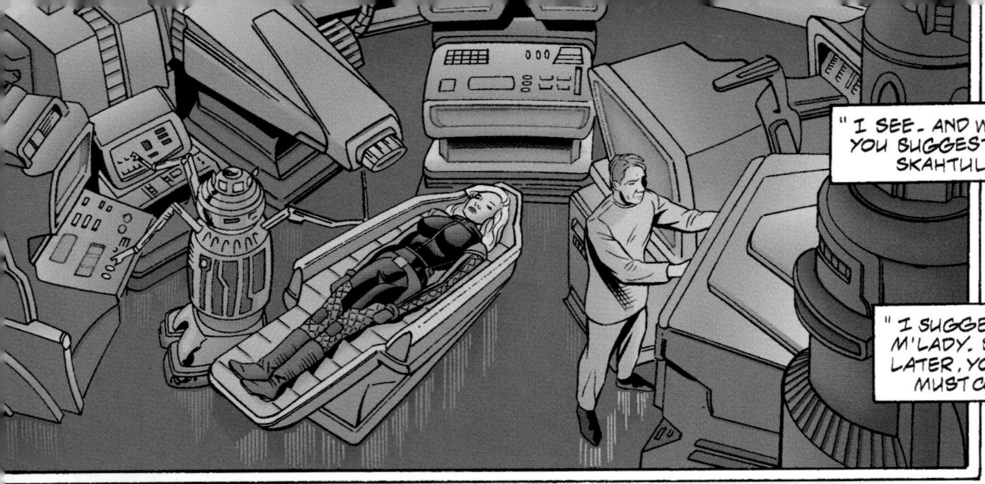
"I SEE. AND WHAT DO YOU SUGGEST WE DO, SKAHTUL?"
"I SUGGEST YOU WAIT, M'LADY. SOONER OR LATER, YOUR QUARRY MUST COME OUT."

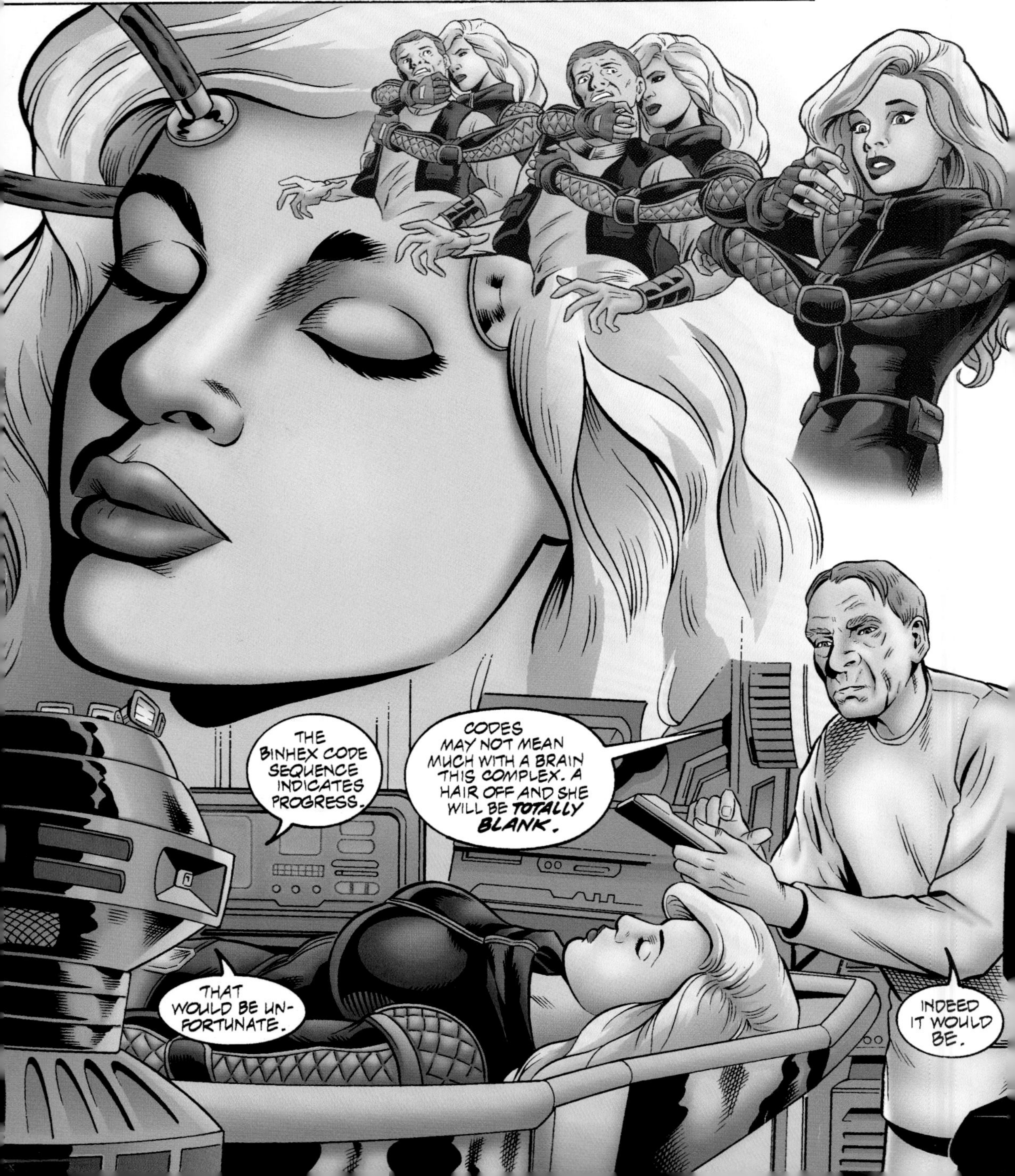
THE BINHEX CODE SEQUENCE INDICATES PROGRESS.
CODES MAY NOT MEAN MUCH WITH A BRAIN THIS COMPLEX. A HAIR OFF AND SHE WILL BE **TOTALLY BLANK**.
THAT WOULD BE UN-FORTUNATE.
INDEED IT WOULD BE.

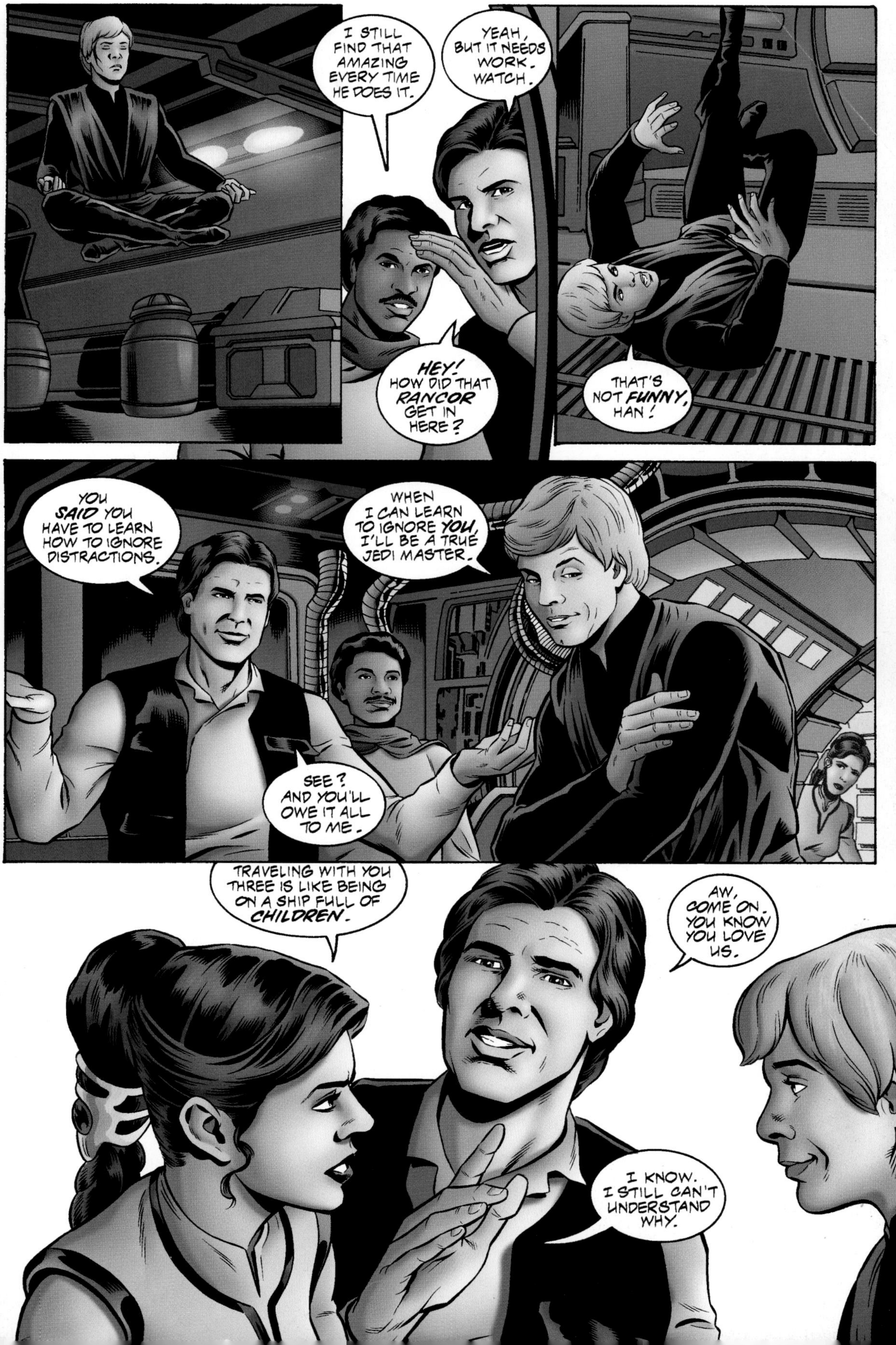
I STILL FIND THAT AMAZING EVERY TIME HE DOES IT.
YEAH, BUT IT NEEDS WORK. WATCH.
HEY! HOW DID THAT RANCOR GET IN HERE?
THAT'S NOT FUNNY, HAN!
YOU SAID YOU HAVE TO LEARN HOW TO IGNORE DISTRACTIONS.
WHEN I CAN LEARN TO IGNORE YOU, I'LL BE A TRUE JEDI MASTER.
SEE? AND YOU'LL OWE IT ALL TO ME.
TRAVELING WITH YOU THREE IS LIKE BEING ON A SHIP FULL OF CHILDREN.
AW, COME ON. YOU KNOW YOU LOVE US.
I KNOW. I STILL CAN'T UNDERSTAND WHY.

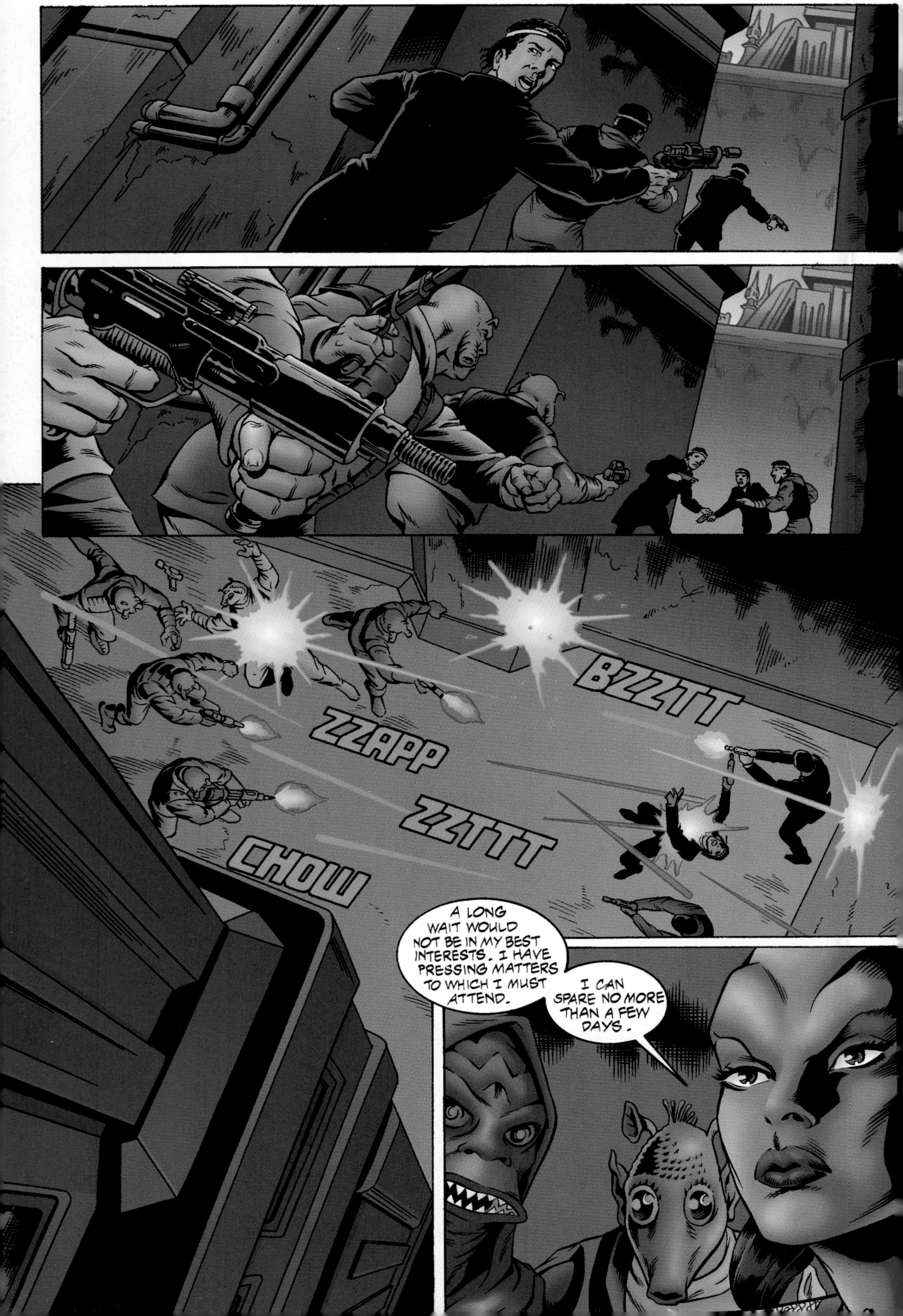
BZZTT
ZZAPP
ZZTTT
CHOW
A LONG WAIT WOULD NOT BE IN MY BEST INTERESTS. I HAVE PRESSING MATTERS TO WHICH I MUST ATTEND.
I CAN SPARE NO MORE THAN A FEW DAYS.

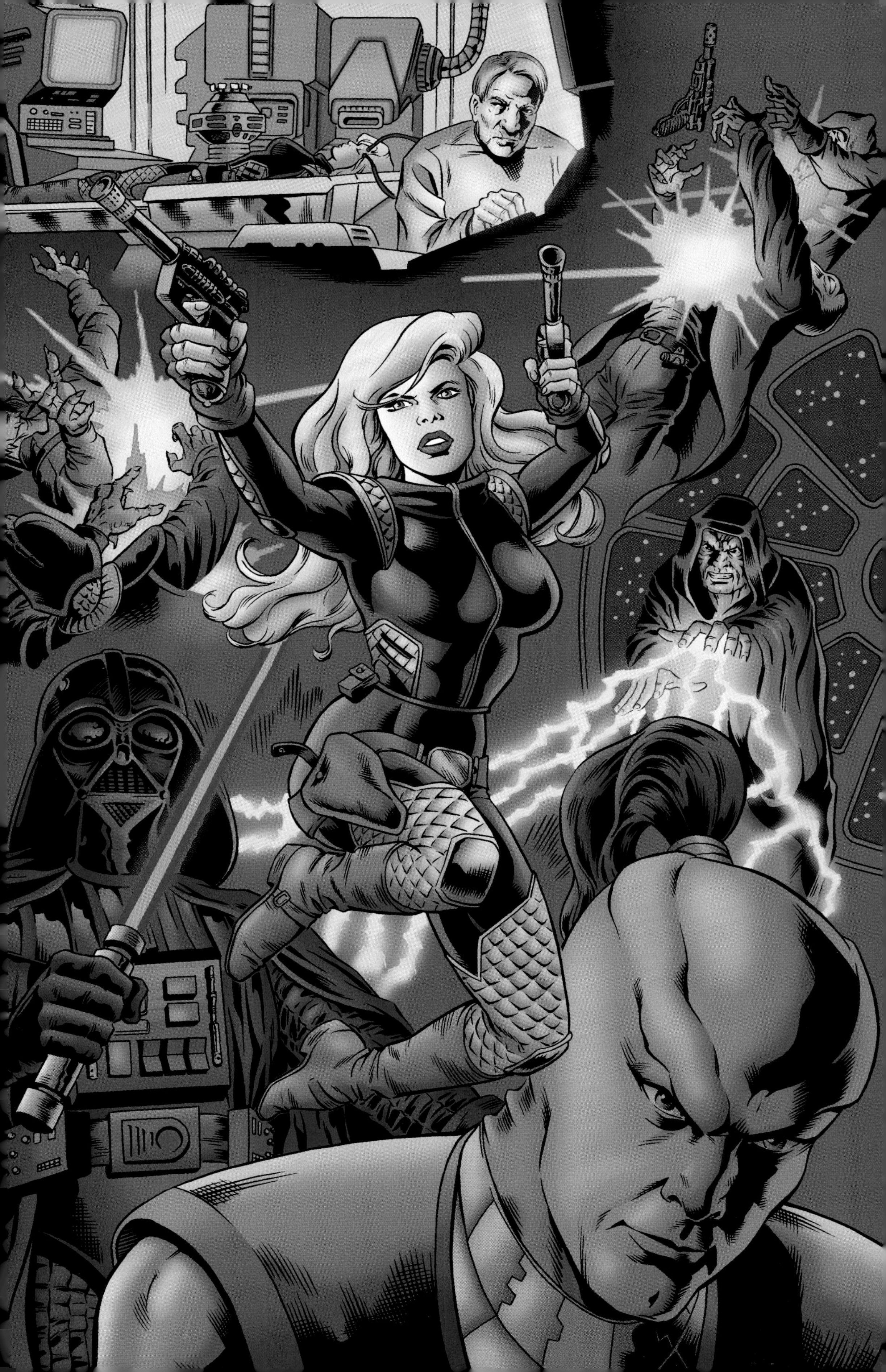

MAYBE HAN IS RIGHT. MAYBE WE SHOULD JUST LET BLACK SUN'S FACTIONS WIPE EACH OTHER OUT.

IF THEY WERE BETTER SHOTS, I MIGHT AGREE. BUT TOO MANY CIVILIANS HAVE GOTTEN CAUGHT IN THE CROSSFIRE.

WE NEED TO FIND SAVAN AND SHUT HER DOWN, LUKE. THE CLOCK IS RUNNING. THE LONGER IT TAKES, THE WORSE THINGS ARE GOING TO GET.

I SURE HOPE I DON'T FIND ANOTHER ONE OF YOUR *MODIFICATIONS*, BUDDY.

HEY, I HAD ALL THAT WORK DONE IN GOOD FAITH. IT'S NOT MY FAULT THE CHIEF MECHANIC HAD A HANGOVER.

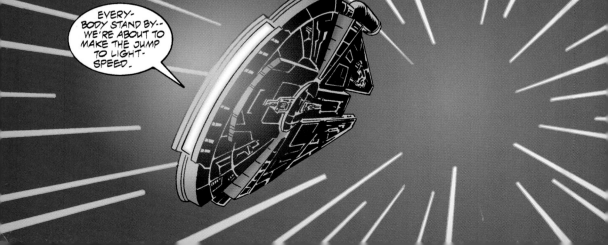

EVERY-BODY STAND BY-- WE'RE ABOUT TO MAKE THE JUMP TO LIGHT-SPEED.

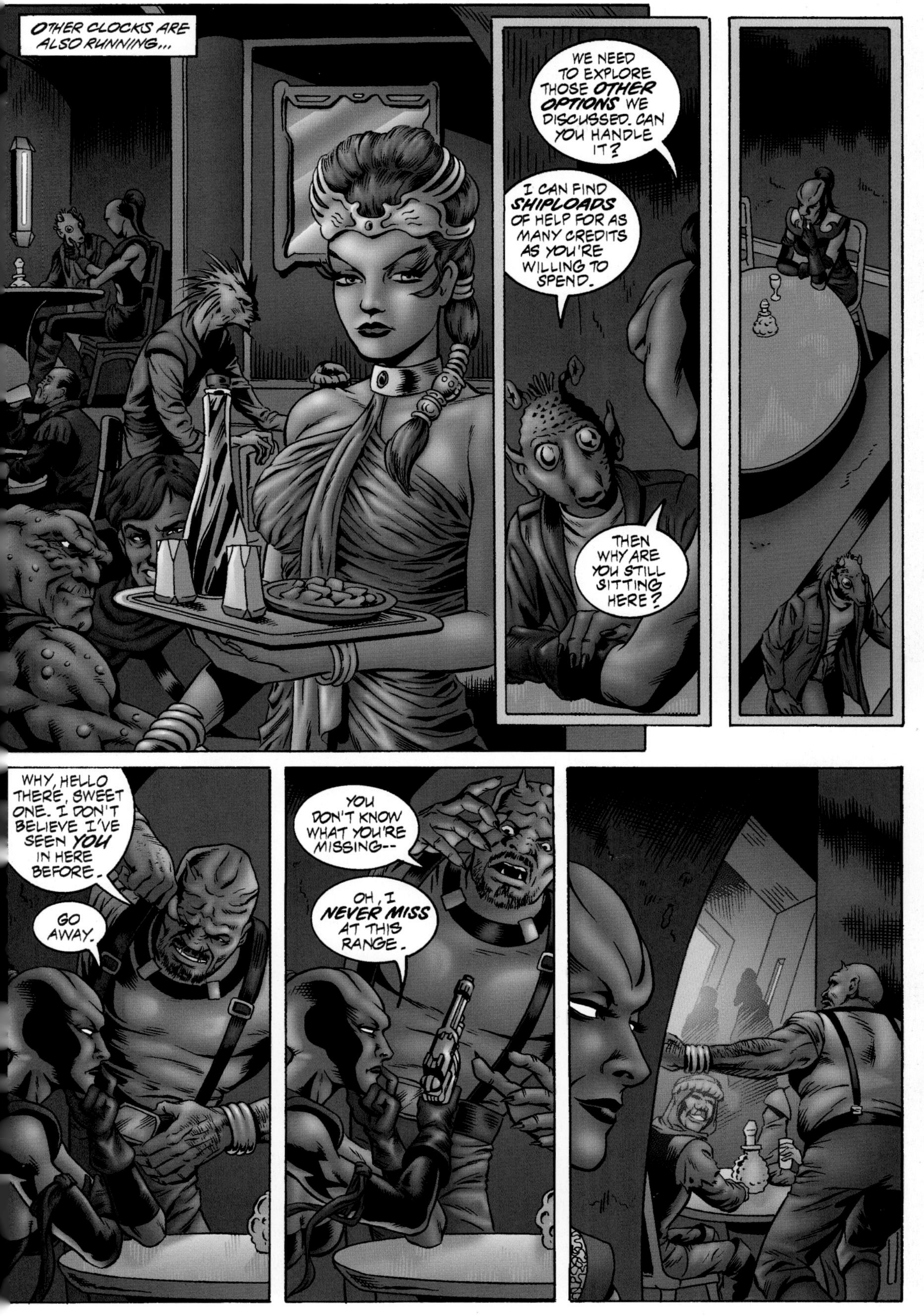
OTHER CLOCKS ARE ALSO RUNNING...
WE NEED TO EXPLORE THOSE **OTHER OPTIONS** WE DISCUSSED. CAN YOU HANDLE IT?
I CAN FIND **SHIPLOADS** OF HELP FOR AS MANY CREDITS AS YOU'RE WILLING TO SPEND.
THEN WHY ARE YOU STILL SITTING HERE?
WHY, HELLO THERE, SWEET ONE. I DON'T BELIEVE I'VE SEEN **YOU** IN HERE BEFORE.
GO AWAY.
YOU DON'T KNOW WHAT YOU'RE MISSING--
OH, I **NEVER MISS** AT THIS RANGE.

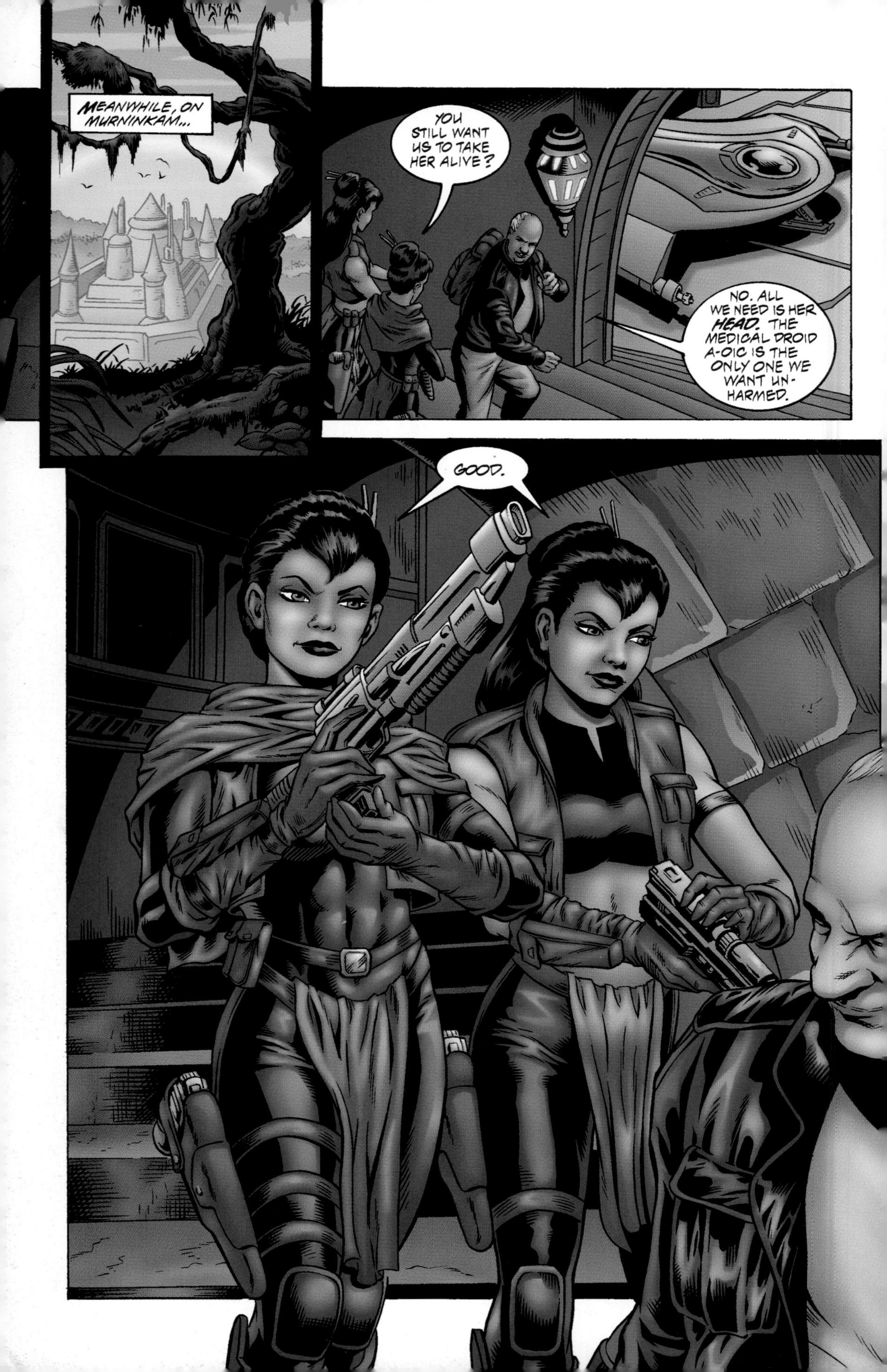
MEANWHILE, ON MURNINKAM...
YOU STILL WANT US TO TAKE HER ALIVE?
NO. ALL WE NEED IS HER HEAD. THE MEDICAL DROID A-OIC IS THE ONLY ONE WE WANT UN-HARMED.
GOOD.

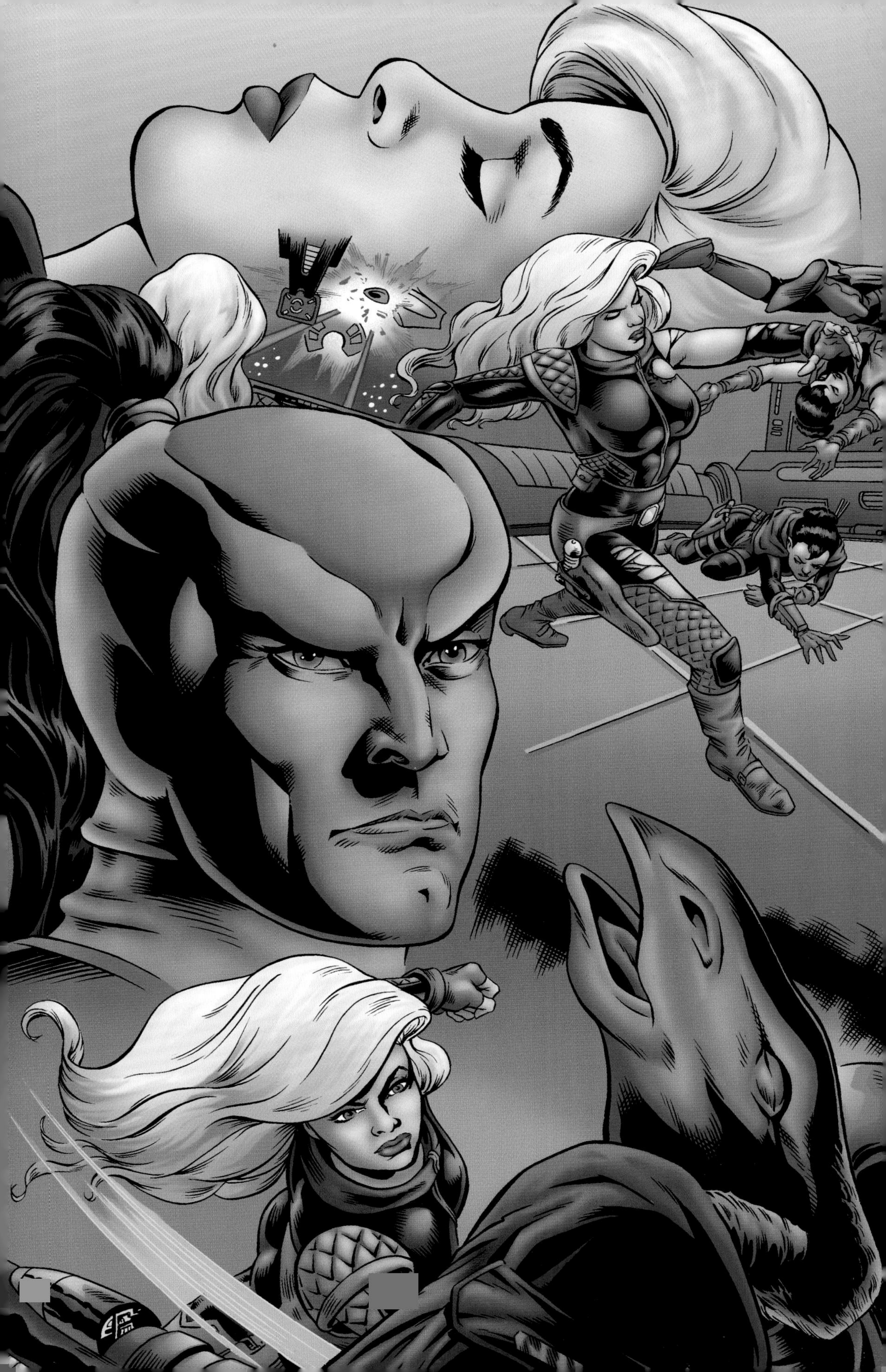

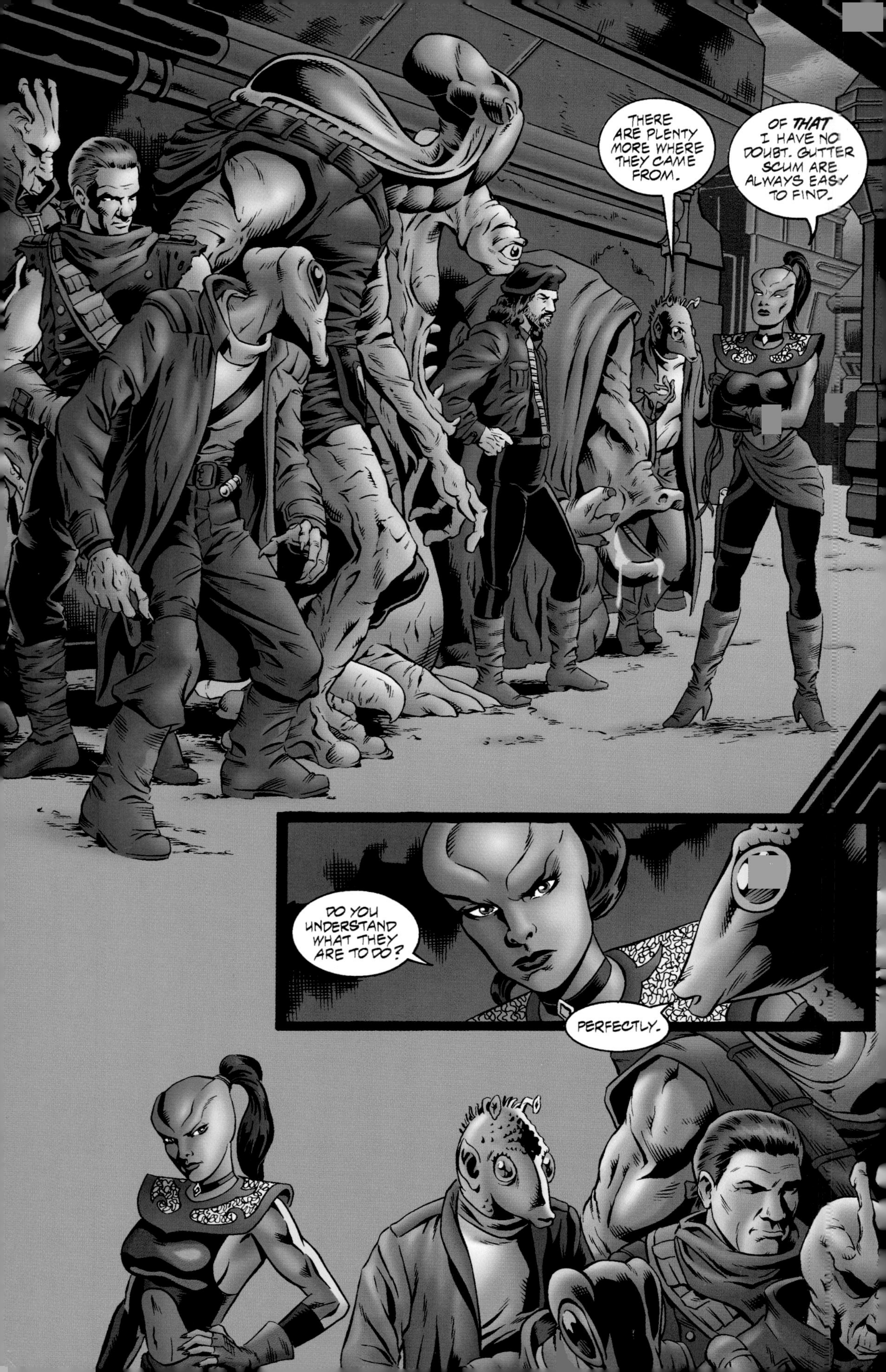
THERE ARE PLENTY MORE WHERE THEY CAME FROM.
OF THAT I HAVE NO DOUBT. GUTTER SCUM ARE ALWAYS EASY TO FIND.
DO YOU UNDERSTAND WHAT THEY ARE TO DO?
PERFECTLY.

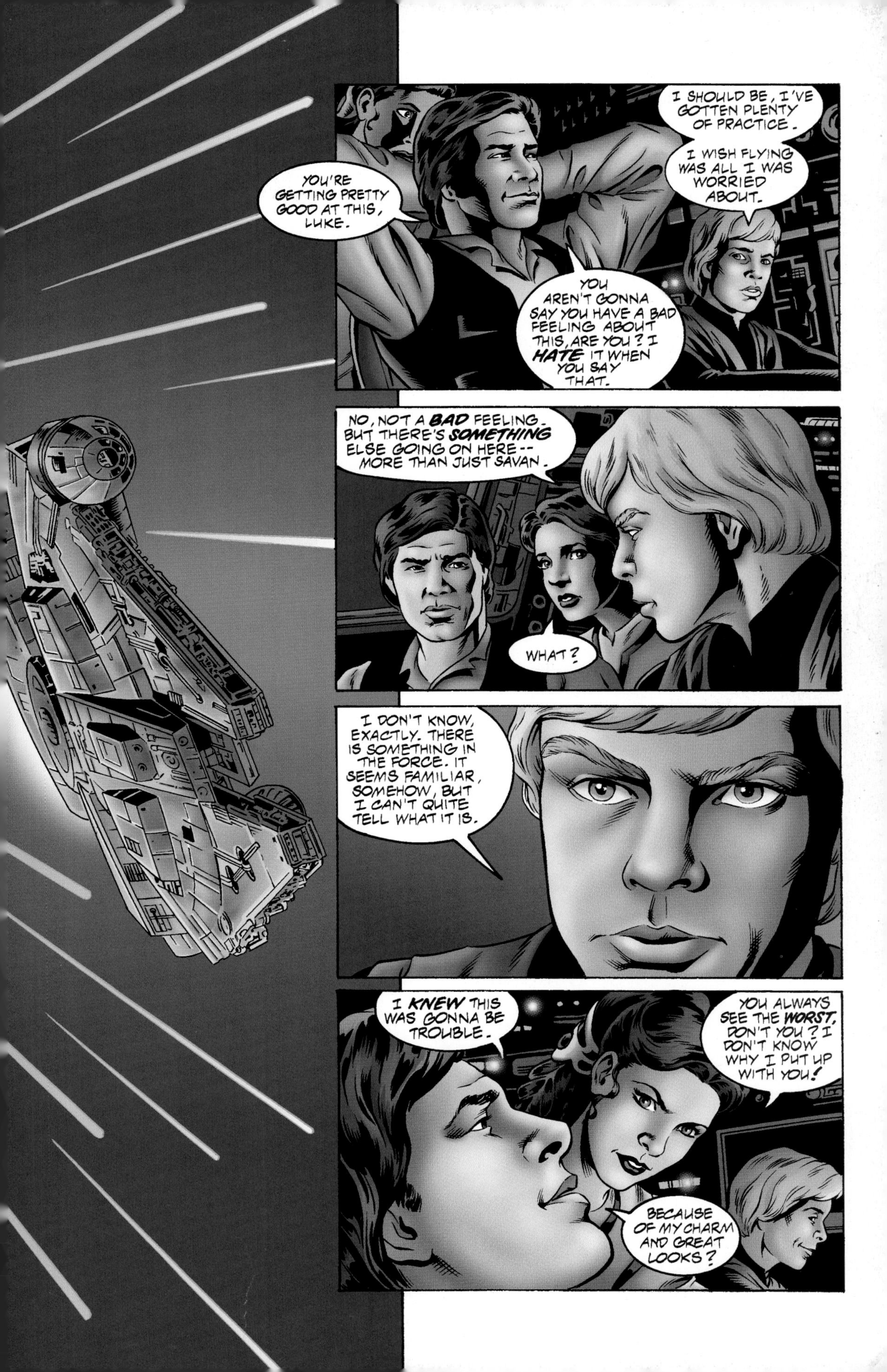

YOU'RE GETTING PRETTY GOOD AT THIS, LUKE.
I SHOULD BE, I'VE GOTTEN PLENTY OF PRACTICE.
I WISH FLYING WAS ALL I WAS WORRIED ABOUT.
YOU AREN'T GONNA SAY YOU HAVE A BAD FEELING ABOUT THIS, ARE YOU? I HATE IT WHEN YOU SAY THAT.
NO, NOT A BAD FEELING. BUT THERE'S SOMETHING ELSE GOING ON HERE -- MORE THAN JUST SAVAN.
WHAT?
I DON'T KNOW, EXACTLY. THERE IS SOMETHING IN THE FORCE. IT SEEMS FAMILIAR, SOMEHOW, BUT I CAN'T QUITE TELL WHAT IT IS.
I KNEW THIS WAS GONNA BE TROUBLE.
YOU ALWAYS SEE THE WORST, DON'T YOU? I DON'T KNOW WHY I PUT UP WITH YOU!
BECAUSE OF MY CHARM AND GREAT LOOKS?

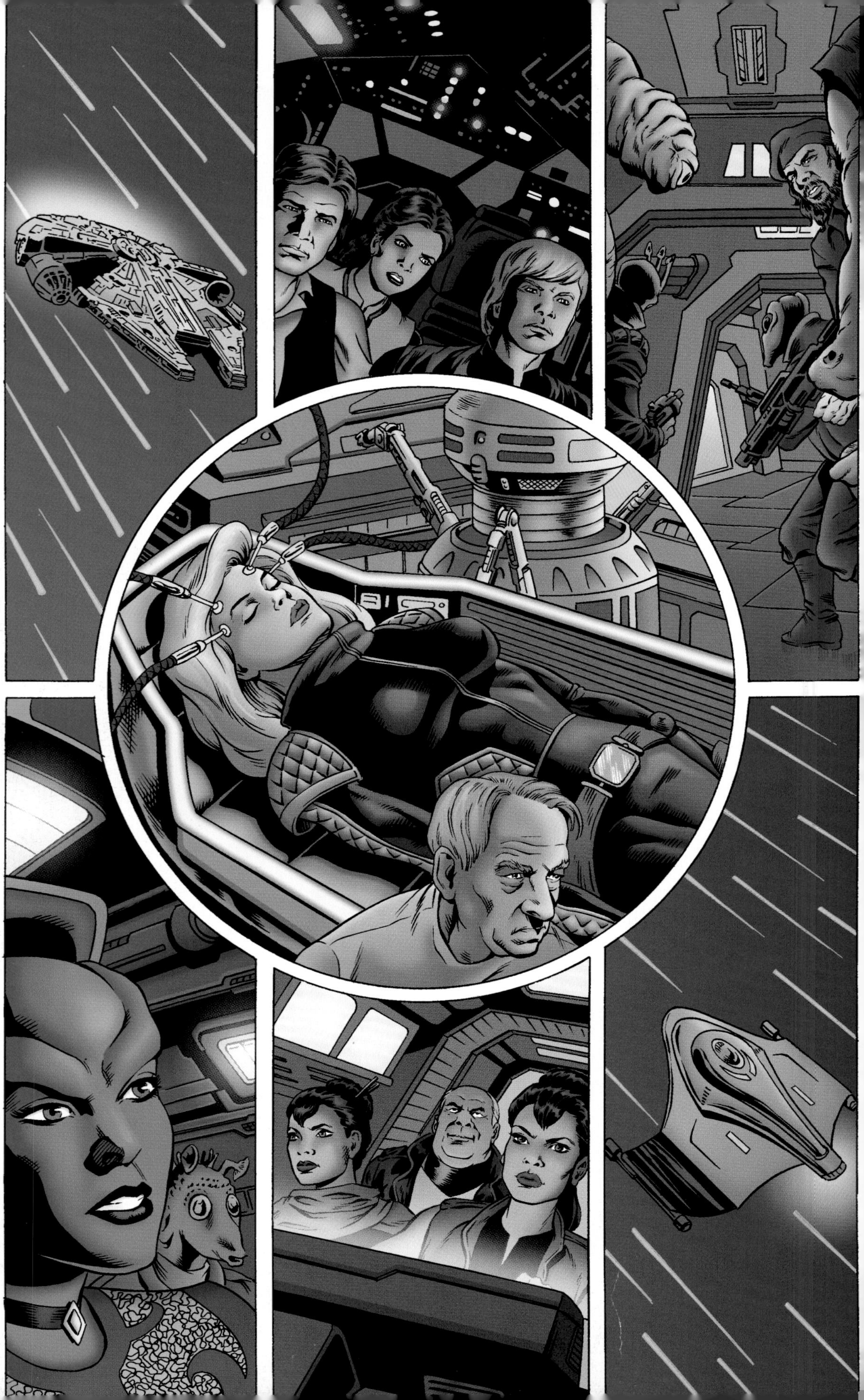

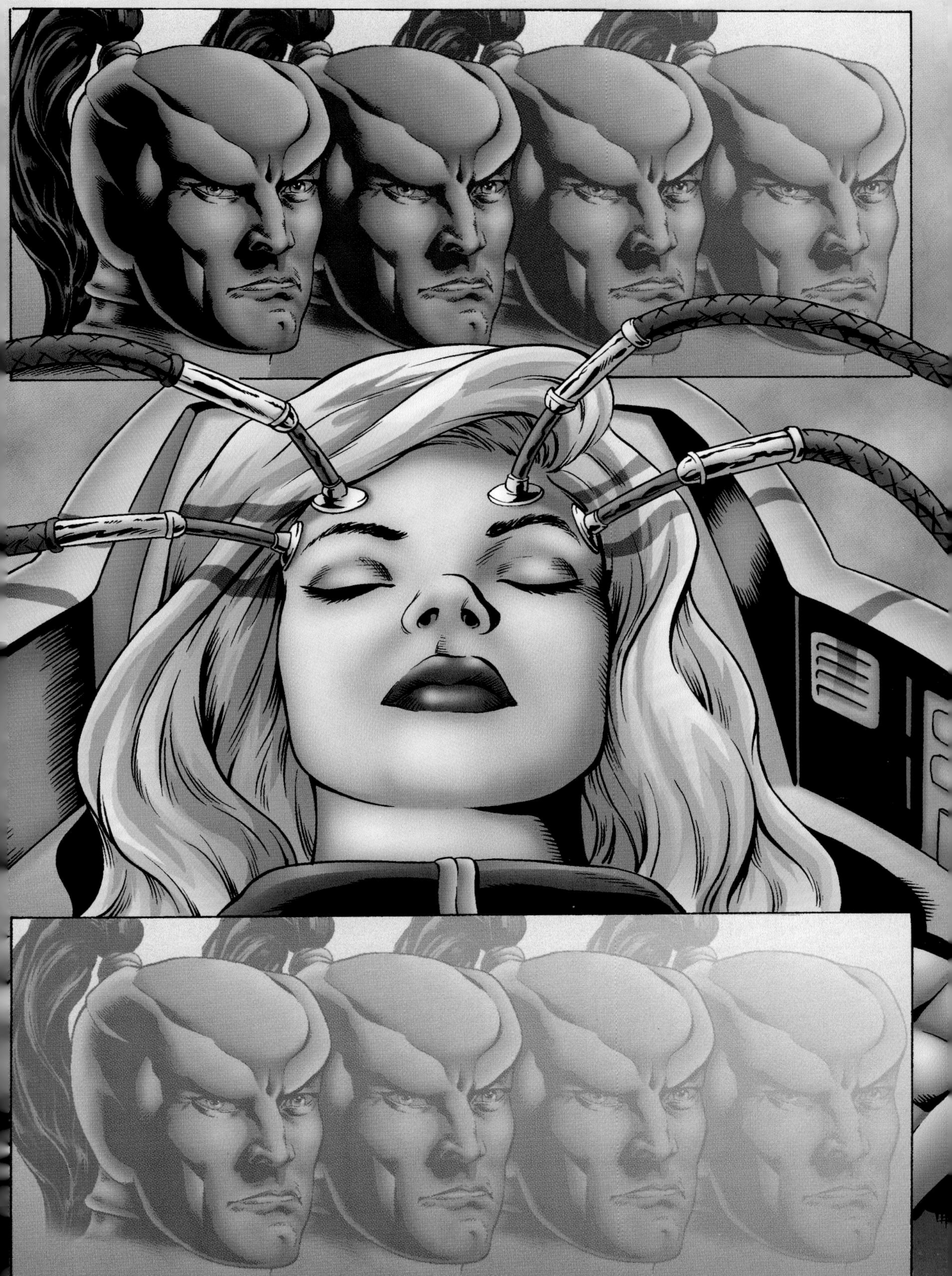

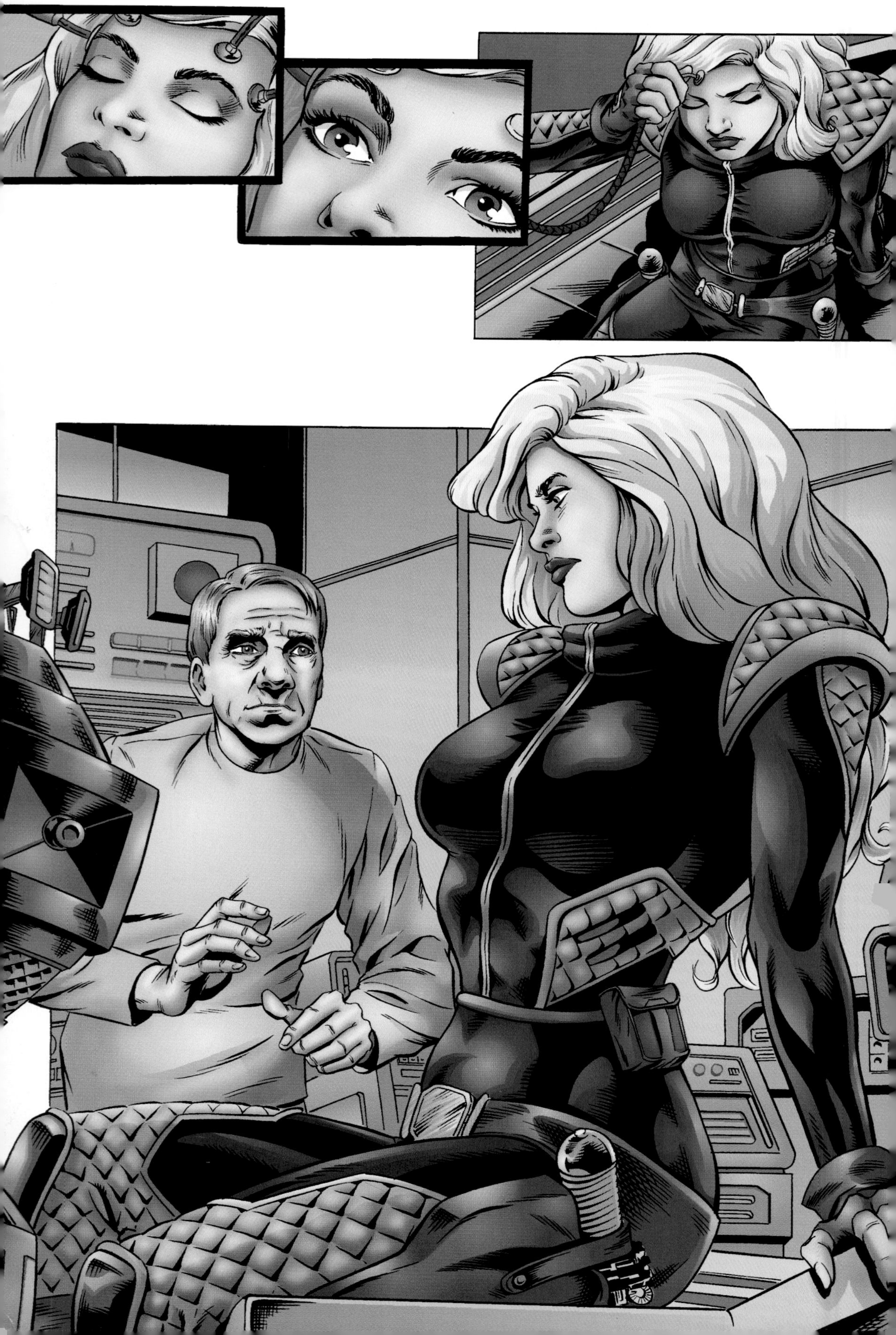

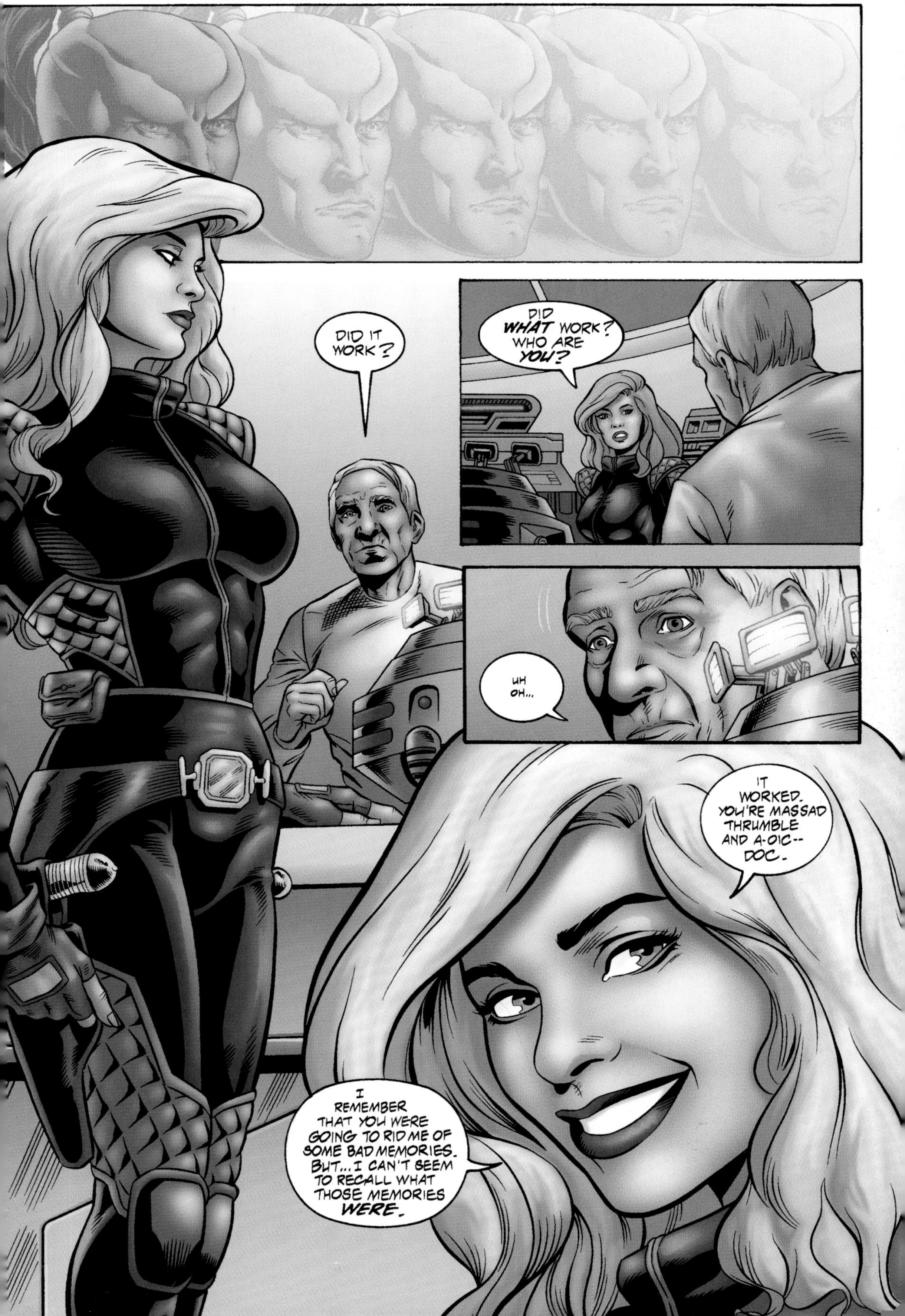
DID IT WORK?
DID WHAT WORK? WHO ARE YOU?
UH OH...
IT WORKED. YOU'RE MASSAD THRUMBLE AND A-OIC--DOC.
I REMEMBER THAT YOU WERE GOING TO RID ME OF SOME BAD MEMORIES. BUT... I CAN'T SEEM TO RECALL WHAT THOSE MEMORIES WERE.

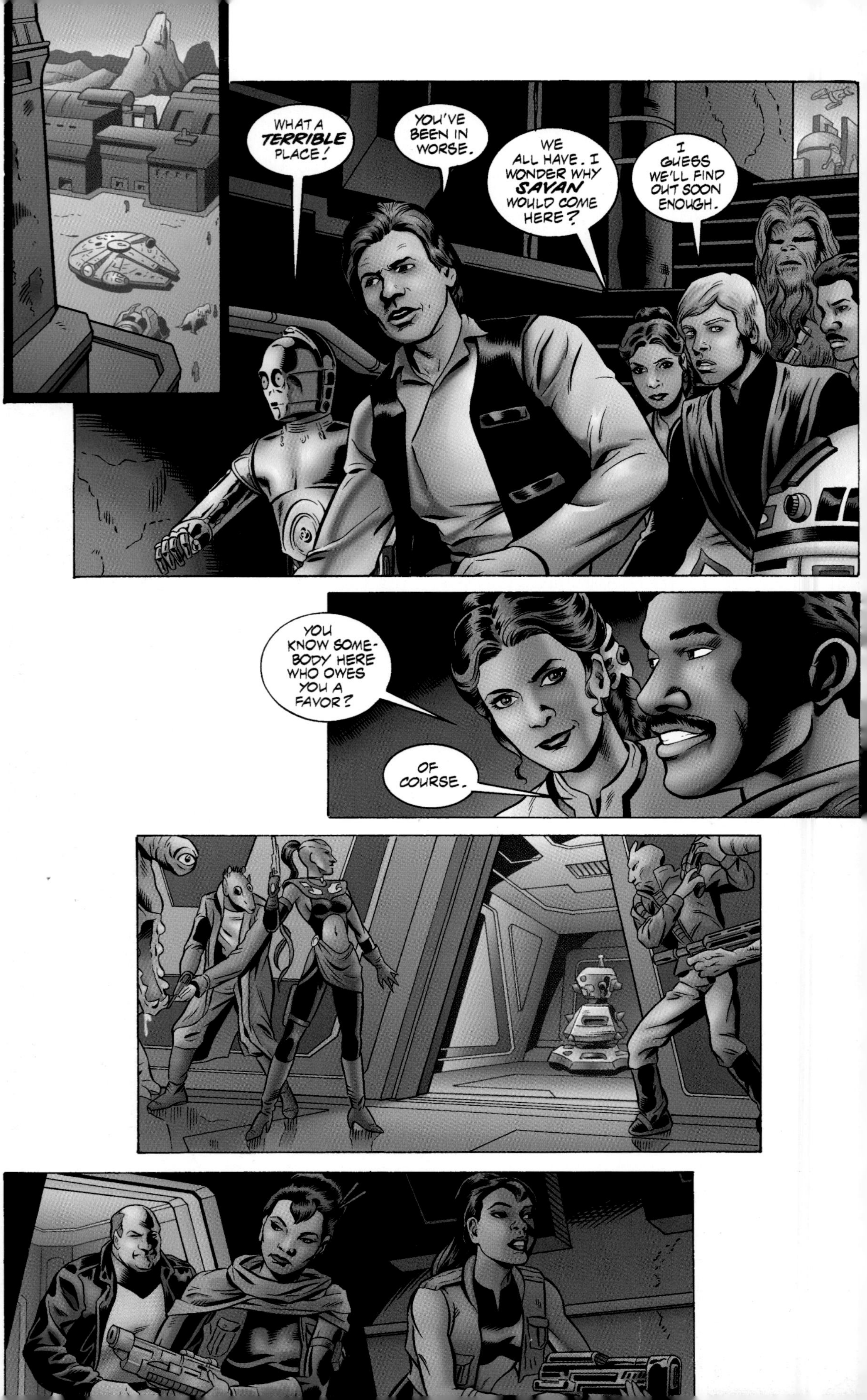
WHAT A TERRIBLE PLACE!
YOU'VE BEEN IN WORSE.
WE ALL HAVE. I WONDER WHY SAVAN WOULD COME HERE?
I GUESS WE'LL FIND OUT SOON ENOUGH.
YOU KNOW SOME-BODY HERE WHO OWES YOU A FAVOR?
OF COURSE.

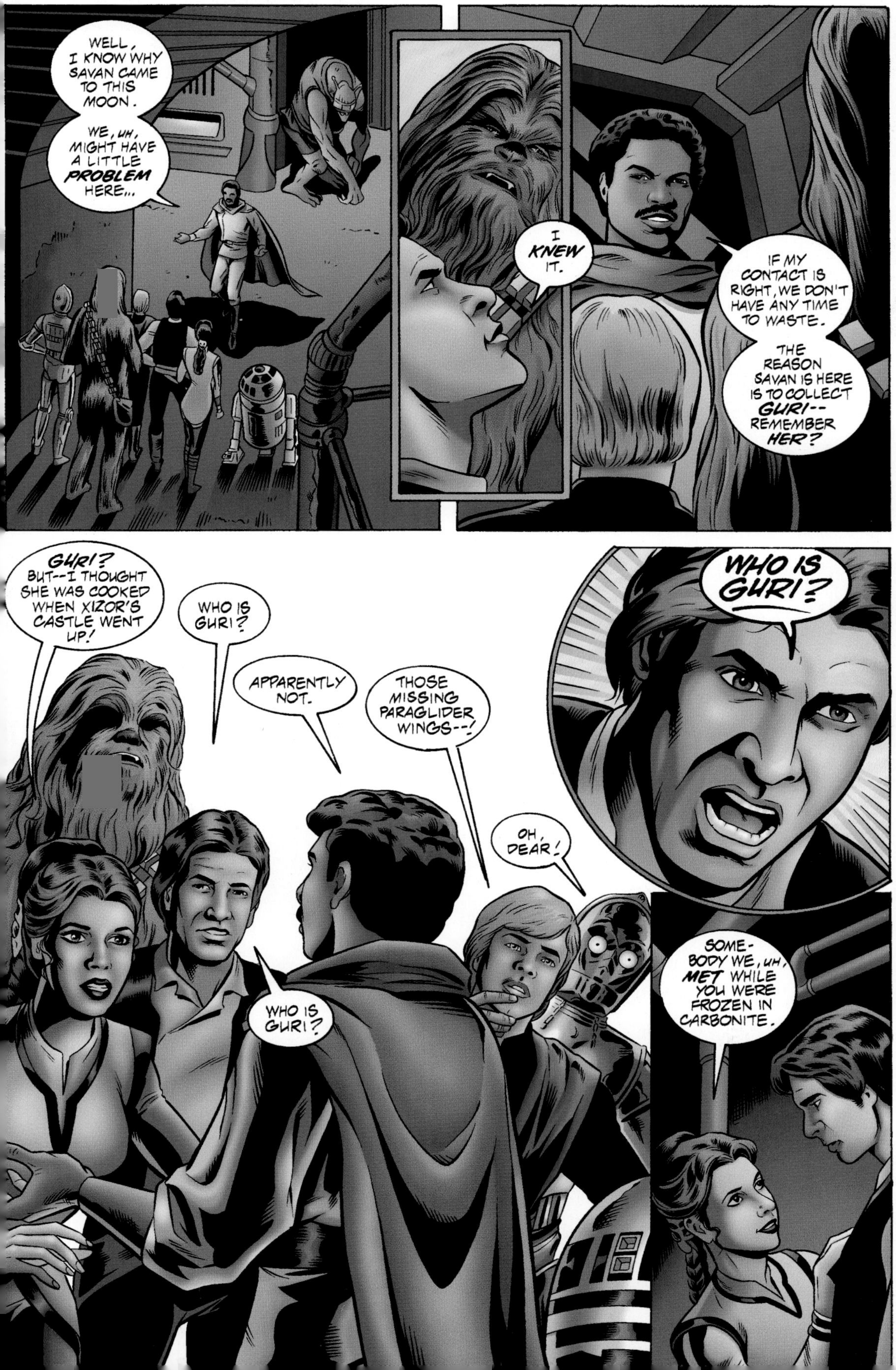
WELL, I KNOW WHY SAVAN CAME TO THIS MOON.
WE, *UH*, MIGHT HAVE A LITTLE ***PROBLEM*** HERE...
I ***KNEW*** IT.
IF MY CONTACT IS RIGHT, WE DON'T HAVE ANY TIME TO WASTE.
THE REASON SAVAN IS HERE IS TO COLLECT ***GURI***-- REMEMBER ***HER***?
GURI? BUT--I THOUGHT SHE WAS COOKED WHEN XIZOR'S CASTLE WENT UP!
WHO IS GURI?
APPARENTLY NOT.
THOSE MISSING PARAGLIDER WINGS--!
OH, DEAR!
WHO IS GURI?
WHO IS GURI?
SOME-BODY WE, *UH*, ***MET*** WHILE YOU WERE FROZEN IN CARBONITE.

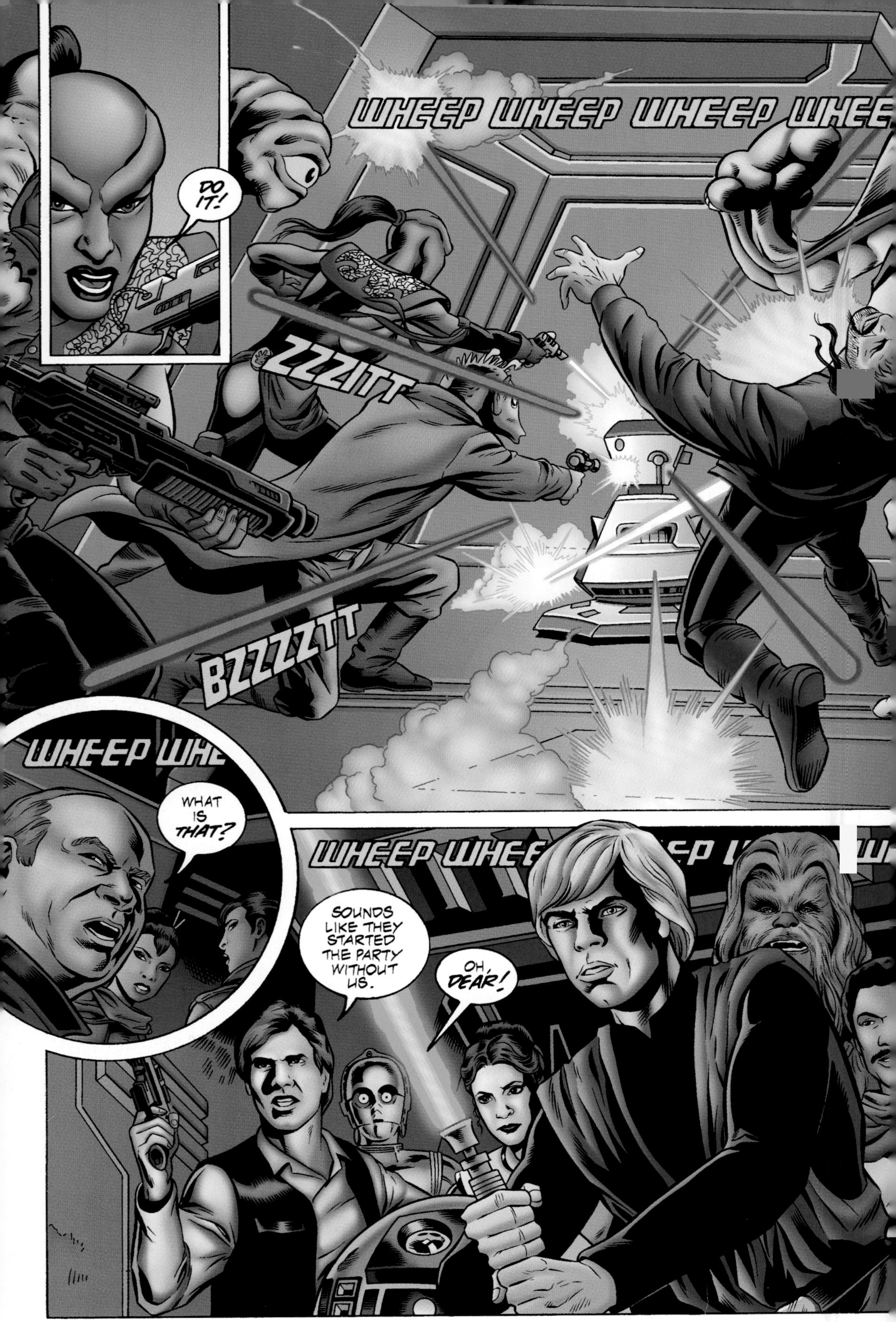
DO IT!
WHEEP WHEEP WHEEP WHEE
ZZZITT
BZZZZTT
WHEEP WHE
WHAT IS THAT?
WHEEP WHEE
SOUNDS LIKE THEY STARTED THE PARTY WITHOUT US.
OH, DEAR!

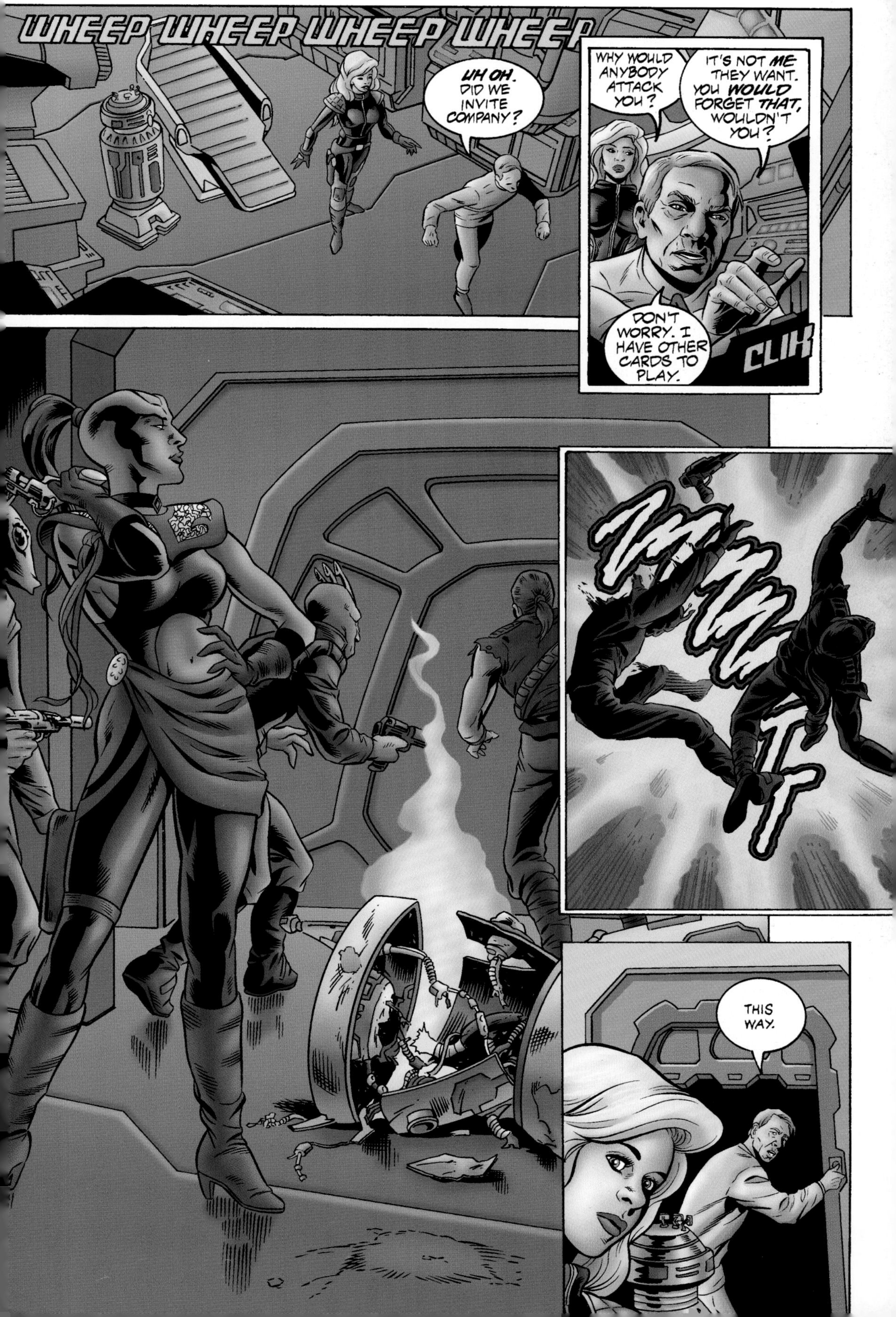
WHEEP WHEEP WHEEP WHEEP
UH OH. DID WE INVITE COMPANY?
WHY WOULD ANYBODY ATTACK YOU?
IT'S NOT ME THEY WANT. YOU WOULD FORGET THAT, WOULDN'T YOU?
DON'T WORRY. I HAVE OTHER CARDS TO PLAY.
CLIK
THIS WAY.

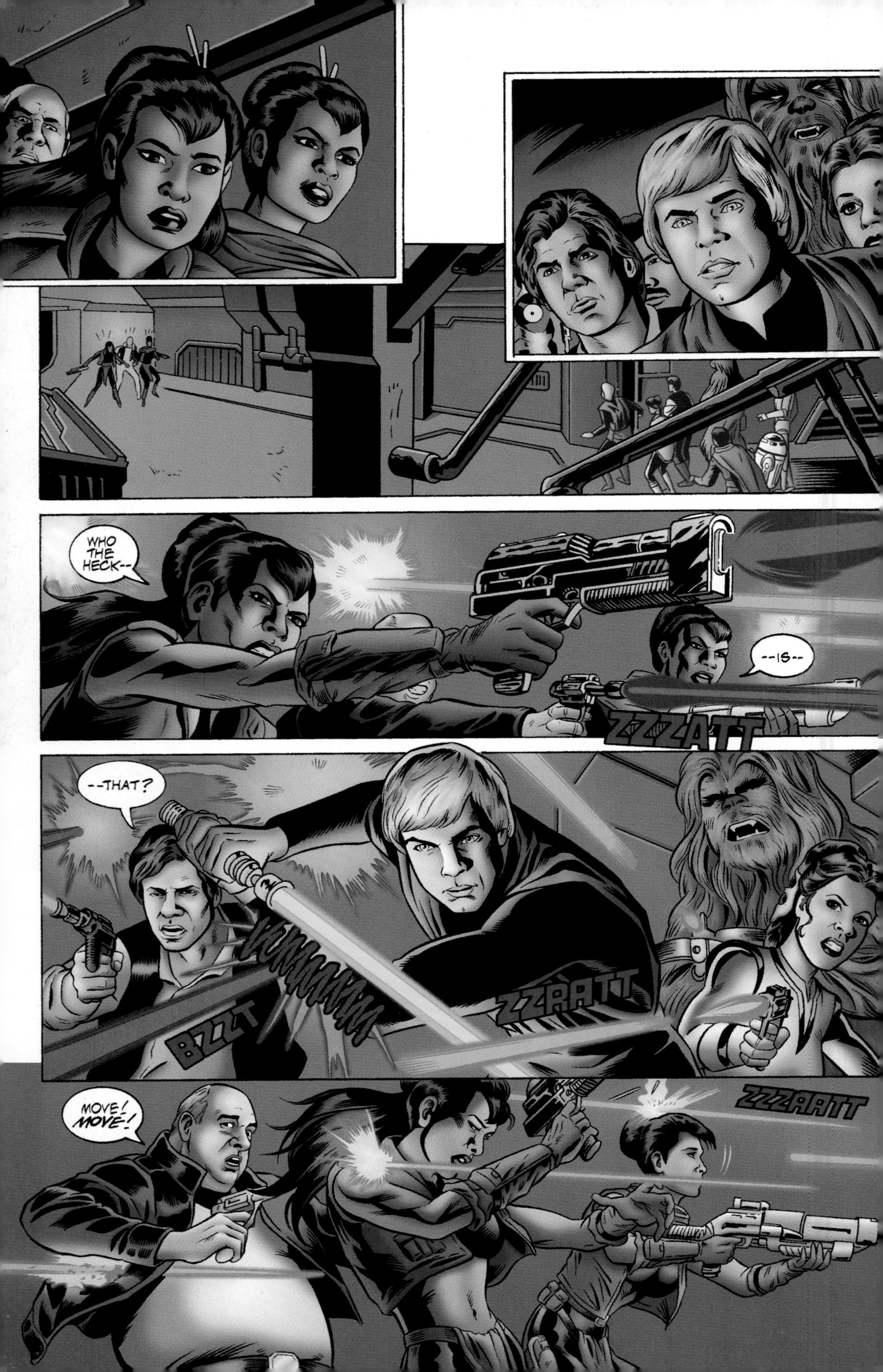
WHO THE HECK--
--IS--
ZZZATT
--THAT?
VVMMMMMM
BZZT
ZZRATT
MOVE! MOVE!
ZZZAATT

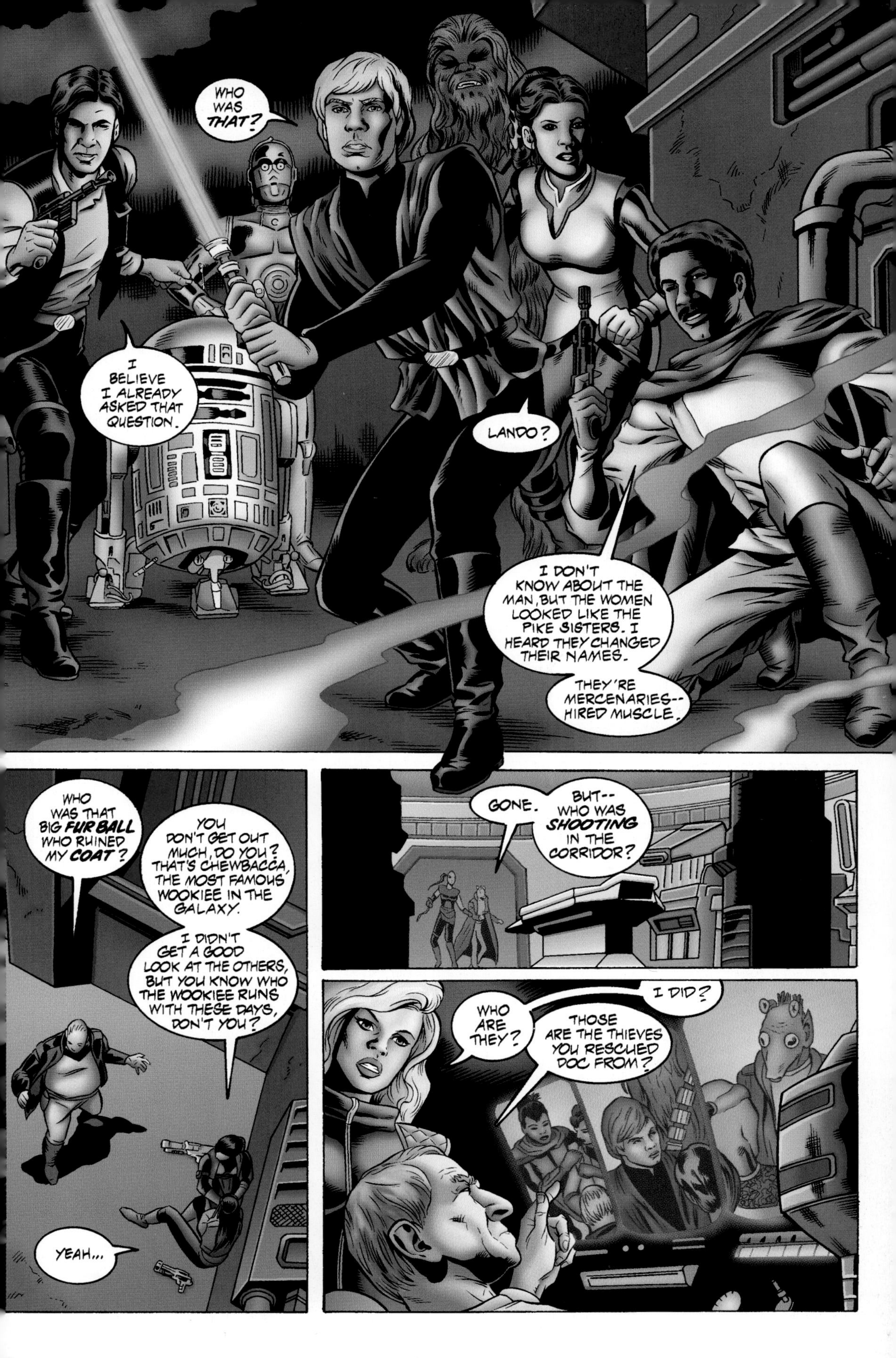
WHO WAS *THAT*?
I BELIEVE I ALREADY ASKED THAT QUESTION.
LANDO?
I DON'T KNOW ABOUT THE MAN, BUT THE WOMEN LOOKED LIKE THE PIKE SISTERS. I HEARD THEY CHANGED THEIR NAMES.
THEY'RE MERCENARIES-- HIRED MUSCLE.
WHO WAS THAT BIG ***FUR BALL*** WHO RUINED MY ***COAT***?
YOU DON'T GET OUT MUCH, DO YOU? THAT'S CHEWBACCA, THE *MOST FAMOUS* WOOKIEE IN THE GALAXY.
I DIDN'T GET A GOOD LOOK AT THE OTHERS, BUT YOU KNOW WHO THE WOOKIEE RUNS WITH THESE DAYS, DON'T YOU?
YEAH...
GONE.
BUT-- WHO WAS ***SHOOTING*** IN THE CORRIDOR?
WHO ARE THEY?
THOSE ARE THE THIEVES YOU RESCUED DOC FROM?
I DID?

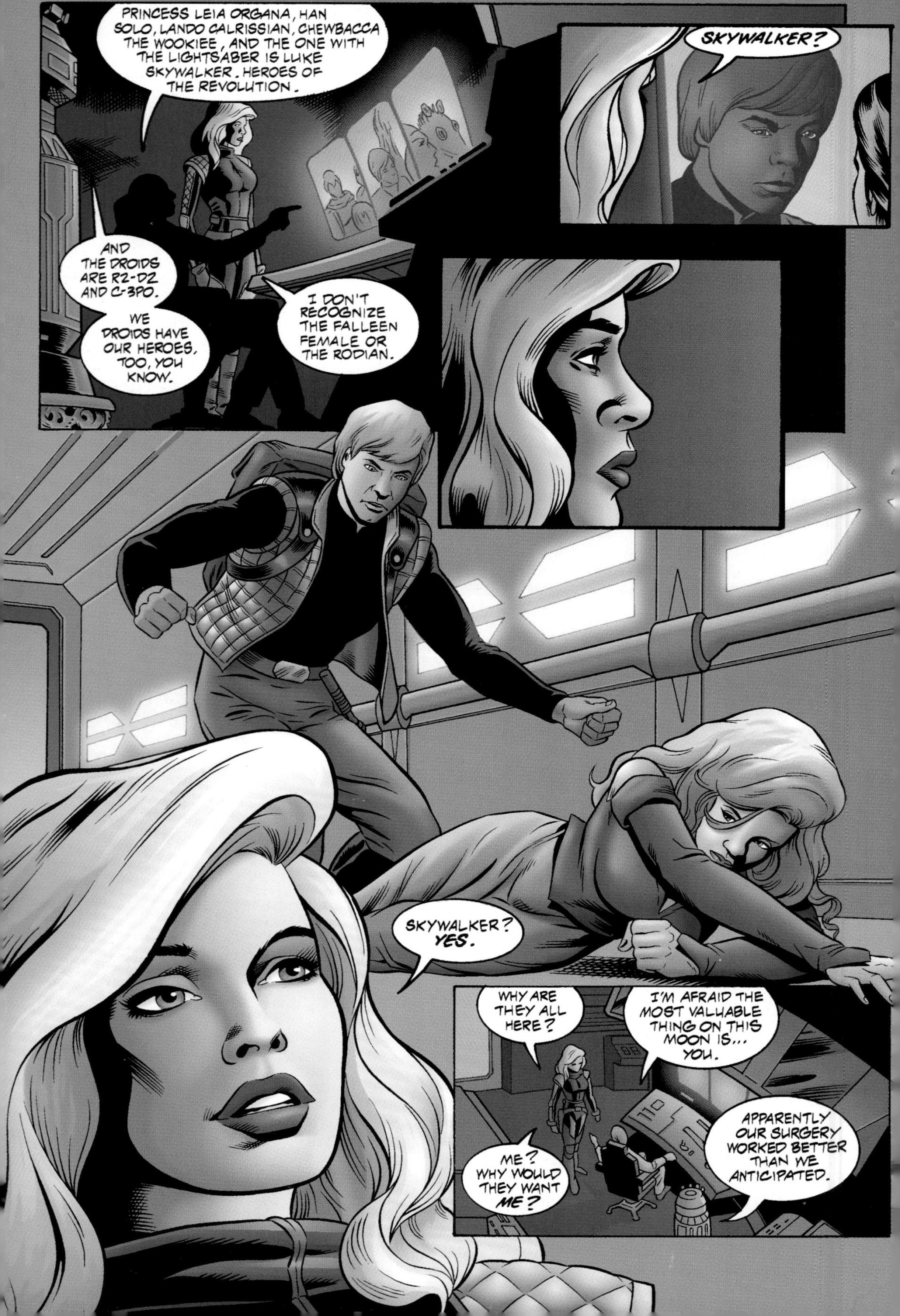
PRINCESS LEIA ORGANA, HAN SOLO, LANDO CALRISSIAN, CHEWBACCA THE WOOKIEE, AND THE ONE WITH THE LIGHTSABER IS LUKE SKYWALKER. HEROES OF THE REVOLUTION.
AND THE DROIDS ARE R2-D2 AND C-3PO.
WE DROIDS HAVE OUR HEROES, TOO, YOU KNOW.
I DON'T RECOGNIZE THE FALLEEN FEMALE OR THE RODIAN.
SKYWALKER?
SKYWALKER? YES.
WHY ARE THEY ALL HERE?
I'M AFRAID THE MOST VALUABLE THING ON THIS MOON IS... YOU.
ME? WHY WOULD THEY WANT ME?
APPARENTLY OUR SURGERY WORKED BETTER THAN WE ANTICIPATED.

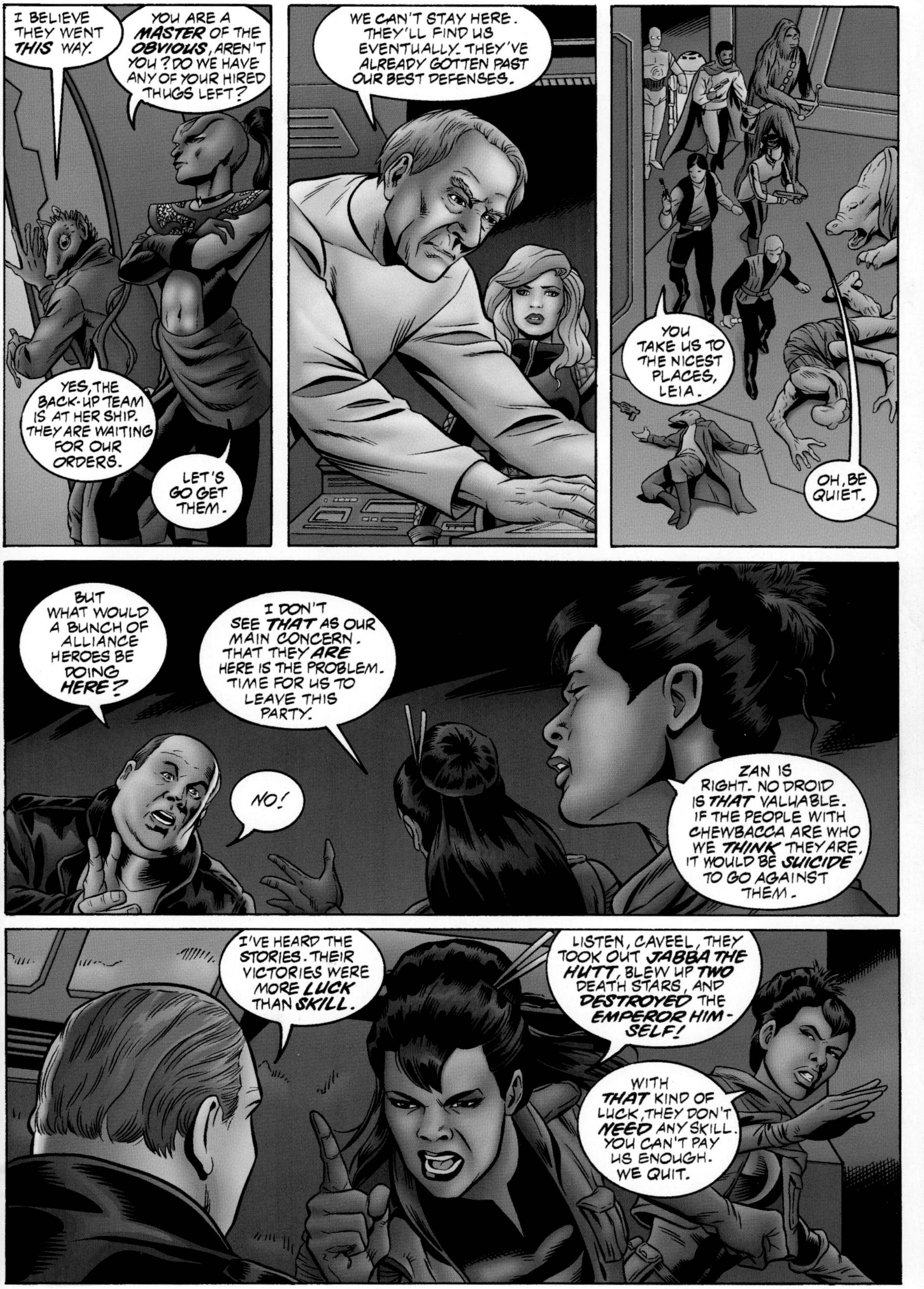
I BELIEVE THEY WENT THIS WAY.
YOU ARE A MASTER OF THE OBVIOUS, AREN'T YOU? DO WE HAVE ANY OF YOUR HIRED THUGS LEFT?
YES, THE BACK-UP TEAM IS AT HER SHIP. THEY ARE WAITING FOR OUR ORDERS.
LET'S GO GET THEM.
WE CAN'T STAY HERE. THEY'LL FIND US EVENTUALLY. THEY'VE ALREADY GOTTEN PAST OUR BEST DEFENSES.
YOU TAKE US TO THE NICEST PLACES, LEIA.
OH, BE QUIET.
BUT WHAT WOULD A BUNCH OF ALLIANCE HEROES BE DOING HERE?
I DON'T SEE THAT AS OUR MAIN CONCERN. THAT THEY ARE HERE IS THE PROBLEM. TIME FOR US TO LEAVE THIS PARTY.
NO!
ZAN IS RIGHT. NO DROID IS THAT VALUABLE. IF THE PEOPLE WITH CHEWBACCA ARE WHO WE THINK THEY ARE, IT WOULD BE SUICIDE TO GO AGAINST THEM.
I'VE HEARD THE STORIES. THEIR VICTORIES WERE MORE LUCK THAN SKILL.
LISTEN, CAVEEL, THEY TOOK OUT JABBA THE HUTT, BLEW UP TWO DEATH STARS, AND DESTROYED THE EMPEROR HIMSELF!
WITH THAT KIND OF LUCK, THEY DON'T NEED ANY SKILL. YOU CAN'T PAY US ENOUGH. WE QUIT.

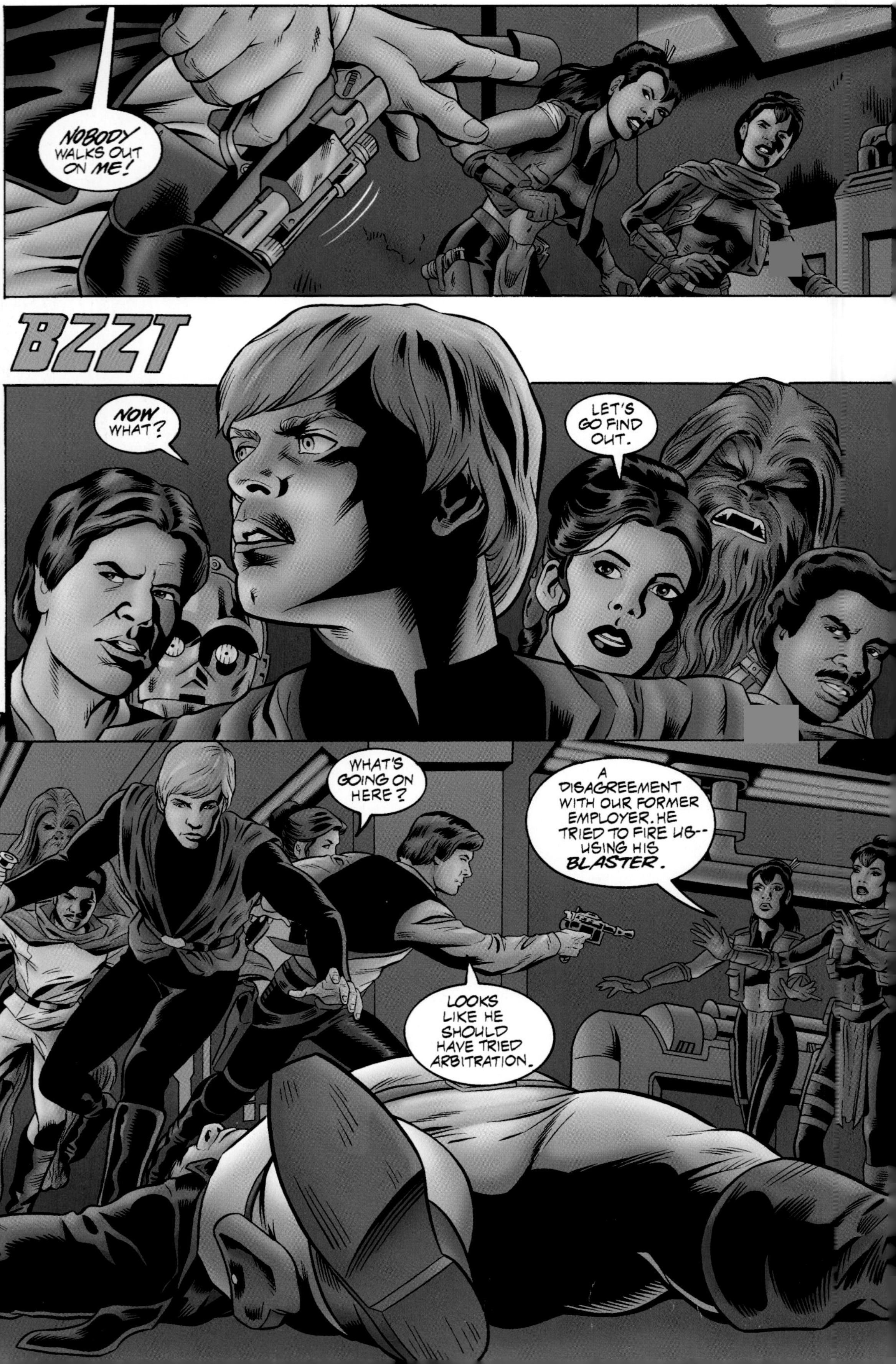
NOBODY WALKS OUT ON ME!
BZZT
NOW WHAT?
LET'S GO FIND OUT.
WHAT'S GOING ON HERE?
A DISAGREEMENT WITH OUR FORMER EMPLOYER. HE TRIED TO FIRE US-- USING HIS BLASTER.
LOOKS LIKE HE SHOULD HAVE TRIED ARBITRATION.

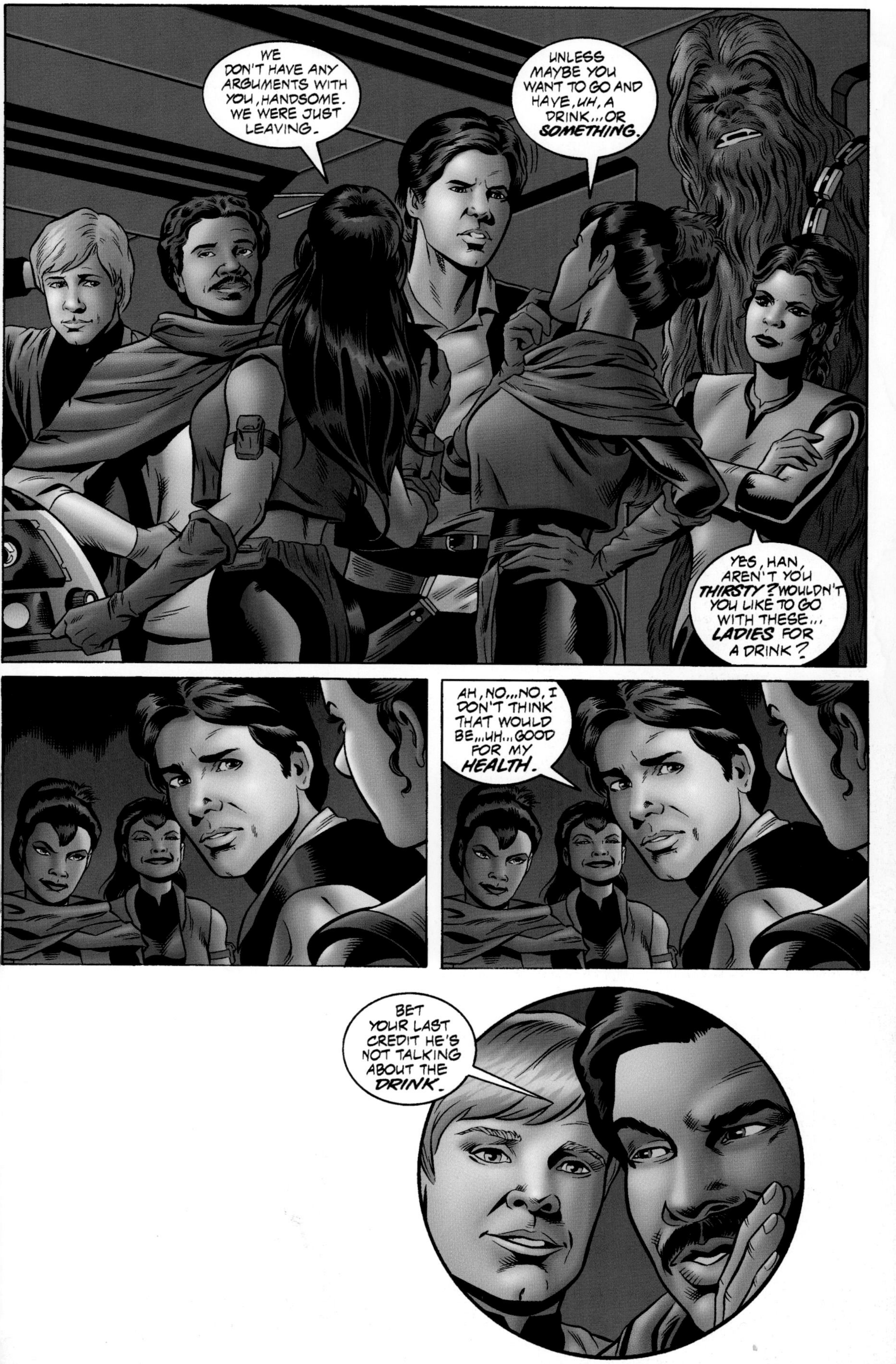
WE DON'T HAVE ANY ARGUMENTS WITH YOU, HANDSOME. WE WERE JUST LEAVING.
UNLESS MAYBE YOU WANT TO GO AND HAVE, UH, A DRINK... OR SOMETHING.
YES, HAN, AREN'T YOU THIRSTY? WOULDN'T YOU LIKE TO GO WITH THESE... LADIES FOR A DRINK?
AH, NO... NO, I DON'T THINK THAT WOULD BE... UH... GOOD FOR MY HEALTH.
BET YOUR LAST CREDIT HE'S NOT TALKING ABOUT THE DRINK.

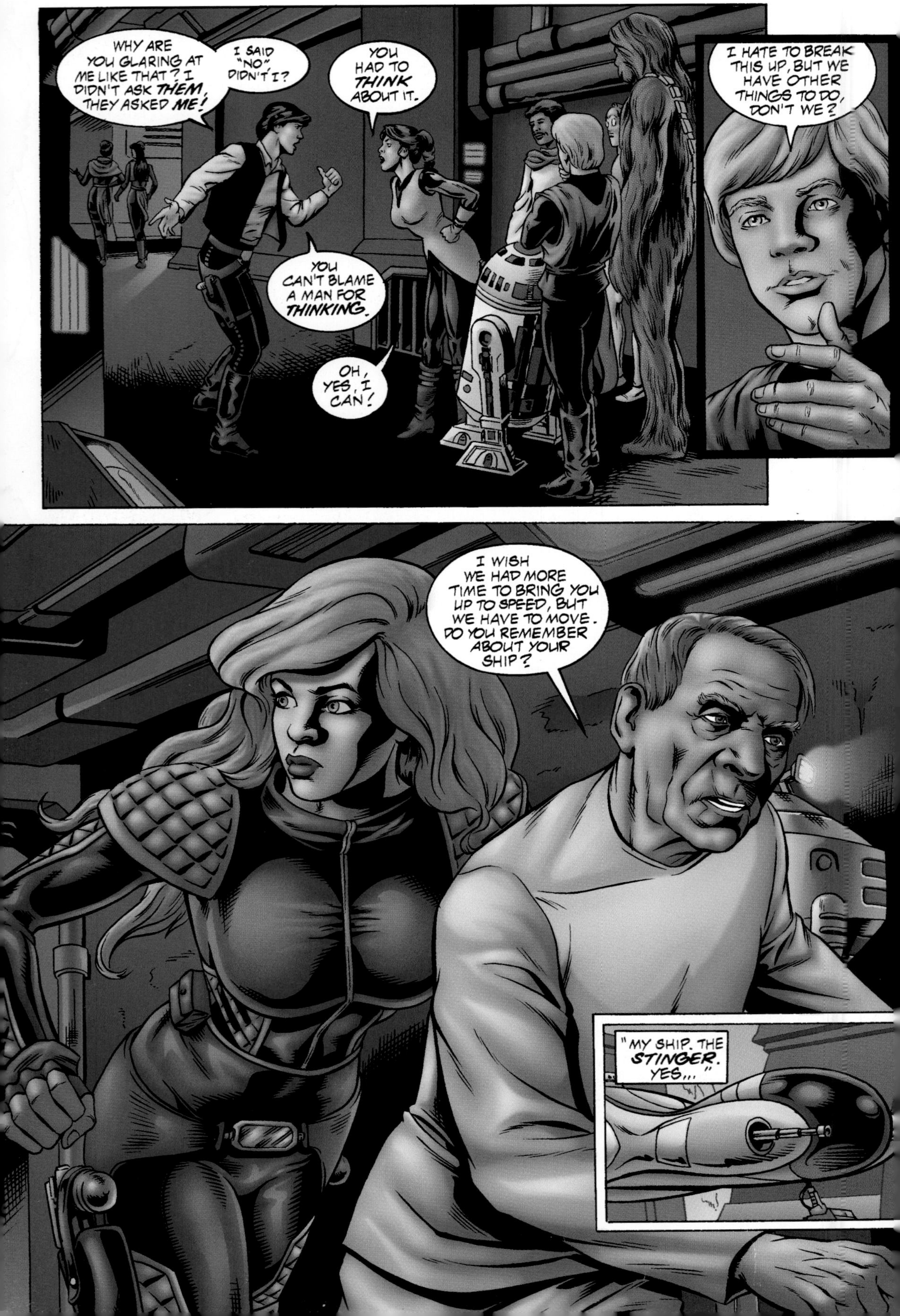
WHY ARE YOU GLARING AT ME LIKE THAT? I DIDN'T ASK *THEM*, THEY ASKED *ME*!
I SAID "NO" DIDN'T I?
YOU HAD TO *THINK* ABOUT IT.
YOU CAN'T BLAME A MAN FOR *THINKING*.
OH, YES, I CAN!
I HATE TO BREAK THIS UP, BUT WE HAVE OTHER THINGS TO DO, DON'T WE?
I WISH WE HAD MORE TIME TO BRING YOU UP TO SPEED, BUT WE HAVE TO MOVE. DO YOU REMEMBER ABOUT YOUR SHIP?
"MY SHIP. THE *STINGER*. YES..."

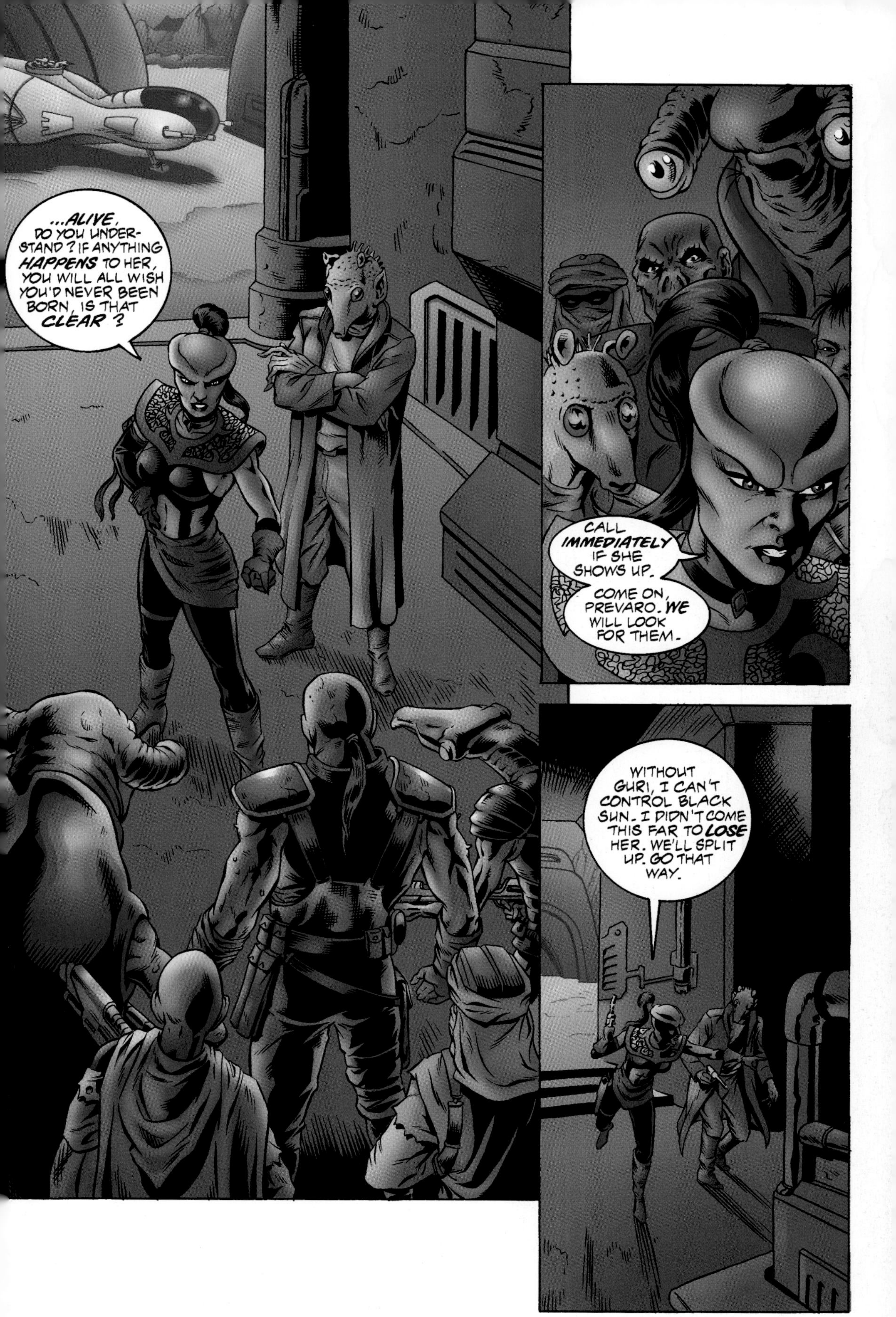
...ALIVE, DO YOU UNDER-STAND? IF ANYTHING HAPPENS TO HER, YOU WILL ALL WISH YOU'D NEVER BEEN BORN, IS THAT CLEAR?
CALL IMMEDIATELY IF SHE SHOWS UP.
COME ON, PREVARO. WE WILL LOOK FOR THEM.
WITHOUT GURI, I CAN'T CONTROL BLACK SUN. I DIDN'T COME THIS FAR TO LOSE HER. WE'LL SPLIT UP. GO THAT WAY.

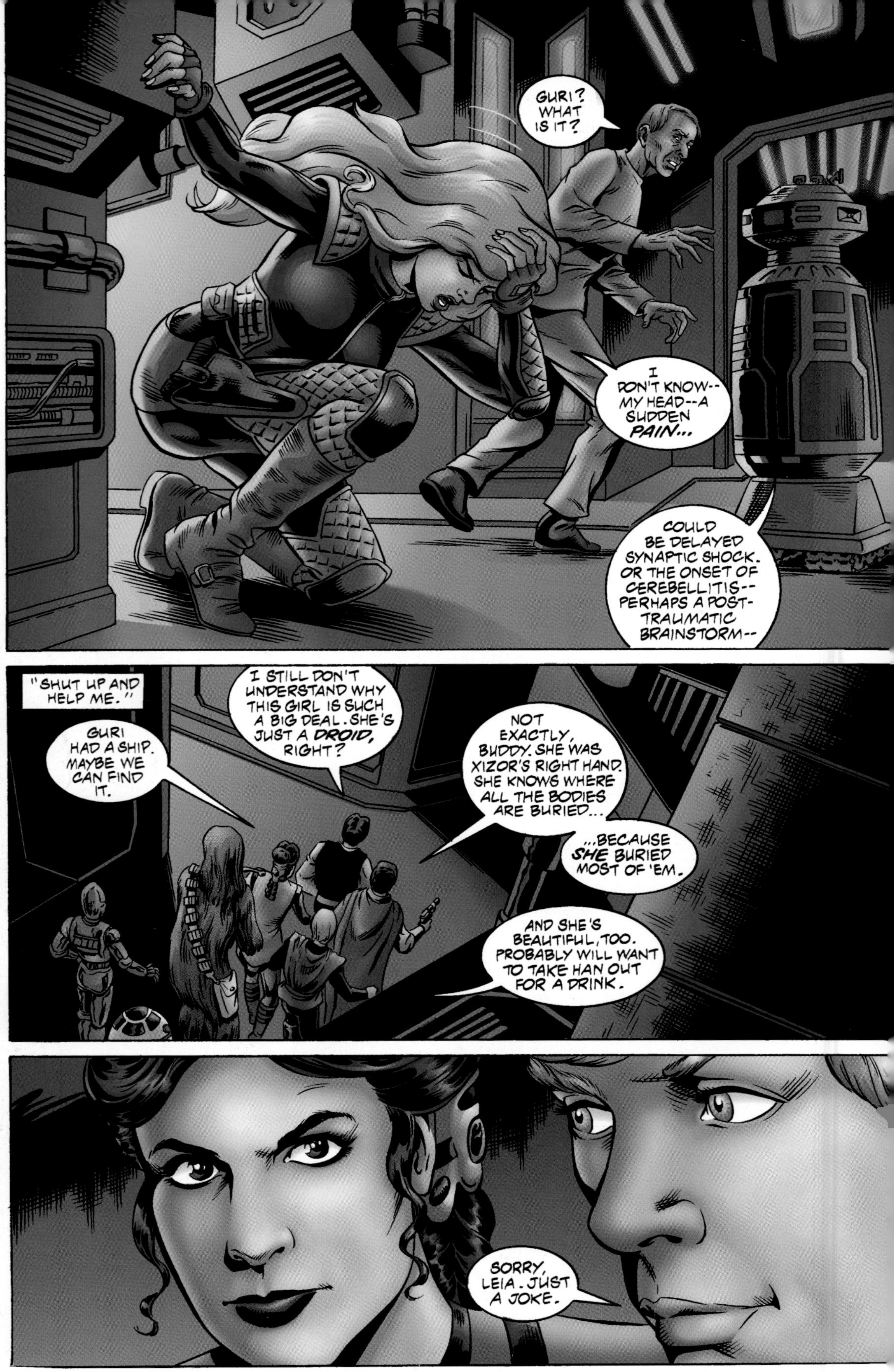
GURI? WHAT IS IT?
I DON'T KNOW-- MY HEAD--A SUDDEN PAIN...
COULD BE DELAYED SYNAPTIC SHOCK. OR THE ONSET OF CEREBELLITIS-- PERHAPS A POST-TRAUMATIC BRAINSTORM--
"SHUT UP AND HELP ME."
GURI HAD A SHIP. MAYBE WE CAN FIND IT.
I STILL DON'T UNDERSTAND WHY THIS GIRL IS SUCH A BIG DEAL. SHE'S JUST A DROID, RIGHT?
NOT EXACTLY, BUDDY. SHE WAS XIZOR'S RIGHT HAND. SHE KNOWS WHERE ALL THE BODIES ARE BURIED...
...BECAUSE SHE BURIED MOST OF 'EM.
AND SHE'S BEAUTIFUL, TOO. PROBABLY WILL WANT TO TAKE HAN OUT FOR A DRINK.
SORRY, LEIA. JUST A JOKE.

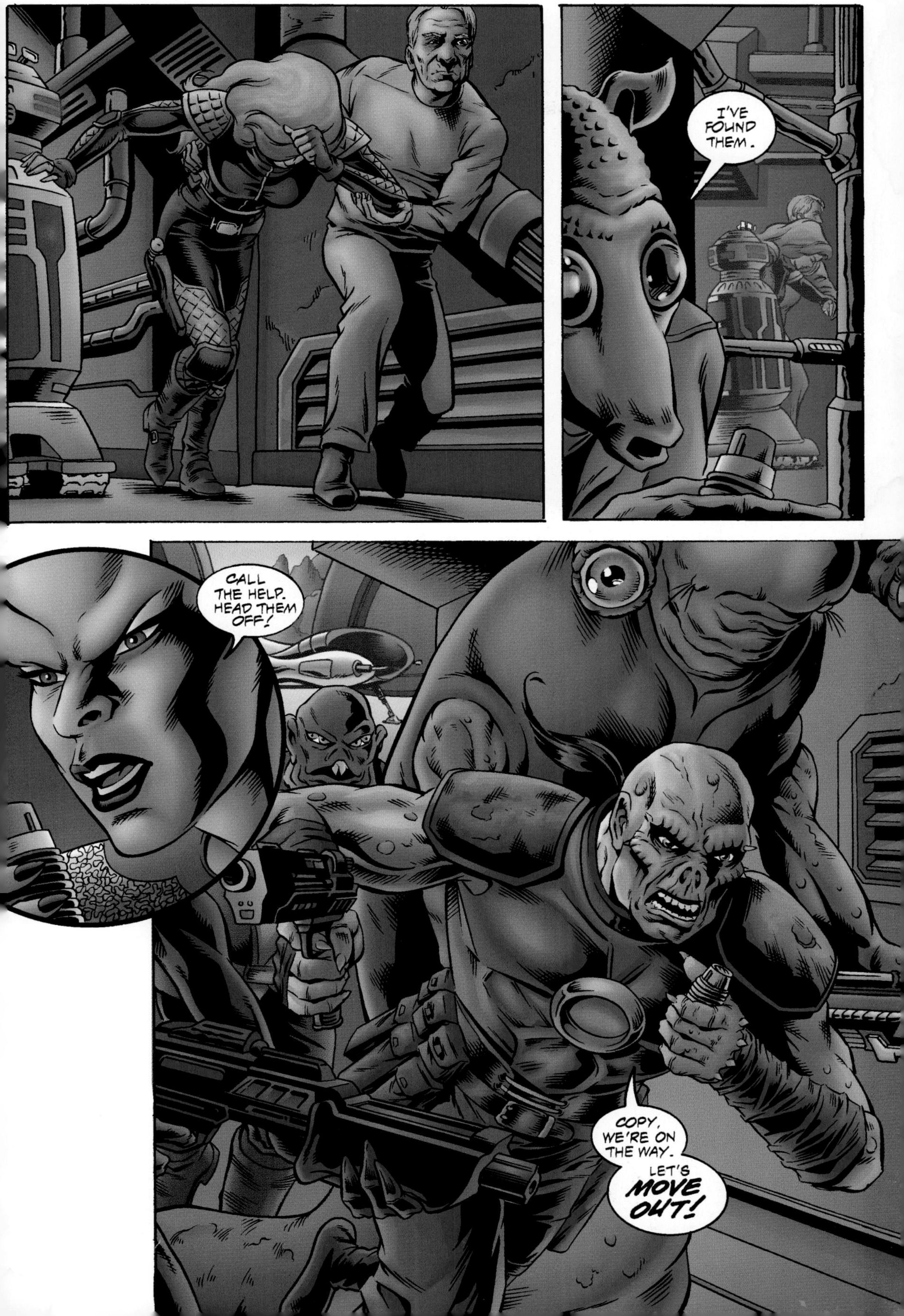
I'VE FOUND THEM.
CALL THE HELP. HEAD THEM OFF!
COPY, WE'RE ON THE WAY.
LET'S MOVE OUT!

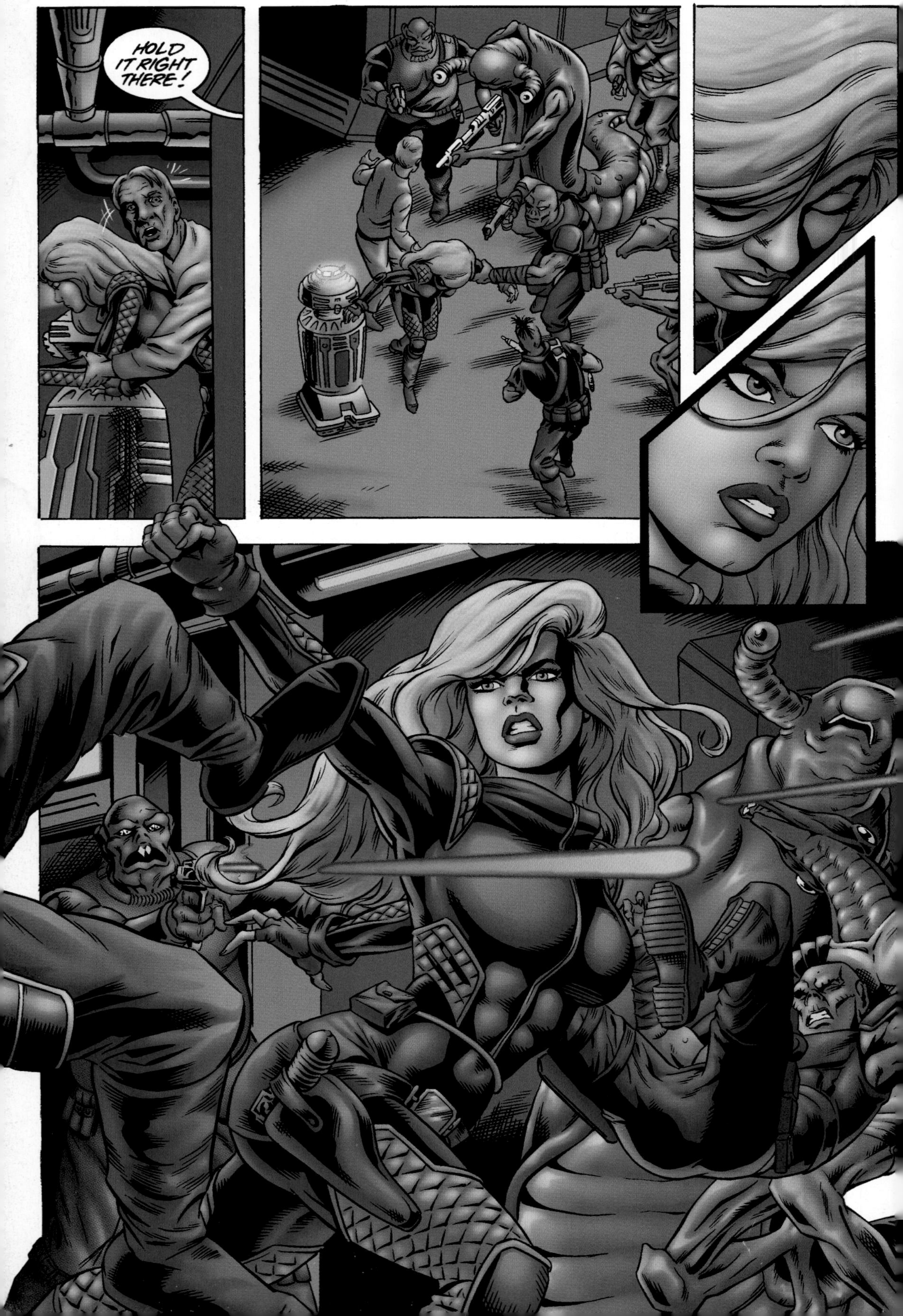
HOLD IT RIGHT THERE!

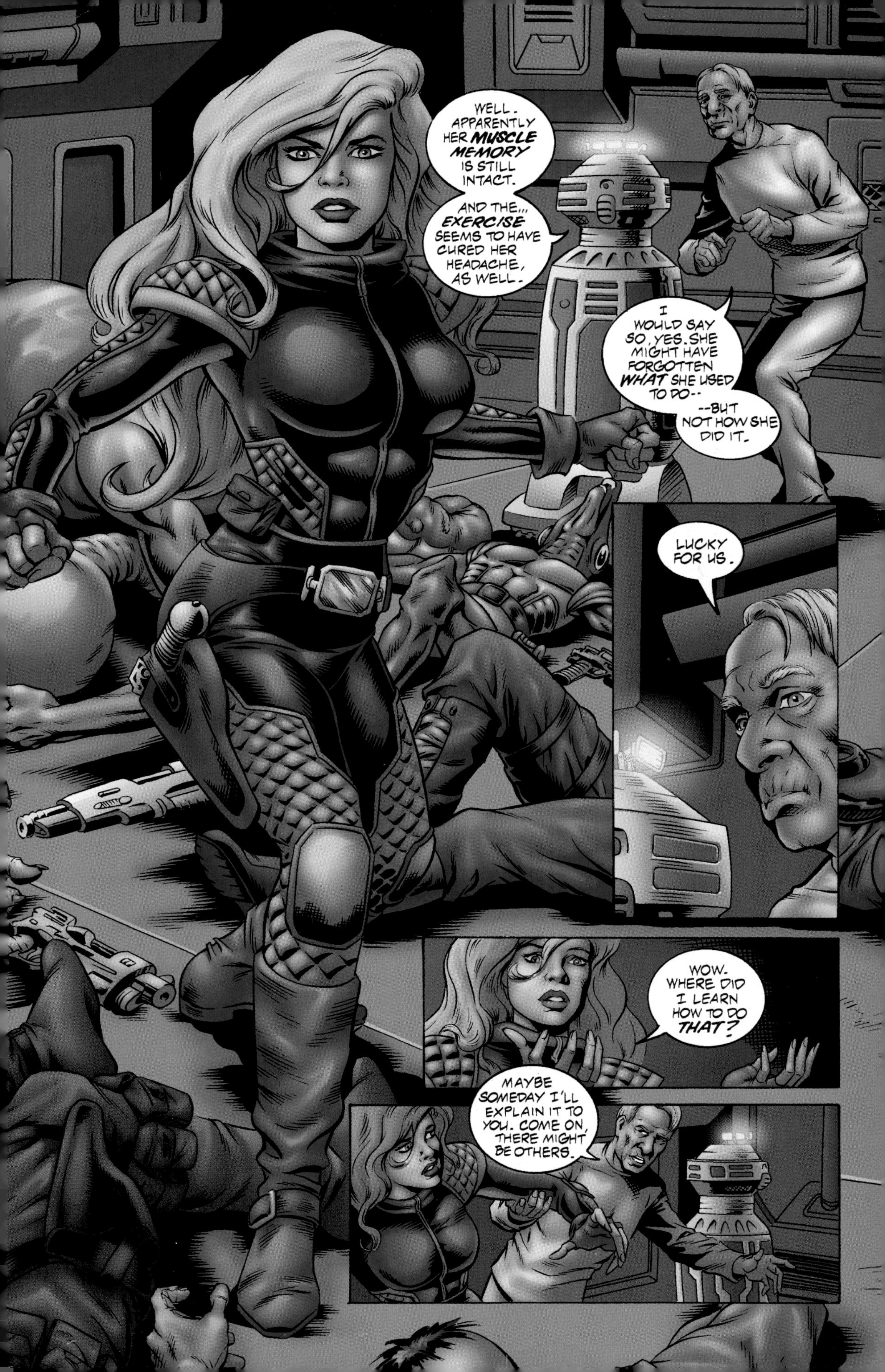

WELL. APPARENTLY HER MUSCLE MEMORY IS STILL INTACT.
AND THE... EXERCISE SEEMS TO HAVE CURED HER HEADACHE, AS WELL.
I WOULD SAY SO, YES. SHE MIGHT HAVE FORGOTTEN WHAT SHE USED TO DO--
--BUT NOT HOW SHE DID IT.
LUCKY FOR US.
WOW. WHERE DID I LEARN HOW TO DO THAT?
MAYBE SOMEDAY I'LL EXPLAIN IT TO YOU. COME ON, THERE MIGHT BE OTHERS.

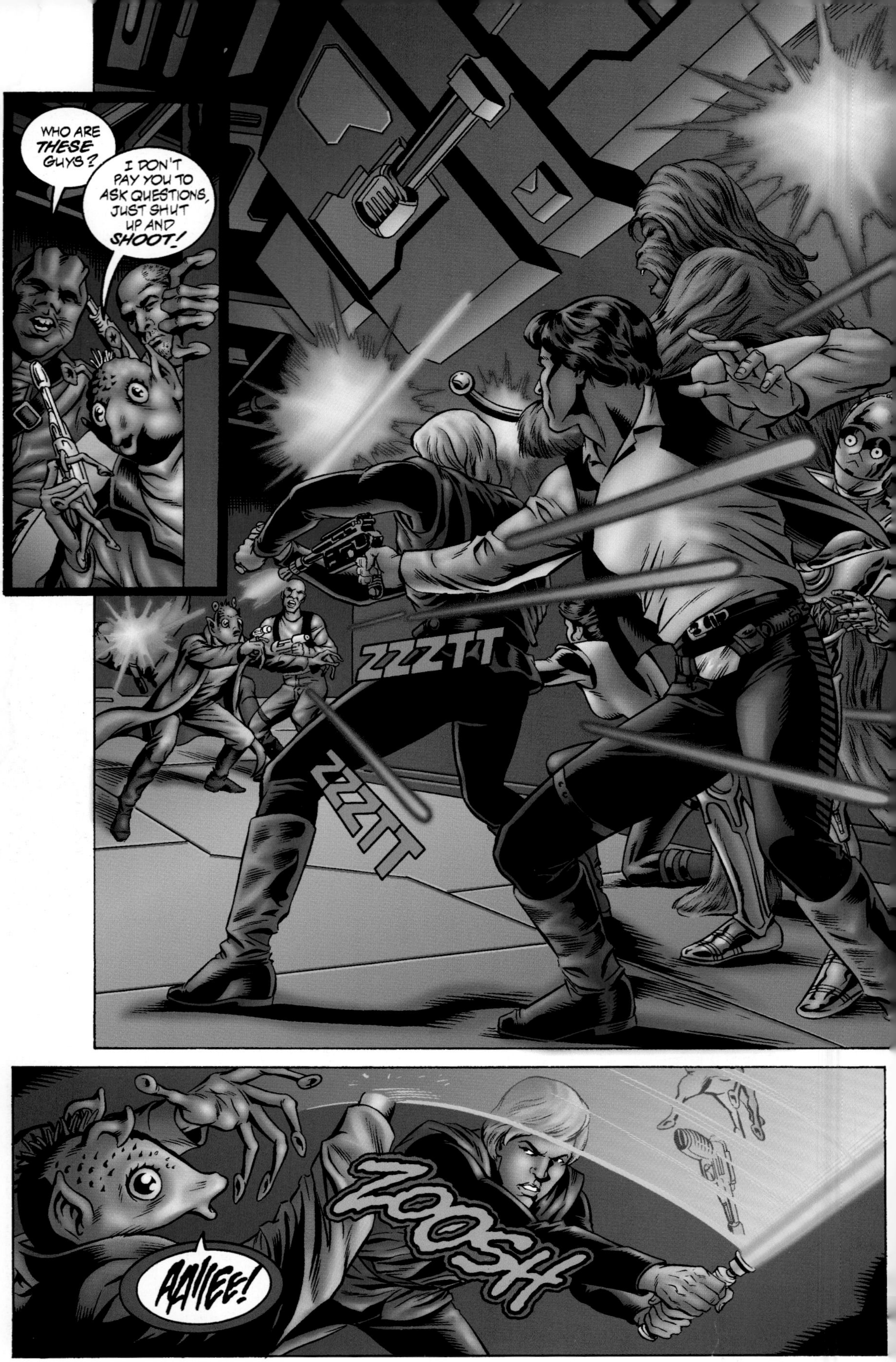
WHO ARE *THESE* GUYS?
I DON'T PAY YOU TO ASK QUESTIONS, JUST SHUT UP AND *SHOOT!*
ZZZTT
ZZZTT
ZOOSH
AAIIEE!

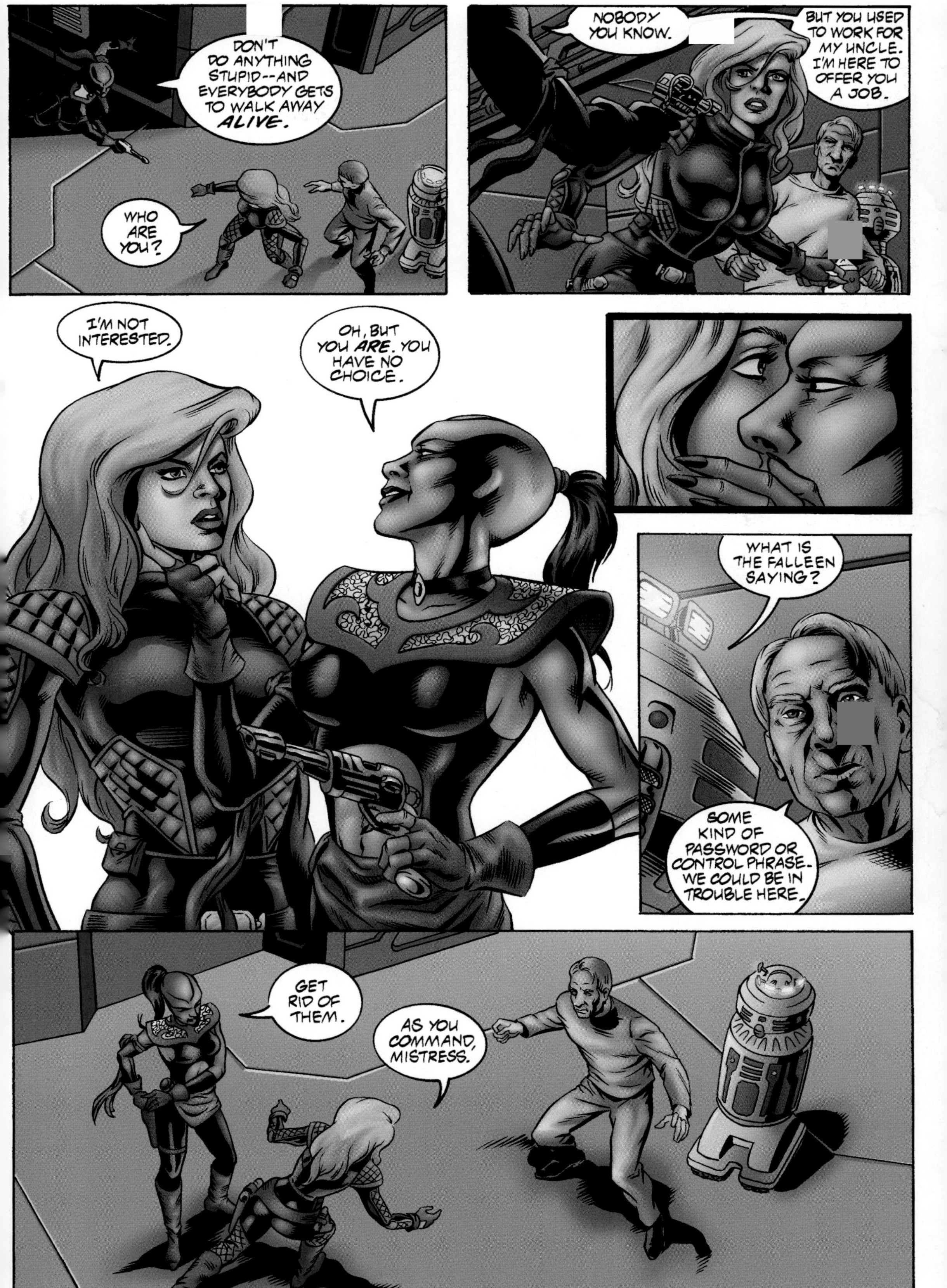
DON'T DO ANYTHING STUPID--AND EVERYBODY GETS TO WALK AWAY ALIVE.
WHO ARE YOU?
NOBODY YOU KNOW.
BUT YOU USED TO WORK FOR MY UNCLE. I'M HERE TO OFFER YOU A JOB.
I'M NOT INTERESTED.
OH, BUT YOU ARE. YOU HAVE NO CHOICE.
WHAT IS THE FALLEEN SAYING?
SOME KIND OF PASSWORD OR CONTROL PHRASE. WE COULD BE IN TROUBLE HERE.
GET RID OF THEM.
AS YOU COMMAND, MISTRESS.

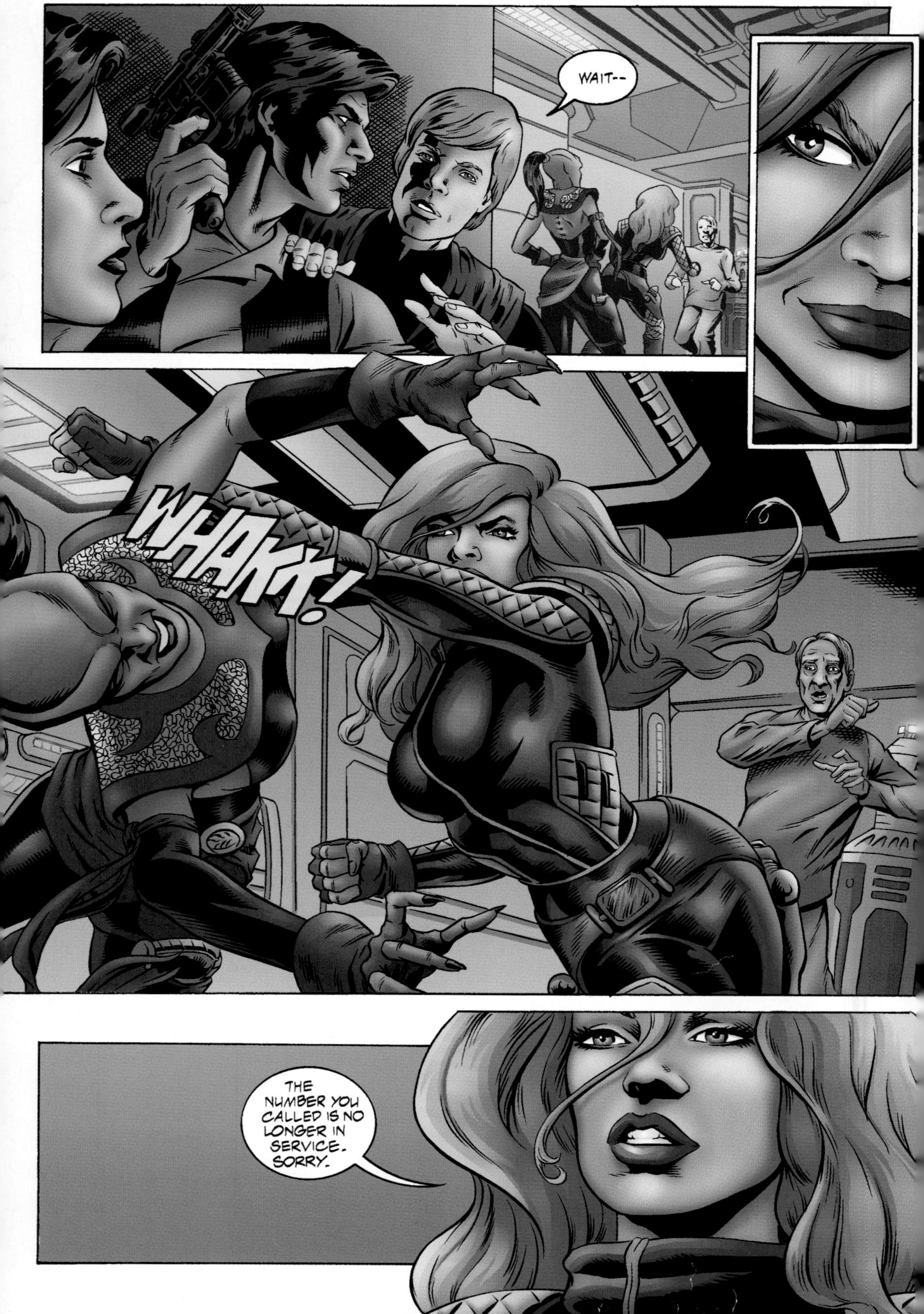
WAIT--
WHAKK!
THE NUMBER YOU CALLED IS NO LONGER IN SERVICE. SORRY.

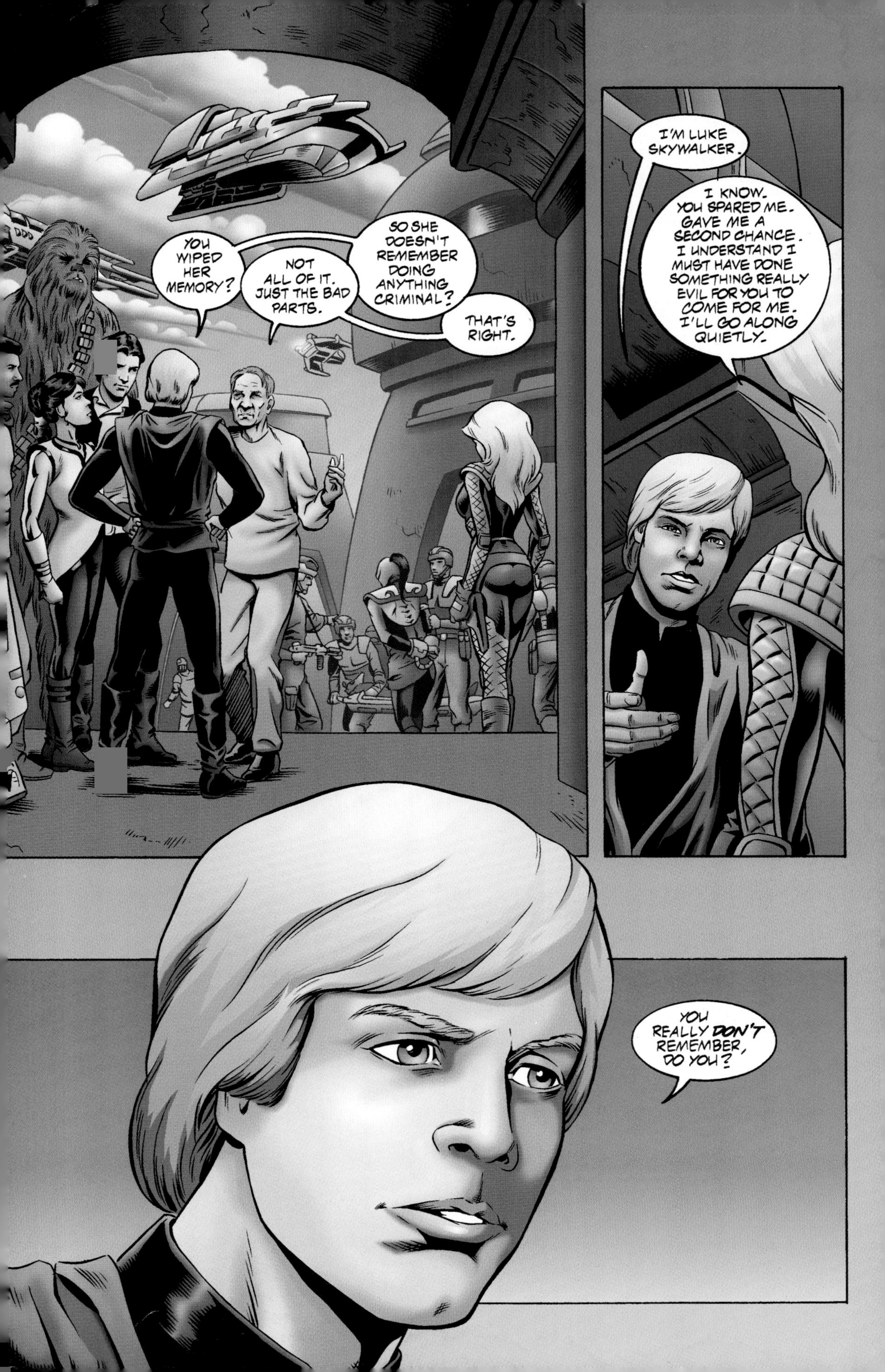
YOU WIPED HER MEMORY?
NOT ALL OF IT. JUST THE BAD PARTS.
SO SHE DOESN'T REMEMBER DOING ANYTHING CRIMINAL?
THAT'S RIGHT.
I'M LUKE SKYWALKER.
I KNOW. YOU SPARED ME. GAVE ME A SECOND CHANCE. I UNDERSTAND I MUST HAVE DONE SOMETHING REALLY EVIL FOR YOU TO COME FOR ME. I'LL GO ALONG QUIETLY.
YOU REALLY DON'T REMEMBER, DO YOU?

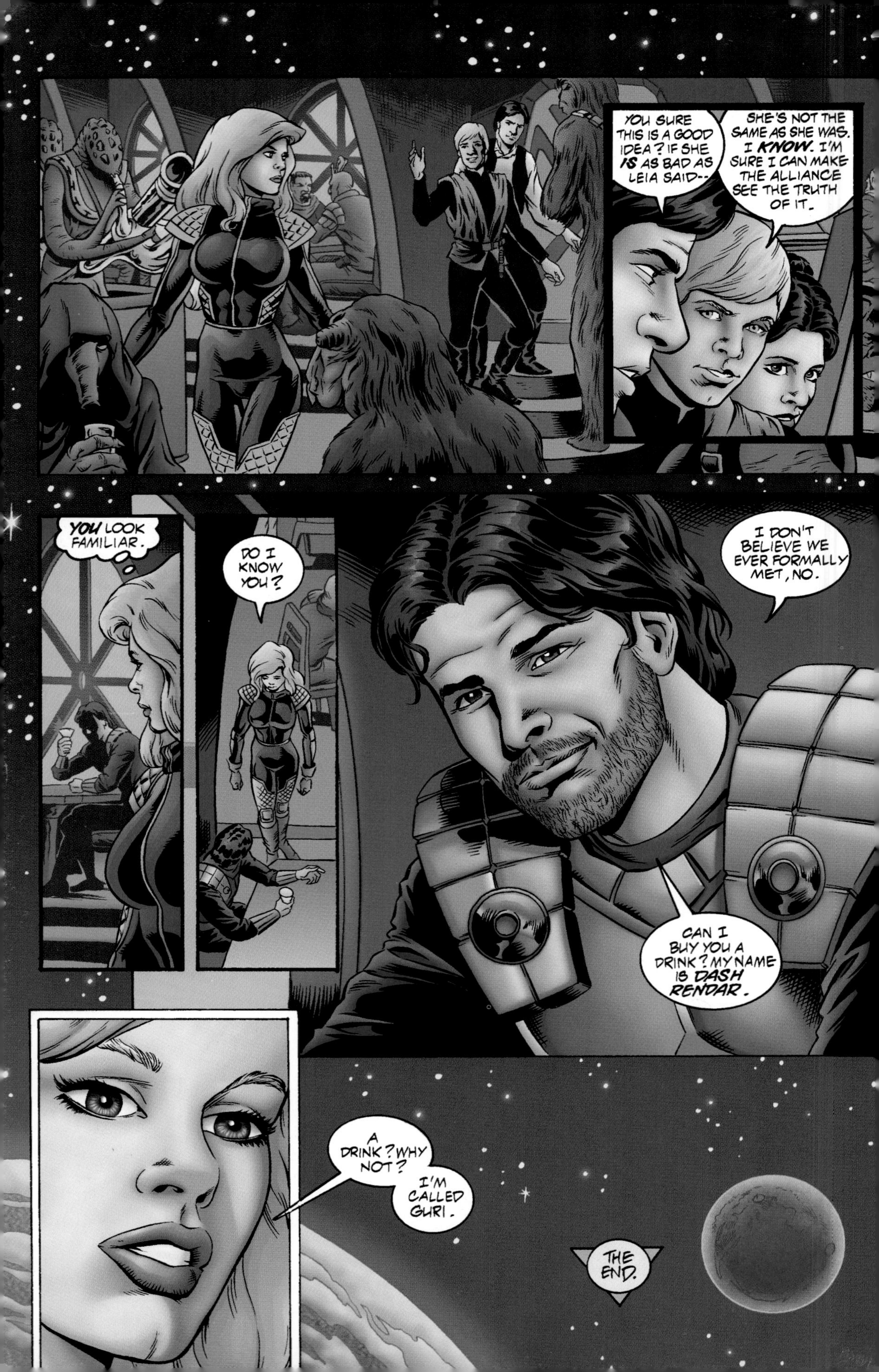

YOU SURE THIS IS A GOOD IDEA? IF SHE IS AS BAD AS LEIA SAID--
SHE'S NOT THE SAME AS SHE WAS. I KNOW. I'M SURE I CAN MAKE THE ALLIANCE SEE THE TRUTH OF IT.
YOU LOOK FAMILIAR.
DO I KNOW YOU?
I DON'T BELIEVE WE EVER FORMALLY MET, NO.
CAN I BUY YOU A DRINK? MY NAME IS DASH RENDAR.
A DRINK? WHY NOT?
I'M CALLED GURI.
THE END.

Steve Perry has sold dozens of stories to magazines and anthologies, as well as a considerable number of novels, animated teleplays, non-fiction articles, reviews, essays, and screenplays. He wrote for *Batman: The Animated Series* during its first Emmy-award winning season, and one of his second-season scripts was nominated for an Emmy for Outstanding Writing. Well-known for his novelizations of popular films (*The Mask*, *Men in Black*) and comic books (including several *Aliens* and *Predator* titles), his *Star Wars: Shadows of the Empire* novel made best-seller lists for *Publishers Weekly*, *USA Today*, *The Wall Street Journal*, and *The New York Times*. A former lifeguard, toy assembler, martial arts instructor, private detective, and nurse, Steve lives in Beaverton, Oregon with his wife, dogs, and cats and is currently working on his 48th novel. *Shadows of the Empire—Evolution* is Steve's first foray into comic-book scripting.

Ron Randall broke into comics after graduating from the Joe Kubert School, working first for DC Comics pencilling *Warlord*, *Arak*, *The Barren Earth*, *Dragonlance*, *Sgt. Rock*, *Justice League Europe*, and *Justice League International*, among others. He has drawn *Venom: Separation Anxiety* and *Star Trek Unlimited* for Marvel Comics as well as producing a variety of work for Image, Tekno, Eclipse, and Malibu. At Dark Horse, Ron created, wrote, and drew *Trekker*, the adventures of a beautiful female bounty hunter in a dystopian future. Ron also pencilled two popular *Predator* miniseries with writer Mark Verheiden, *Cold War* and *Dark River*. Also a well-respected inker, Ron has lately been delineating Paul Chadwick's *The World Below* for Dark Horse Maverick and *The Dreaming* and *Proposition Player* for Vertigo. Ron lives in Portland, Oregon with his wife and two children, all of whom lead more interesting lives than he does.

Tom Simmons was born in Colorado but was transplanted to the arid wilds of southeastern New Mexico at age ten. After high school, Tom enrolled in the commercial art program at Eastern New Mexico University. Realizing that drawing comics beat drawing vacuum cleaners for a living, Tom dropped out to pursue a career in comics. Since then, his inks have appeared in *Ghost*, *Mecha Special*, *Doc Savage: Curse of the Fire God*, *The Dirty Pair: Fatal but Not Serious*, *X*, *Legion of Super-Heroes*, *Legionnaires*, *Excalibur*, *Xero*, and *Titans: Scissors, Paper, Stone*. Tom's most recent work includes *The Kingdom: Nightstar*, *Elseworld's Finest: Supergirl & Batgirl*, and *Gen 13: Magical Drama Queen Roxy*. Tom currently resides in San Antonio, Texas, where he occupies himself inking *Wonder Woman* for DC Comics.

STAR WARS
SHADOWS OF THE EMPIRE
EVOLUTION

Gallery

Featuring the original comic-book series cover paintings by Duncan Fegredo

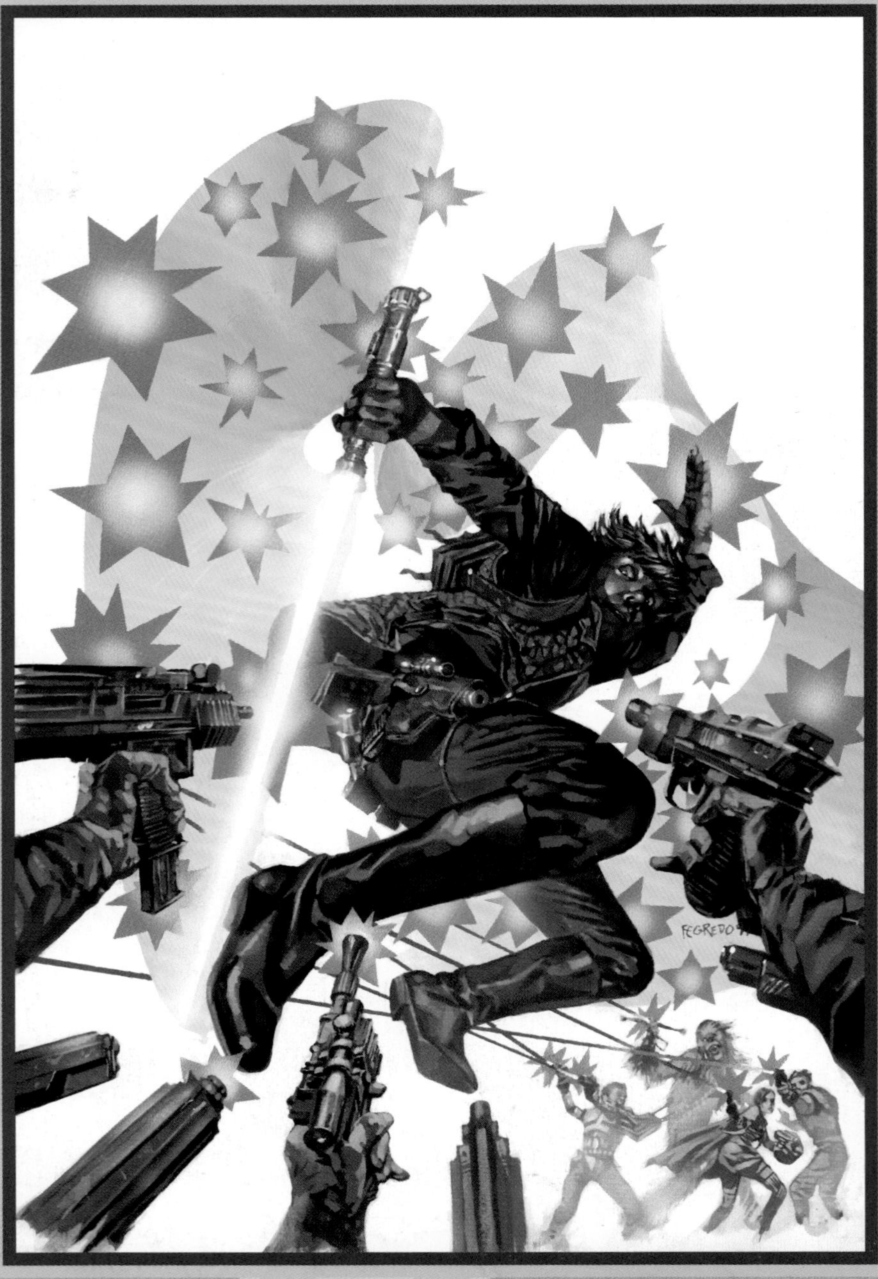
FEGREDO

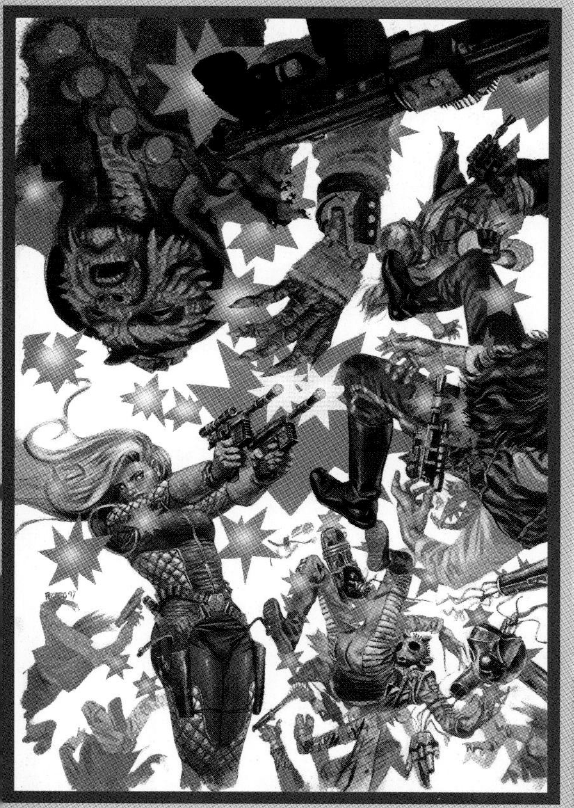

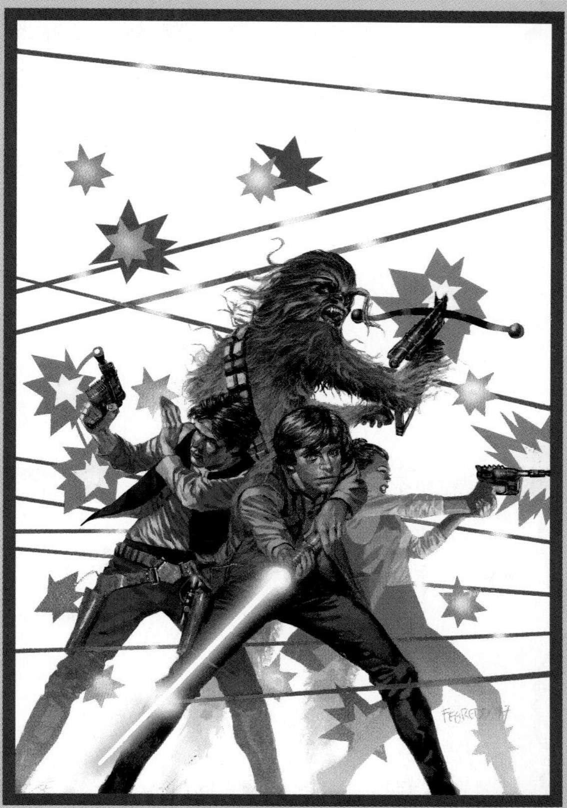

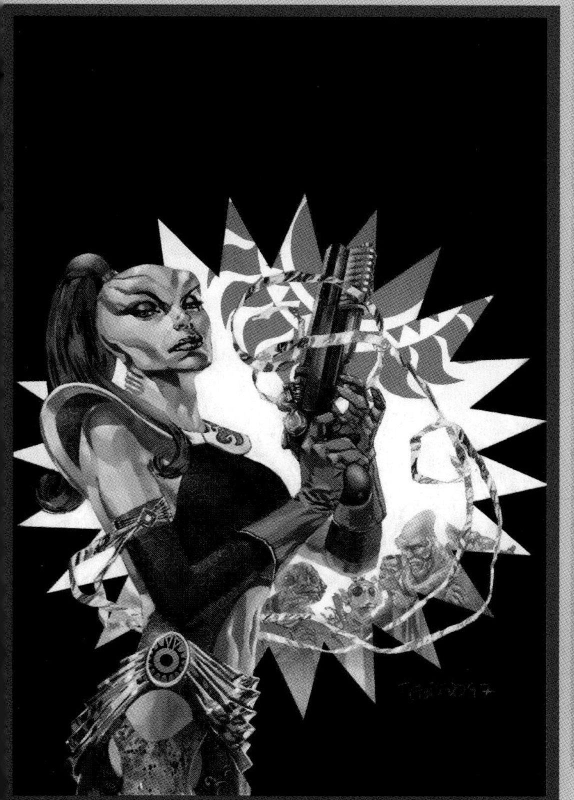

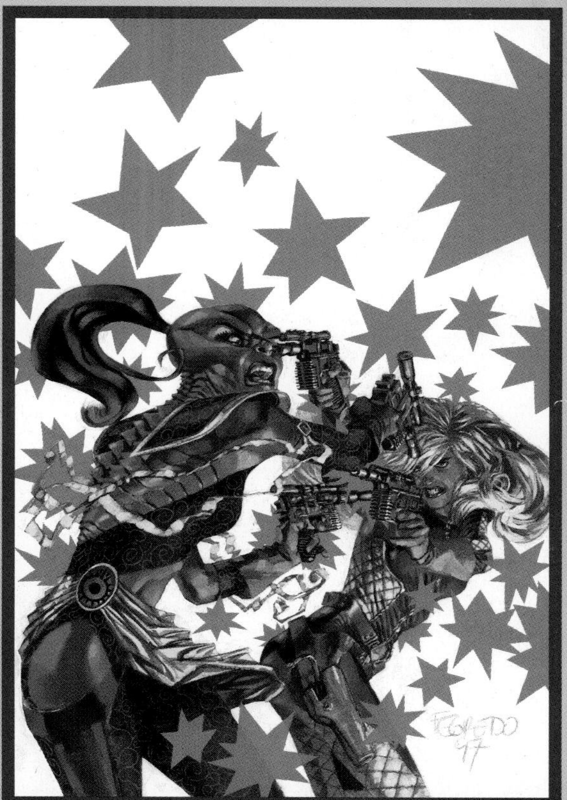
FEGREDO
97